MORE E-PRIME:
TO BE OR NOT II

MORE E-PRIME:
To Be or Not II

Edited by
Paul Dennithorne Johnston
D. David Bourland, Jr.
Jeremy Klein

Foreword by
Albert Ellis

INTERNATIONAL SOCIETY FOR GENERAL SEMANTICS

Concord, California

INTERNATIONAL SOCIETY FOR GENERAL SEMANTICS
P. O. Box 728
Concord, CA 94522

Library of Congress Cataloging-in-Publication Data

More E-prime: to be or not II / edited by Paul Dennithorne Johnston,
D. David Bourland, Jr., Jeremy Klein ; foreword by Albert Ellis.
     p.   cm.
    Includes bibliographical references.
    ISBN 0-918970-40-7
    1. English language — Reform. 2. English language — Verb.
I. Johnston, Paul Dennithorne, 1942– . II. Bourland, D. David
(Delphus David), 1928– . III. Klein, Jeremy, 1945– .

IV. Title: To be or not II.
PE1585.M63 1994
420' . 1—dc20   94-16584
                                        CIP

CONTENTS

Part One: THE FIRST E-PRIME SYMPOSIUM

Part Two: THE SECOND E-PRIME SYMPOSIUM

Part Three: Applications

Dedicated to the memory of
Alfred Korzybski

ACKNOWLEDGMENTS

OUR SINCERE THANKS to the authors who have generously allowed us to publish their work in this anthology. Without their passion for debate and their dedication to effective writing, we would not have had the rich textured discourse that fills these pages.

THE EDITORS

ALBERT ELLIS* **FOREWORD**

E-PRIME — the use of English without the verb *to be* — has generated controversy since D. David Bourland, Jr., formulated it in 1965. Good! If we dogmatically and unthinkingly accept or rigidly reject E-Prime we would defy the fundamental teachings of the founder of general semantics, Alfred Korzybski, and of Bourland himself. E-Prime has its advantages and its limitations. Had we better not, then, acknowledge *both*, and not insist on an *either/or* attitude toward its use?

I got excited about general semantics in the 1940s when I read Stuart Chase's and S. I. Hayakawa's popularizations of some of its principles. So when I formulated rational-emotive therapy (RET) in 1955 I incorporated some of these principles into RET's theory and practice. Thus, I noted in *Reason and Emotion in Psychotherapy* (Secaucus, NJ: Citadel, 1962):

"...rational-emotive psychotherapy...parallels much of the thinking of the General Semanticists."

* Dr. Albert Ellis, founder and president of the Institute for Rational-Emotive Therapy in New York, has published numerous books about RET, some written in E-Prime. Recently, he renamed RET to Rational-Emotive Behavior Therapy (REBT).

xiii

Both RET and general semantics hold that people largely (not completely) *disturb themselves* (as opposed to *get* disturbed) by their thinking, their over-generalizing, and their use of rigid language. They have innate and learned self-changing and self-actualizing tendencies. But they also easily and forcefully take their healthy preferences, wishes, and desires and (consciously and unconsciously) raise them to unhealthy, absolutist musts, shoulds, oughts, necessities, and demands. They thereby neuroticize themselves — or, as Korzybski sometimes put it, often render themselves "unsane."

As Korzybski indicated, and as Bourland, Johnston, and Klein show in this book, imprecise and over-generalized language has much to do with *exacerbating* self-disturbing human behaviors.

When I read Bourland's "A Linguistic Note: Writing in E-Prime" (*General Semantics Bulletin*, 1965/1966, Vols. 32-33, pp. 111-114) and "The Semantics of a Non-Aristotelian Language" (*General Semantics Bulletin*, 1968, Vol. 35, pp. 60-63) it reinforced my conviction regarding the importance of using E-Prime. For several years I discussed E-Prime with one of the pioneering RET practitioners, Robert H. Moore.

After I read Moore's Ph.D. dissertation, *Alienation in College Students: A Rational and Semantic Analysis* (Walden University, Tallahassee, FL, 1977), I decided to write in E-Prime. The resulting E-Prime books include: *How To Live With A "Neurotic"* (Rev. ed., North Hollywood CA: Wilshire Books, 1975; with Robert A. Harper), *A New Guide to Rational Living* (North Hollywood, CA: Wilshire Books, 1975); *Sex and the Liberated Man* (Secaucus, NJ: Lyle Stuart 1976); *Anger — How To Live With And Without It* (Secaucus, NJ: Citadel, 1977; with William Knaus) *Overcoming Procrastination* (New York: Signet, 1977).

My RET associate, Dr. William J. Knaus, has also written several articles and a book, *How to Conquer Your Frustrations*, (Englewood Cliffs, NJ: Prentice-Hall, 1983) in E-Prime.

When I gave the Alfred Korzybski Memorial Lecture recently (*General Semantics Bulletin 57*) I pointed out that thinking in E-Prime and thereby minimizing the use of the is-of-identity and the is-of-predication helps keep us emotionally healthy and free from disturbance, because these two uses of the verb *to be* constitute (as Korzybski indicated) two of the main cores of self-disturbance.

To put this again in RET terms, humans mainly neuroticize themselves by taking their healthy preferences, wishes, and desires — especially their preferences for approval, competence, comfort, and safety — and *unhealthfully making them into absolutist, over-generalized shoulds, oughts, and musts.* For example:

"Under all conditions and at all times,
(1) I *must* perform well and *must* gain the approval of all significant others; and
(2) I *have to* have people treat me fairly and considerately and I *need* comfortable and safe conditions to live under."

The first of these absolute "necessities" leads to the is-of-identity: "If my thoughts, feelings, and actions make me fail and lose the approval of significant others, I *am* no good and I *am* undeserving of human happiness."

The second of these "necessities" leads to the is-of-predication: "If people and/or conditions treat me unfairly or uncomfortably it *is* bad and this badness *is* awful and horrible (meaning, *more than* bad)."

The is-of-identity constitutes a core of self-denigration and concomitant feelings of worthlessness; and the is-of-predication constitutes a core of devaluing other people, one's own life, and the world.

Rational-emotive therapy, therefore, tries to show people how to understand and uproot their self-deprecation and their feelings of worthlessness and to surrender their awfulizing and their feelings of low frustration tolerance and self-pity.

Rational-emotive therapy has many cognitive, emotive, and behavioral methods of helping people to do this — especially those of showing them how to give up their is-of-identity and their is-of-predication.

Let me give a specific case illustration. Several years ago I saw Keva, a 34-year-old teacher, for severe depression which

struck when she did poorly in college. At the same time, a
fellow student whom she loved madly had rejected her for
neglecting her studies and for getting poor marks. She concluded, with some reason, that her work really *was* bad, that
she hadn't sufficiently pushed herself when she could have
done better, and that she had thereby helped ruin her
relationships.

At the time, as she acknowledged in her therapy with me,
she told herself, "Seeing how badly I am doing, especially
when I could do much better, I am worthless and don't deserve a good relationship." Since that time, she continued to
hold to the same dysfunctional belief system, to do badly
partly because of it, and to not even try to get into a good
relationship.

When I saw Keva I tried to help her see and dispute her
irrational demands on herself:

"I absolutely *must* do better at school, at work, or anything
important that I try to do, and I *have to* win the approval of
those I really like, or else I *am* no good!"

But she kept insisting that not only did she desire to do
well at her teaching, as well as socially, but that she *had* to do
so because:

(1) she did have the ability to do well *if* she worked hard
enough; and,
(2) therefore she *had* to use this ability.

She refused to change her dire *needs* back into strong *preferences*, as I try to help almost all my clients to do when we are
working with RET.

I finally tried some general semantics methods, to show
Keva that although she often *acted* badly in some ways, she
wasn't, she didn't *equal*, her bad acts. I said,

"If you *are* bad, as you claim, you would *always* and
only do bad deeds. You would have a rotten *essence* or
soul. But you, your youness, does millions of acts during
your lifetime — good, bad, and indifferent. And even if
you *only* acted badly right now — which is unlikely — if
you *are* bad you would have to *continue* to only behave

badly forever. Moreover, if you think that you *are* a bad *person*, you will usually not only rate, evaluate your entire self — which leads to an arrant over-generalization — but you will tend to *damn* that self and consider it unworthy of any pleasure or goodness. People who presumably *are* bad ostensibly *deserve* only bad things. Now, where will *that* idea get you?"

Also, I pointed out to Keva, if she *were* a bad *person*, how could she change and do any good deeds in the future? How could she, a no-goodnik, *change* her poor performances? And how could she be lovable at all, if *she* were so rotten?

Finally, after I persisted in showing Keva the error and the inevitable poor effects of her over-generalizing and self-damnation, she kept rating her lack of effort and her teaching *performances* as "bad," when they were less desirable, but agreed to accept her *self*, her *personhood*, with this poor behavior.

When asked what she told herself to make herself change and feel self-accepting, she said,

"The most valuable thing I learned in therapy, in addition to the needless *musts* I put on myself and that I still have trouble changing, consisted of seeing that I may *be* me, may *be* a human, but I 'am' only a person who *does* many good and bad things. Although I can evaluate these things in accordance with whether they help or hinder my chosen goals, I cannot legitimately rate my *being*, my *self*, my *totality*. That leads to overgeneralizing; and that, to use a dangerous word, is too much. That will get me into serious trouble!"

With this conclusion, and with other RET work, Keva lost her depression, worked better at school, and finally achieved a good relationship with the same lover who had previously rejected her.

Using E-Prime, as shown in this book, will not in itself stop us completely from using all mechanisms of identity and predication, nor from employing other forms of illogical, over-generalizing, inflexible, and unrealistic thinking by which we often make ourselves self-defeating or neurotic. But it can help greatly in these respects. Humans easily and forcefully think and communicate crookedly and thereby help upset themselves and their social relationships. Using E-Prime helps to remind us that we keep doing this and helps us communicate more effectively and less disturbedly. Try it and see for yourself!

ALBERT ELLIS, PRESIDENT
INSTITUTE FOR RATIONAL-EMOTIVE THERAPY
NEW YORK

PAUL DENNITHORNE JOHNSTON   *INTRODUCTION₁*

T HE SUCCESS of our first E-Prime collection, *To Be or Not: An E-Prime Anthology*, encouraged us to bring out another. Why has E-Prime caught the imagination of so many people? I can only speculate.

It seems simple enough. Just stop using all forms of the verb *to be*. The results can astonish you: anything from clearer thinking, or improved writing, to a change in epistemology that can enhance how well you function in the world.

The success of our first book surprised us. Perhaps part of that success came as a result of the efforts of one of our E-Prime "dissenters." Emory Menefee wrote an article in protest of the *absolute* use of E-Prime, saying he preferred *choosing* when to omit various usages of *to be*. He named his method E-Choice. His article appeared in the Summer 1991 issue of *ETC: A Review of General Semantics (Et cetera)* (Vol. 48, No. 2) with the title "E-Prime or E-Choice?"

The Managing Editor of *The Atlantic Monthly* magazine, Cullen Murphy, intrigued by apparent rebellion in the general semantics ranks, wrote a piece in his magazine called "'To Be' in Their Bonnets: A Matter of Semantics," which appeared shortly after the publication of *To Be or Not*. Also at about that time, E-Prime author Dr. E. W. Kellogg III had interviews on local and national public radio.

Subsequently, the Editor-in-Chief of *Et cetera*, Jeremy Klein, put together two symposia on E-Prime which appeared in the Summer 1992 and Fall 1993 issues.

This much publicity seems small by mainstream publishing standards. However, two printings of *To Be or Not* have sold out and we've done a third. Something struck a chord with people who think. I'll leave it to you to ponder the reasons for this as you read more about E-Prime.

The first sections of this book consist of an historical record of these publishing events. In the Prologue we reprint Emory Menefee's dissenting article and the replies from E-Prime supporters which followed. Part One and Part Two contain the two symposia as they appeared in *Et cetera*.

Part Three contains a paper by the noted psychotherapist Dr. Albert Ellis, "General Semantics and Rational Emotive Behavior Therapy," his 1991 Alfred Korzybski Memorial Lecture, which shows some of the relationships between general semantics, E-Prime, and Dr. Ellis' therapy. Part Three also includes a piece of interest to writers and thinkers, D. David Bourland Jr.'s "E-Prime and the Crispness Index," which discusses how E-Prime can tighten your writing and your thinking. Some detractors have complained that E-Prime doesn't solve all linguistic and semantic problems; in response, we've included "The Rise of Nopanaceism," by C. W. Griffin, Jr. I wondered if E-Prime would help produce the tight style of many contemporary mysteries, and wrote "Boiling Creek: The G.S. Detective," perhaps the first mystery written in E-Prime. The final piece in this book, Bourland's "Changing 'Human Nature,' " offers some encouraging notes on using Alfred Korzybski's general semantics to help create a saner world.

I'd call this particular feast more of a smorgasbord than a formal dinner — something for everyone who wants to learn more about E-Prime. I hope you enjoy it.

PAUL DENNITHORNE JOHNSTON
CONCORD, CALIFORNIA
MARCH, 1994

D. David Bourland, Jr. *INTRODUCTION₂*

1. *About Some Beginnings*

WHEN I CONSCIOUSLY exercised E-Prime in a paper for the first time, 45 years ago, I felt confident that many belonging to the general semantics community, and most particularly the "Institute Crowd," as I thought of them, would immediately perceive what I had done. I had even given them a strong clue in a footnote. I now suspect that probably very few people read that footnote. But at the time I supposed that, seeing how easily one could write in E-Prime (and conscious of the obvious epistemological benefits), I felt that surely others would try it out and very likely proceed to do it much better than I had. Smoother. More articulately.

Imagine my surprise! Over 15 years and several papers later, I finally wrote about E-Prime as such. No response. Four years after *that* came the piece in *Time* magazine, thanks to a mention of E-Prime as an oddity in a footnote of an article by Dr. Allen Walker Read. At least one person read *his* footnotes. I regarded the *Time* piece as somewhat foolishly written, for it included two manufactured quotes attributed to me. The silliness of one of those bogus quotes rated an appearance at the end of a story in *The New Yorker* magazine in the fall of 1969; of course *The New Yorker* obviously thought the blame belonged to *me!* The *Time* article did generate a certain amount of mail. It also brought general semantics and E-Prime to the attention of various people, most prominently including Mr. Earl Hautala, the current President of the International Society for General Semantics, who today writes in E-Prime. It also caught the eye of a graduate student at the University of Chicago, Luis Camacho, who subsequently returned to the Universidad de Costa Rica with his doctorate in philosophy. This circumstance generated one of my peak life experiences when I went to him as one of the possible advisors for my *licenciatura* thesis a few years later, and he said, "Are you the guy who...." "Yes."

Quite apart from the struggles with E-Prime, my professional lives (general semantics, operations research, and linguistics) and my personal lives (we won't go into that) have provided me with more than enough conflict, controversy, and drama. Those emotional miseries seem to overlap so much that one would inevitably regard much of them as surface aspects of the same underlying dynamics, as one would expect from taking an organism-as-a-whole-in-an-environment orientation. In any event, I do not, in these sunset years, need more controversy to keep me warm.

Nevertheless, I cannot deny that publicized controversy *has* stimulated a certain amount of interest in E-Prime and hence in the field of general semantics from whence it sprang, and of which it amounts to a very small part. I refer specifically to comparatively recent papers by Dr. Emory Menefee (1) and Mr. Cullen Murphy (2).

One more reminiscence, please. In 1980 when I saw my dear friend Mary Morain again for the first time in many years, she said, commenting on a paper I planned to present at the Toronto Conference on General Semantics, "Have you gone beyond E-Prime?" I felt astonished! I had had no idea that at least some people in the "Society Crowd" thought highly enough of E-Prime that it amounted to something one could "go beyond." I still believed, after three papers on E-Prime *per se*, that I had made the whole thing sufficiently obvious and clear. When a well-wisher some time later encouraged me to do a book on E-Prime, I replied, "How can you write a book about something as straightforward as *How to Assemble a Lawn Chair?*"

Now I finally — after almost 50 years, *finally* — understand what at least some parts of the intellectual world wants from me: (i) not some fiddling about with the formalities of non-Aristotelian postulates (3) (anyway, Dr. C. A. Hilgartner has dealt effectively with those matters); (ii) not the conjugations of a general model for Information Transfer Systems (4) (which never really got off the ground); (iii) not a polished-up version of ΣEOS Theory (5) (but which I have in fact begun to polish up anyway). No, not those pretty and glittery contributions: just that old lawn chair, E-Prime! So let's continue to have at it.

2. Reiterated Iterations

As you will see in my (sometimes, I *hate* to admit it, ill-tempered) comments in the two *Et cetera* Symposia that appear in Parts One and Two of this book, I have often felt that I have preached to the choir whilst those rascals comported themselves naughtily and did not pay attention. How depressing!

Some critics as they reveal themselves in their papers contained in this book cannot seem to bring themselves to recognize that the most semantically insidious aspects of the verb "to be" lie *precisely* in the Auxiliary and Existence usages of that heinous verb. This circumstance proceeds from the fact that those supposedly benign usages facilitate and practically insure our continued employment of "to be" in the Identification and Predication usages. Friends, please try to pay attention: even Korzybski could not eschew the uses of Identification and Predication, while retaining the Auxiliary use (which includes the passive voice with its inherent elementalism) and the Existence use (see the paper by Ms. Wedge in Part Two). Neither could many noted workers in the field of general semantics. Only those of us who have adopted E-Prime manage to avoid the "is" of Identity and the "is" of Predication. Doesn't that give you pause? If not, why not?

Now please do not try to shift the ground on me and say, implying that I may never have heard it before, that E-Prime does not clear up *all* problems of identification. See, in this regard, the delightful article in Part Three by Griffin on "The Rise of Nopanaceism," and reflect on how much, realistically, one can expect of any single extensional device. You will find more on this specific matter in my paper in Part Two, "Too Far?"

3. *Messy Matters*

From the middle 1920s to 1950, Korzybski *insisted* on bringing his methodology to the general attention of the intellectual world, which rarely had any interest in hearing from him. The man had no Ph.D., after all, and he never had a "proper" association with an academic institution. In my opinion, this undoubtedly provided a basic, but forever irreconcilable, bone of contention between him and Hayakawa. Of course, many other matters (and people) muddied their waters. I assert, however, that their conflicts certainly had nothing to do with the financial success of Hayakawa's main book, and/or his personal notoriety, as some have suggested. Furthermore, and most damning, Korzybski tended to dwell on matters that some have regarded as better left to the laboratory, the psychoanalyst's couch, or even the dust bin.

Perhaps more precisely, Korzybski studied and discussed a number of unpopular matters because he perceived their importance, despite their neglect by most academics. Korzybski and his followers have tried to come to grips with a variety of messy matters that have not yet had appropriate numerical measures associated with them. Please join me in considering the examples given below:

Example from Korzybski's seminars: Once, he said, several noted philosophers attended a seminar. Korzybski mentioned, as a consequence of the insights provided by Einstein's general theory of relativity, the indivisibility of space-time. The *non-elementalistic* indivisibility of space-time.

He noticed a hand raised by one of the special guests. He asked if the philosopher wanted to make a comment. "You said we cannot split space *and* time. *I* can." Korzybski replied, "All right. Go ahead and show us. Do it." The philosopher said, "I can do it, but I won't do it for you!"

Another seminar example: Trying to help his students understand, viscerally, the crucial notion of object level/symbolic level non-identity, Korzybski said, "Pinch your finger [illustrating it himself]. Go on, pinch your finger. Whatever you say about it, *is not* what you feel when you pinch that finger."

A third example (one of my all-time favorites) comes from the Introduction to the Second Edition of *Science and Sanity*: "Even a gramophone record undergoes some physical changes before words or phrases can be 'stored' and/or reproduced. Is it so very difficult to understand that the extremely sensitive and highly complex human nervous system also undergoes some electro-colloidal changes before words, evaluations, etc., are stored, produced, or reproduced? In the work of general semantics we deal with the *living neuro*-semantic and *neuro*-linguistic reactions, not mere detached verbal chatter in the abstract." (6, p. xxviii) Korzybski's basic point seems quite valid whether one subscribes to an electro-colloidal theory of the brain (7), a computer-oriented model of brain processes (8), or the Neural Darwinism of Edelman (9).

A fourth example comes from Korzybski's Preface to the First Edition of *Science and Sanity*: "Few of us realize the unbelievable traps, some of them of a psychopathological character, which the structure of our ordinary language sets before us." (6, p. lxxxii) Dr. Albert Ellis has seen this assertion frequently confirmed in his clinical practice of psychotherapy, with particular focus on the verb "to be," as described in his Foreword to this book.

A fifth example appears in Dr. Albert Ellis's paper that begins Section Three of this book. Early in that paper he stated that, during his beginning days as a psychoanalyst, using then-conventional psychoanalytic procedures, "I saw that most of my clients *felt* better as a result of my psychoanalytic sessions with them, but virtually none of them *got* better.

Why? Because they still strongly believed in the same basic, largely self-created *philosophies* that originally made them and now kept them neurotic."

For a final example, let us review Korzybski's semantic experiment to seek undefined terms in our standard language of discourse. He described his experiment as follows: "We begin by asking the 'meaning' of every word uttered, being satisfied for this purpose with the roughest definitions; then we ask the 'meaning' of the words used in the definitions, and this process is continued usually for no more than ten to fifteen minutes, until the victim begins to speak in circles — as, for instance, defining 'space' by 'length' and 'length' by 'space.' When this stage is reached, we have come usually to the *undefined* terms of a given individual. If we still press, no matter how gently, for definitions, a most interesting fact occurs. Sooner or later, signs of *affective disturbances* appear. Often the face reddens; there is a bodily restlessness; sweat appears — symptoms quite similar to those seen in a schoolboy who has forgotten his lesson, which he 'knows but cannot tell.'....Here we have reached the bottom and the foundation of all *non-elementalistic meanings* — the meanings of *undefined terms*, which we 'know' somehow, but cannot tell. In fact, we have reached the un-speakable level." (6, p. 21) Some years ago two associates and I conducted a series of such interviews, and obtained results that confirmed Korzybski's assertions. (10)

The six examples cited above provide slightly different slants on several inter-related issues which we can summarize as follows: *the way we use language affects our brains.* Psycho-physiologically. Unfortunately, semantic processes do not readily fit into antiseptically clean, discrete little compartments; we still must help one another to remember the sharp distinctions between related event level structures, object level structures, and symbolic level structures, i.e., focus on a consciousness of abstracting; relative to the complexities of "meaning," some people evidently continue to yearn for an academic tidiness that never really existed, even in the past. An inadequate appreciation of those points seems manifested in the recent papers by the various students of Lieutenant Semantics. (See the discussion of this practical discussion as provided by Schnapps in the Prologue.) Consider yourself warned!

Perhaps predictably, E-Prime may pose more of a problem to some older scientists than to younger scientists or even those who lack very much scientific training. I try to understand in this way the peculiar positions against E-Prime taken by some otherwise brilliant individuals. Perhaps they unconsciously strive for a Newtonian determinism that one cannot always produce when dealing with semantic processes of the kinds just illustrated above. Perhaps the benefits offered by E-Prime have a closer relation to the lower degrees of determinism developed by such greats as Werner Heisenberg, P.A.M. Dirac, Kurt Gödel, etc., that characterize many advancements in twentieth century physics and mathematics. When one really gets down to it, I believe that we can not hope to go beyond saying, with Dr. Albert Ellis, that E-Prime, like the latter's Rational Emotive Behavior Therapy, "becomes and remains effective with many (not all) people much (not all) of the time." This probably will not satisfy some people. Sorry about that.

4. Future Steps in the Application of E-Prime

I can visualize three particularly fruitful regions for future work involving E-Prime: (i) literary studies; (ii) support for various research projects pertaining to general semantics; and (iii) inquiries into the effects on the brain (if any) of using E-Prime, employing EEG or similar, but more advanced, technology. Russell Joyner has recently brought to my attention a procedure that seems to me highly promising for this kind of inquiry, the H_2 ^{15}O method for studying regional cerebral blood flow. (11)

I have recently developed a new tool that should see a variety of applications, called the Crispness Index. This matter receives extensive treatment in my paper, "E-Prime and the Crispness Index," which finally appears in Part Three of this book. The Crispness Index equals the ratio of the number of E-Prime sentences (sentences without any form of the verb "to be") to the total number of sentences in a sample of spoken or written material. Due to the obvious difficulties and, indeed, the expense, of coping with the complete sequence of (a) eliciting, (b) recording, (c) transcribing, and (d) analyzing an extensive spoken utterance, no body of material has yet received such study. I hope that someone soon will look into this, perhaps in a MA thesis. The Crispness Index could also provide the basis for quantitative studies to correlate various aspects of speech with the consequences of using the verb "to be," with its attendant burdens of identification, predication, elementalism, static constructions, etc.

In addition to serving as a method for introducing a group of students, on whatever level, to the many other facets of general semantics and providing a certain amount of semantic catharsis, E-Prime and particularly the Crispness Index have the potential of offering an important tool for research related to general semantics. Consider the following, from Alvin A. Goldberg: "Experimental research dealing with the effectiveness of general semantics has many pitfalls. Among other things, it is difficult to randomly assign subjects to control and experimental groups; keeping everything the 'same' in the experimental groups and control groups except for the independent variable is almost impossible; determining exactly what the independent variable — the training approach — should consist of is a major problem; and subject improvement or change is very difficult to measure. Nevertheless, such research is vital if the value of general semantics as a methodology or therapy is to be determined on the basis of anything other than a priori grounds." (12, p. 16) Or, we would probably add today, other than *anecdotal* grounds.

Let me now close by offering *Bourland's Conjecture*: The careful study of brain activity when hearing, speaking, writing, and/or "thinking" in E-Prime will show measurable differences in comparison with brain functioning using standard English (with 50% or so of the sentences bristling with forms of the verb "to be"). Please telephone me, collect, at (817) 767-9290 when you obtain results...either positive or negative.

—D. DAVID BOURLAND, JR.
WICHITA FALLS, TEXAS
March 1994

REFERENCES

1. Emory Menefee. "E-Prime or E-Choice." *Et cetera: A Review of General Semantics*, Vol. 48, No. 2, 1991, p. 136-140. Reprinted in the Prologue to this book.
2. Cullen Murphy. " 'To Be' in Their Bonnets: A Matter of Semantics." *The Atlantic Monthly* magazine, February 1992. Reprinted in *Et cetera: A Review of General Semantics*, Vol. 49, No. 2, p. 125-130. Also reprinted in Section One of this book.
3. D. David Bourland, Jr. "Introduction to a Structural Calculus: A Postulational Study of Alfred Korzybski's Non-Aristotelian Linguistic System." Presented at the Third Congress on General Semantics, University of Denver, 22-24 July 1949. Published in the *General Semantics Bulletin*, Nos. 8 & 9, 1952, p. 16-22.
4. D. David Bourland, Jr., and Robert P. McManus. "A General Model for Information Transfer Systems." Presented at the International Conference on General Semantics, San Francisco State College, 9-13 August 1965. Published in the *General Semantics Bulletin*, Nos. 32 & 33, 1965-1966, p. 72-77.
5. D. David Bourland, Jr. "Preliminary Notes on ΣEOS Theory: Epistemological Foundations for a Non-Korzybskian System." Presented at the International Conference on General Semantics, University of Toronto, August 1980. Published in *Comunicación: Revista del Instituto Tecnológico de Costa Rica*, Vol. 1, No. 3, 1979, p. 19-36.
6. Alfred Korzybski. *Science and Sanity: An Introduction to Non-Aristotelian Systems and General Semantics.* Lakeville, Conn.: International Non-Aristotelian Library Publishing Co. 1933. Fourth Edition, 1958.
7. Marjorie Swanson. *Scientific Epistemologic Backgrounds of General Semantics: Lectures on Electro-Colloidal Structures.* General Semantics Monograph IV. Lakeville, Conn.: Institute of General Semantics. 1959.
8. P. N. Johnson-Laird. *The Computer and the Mind.* Cambridge, Mass.: Harvard University Press. 1988.
9. Gerald M. Edelman. *Neural Darwinism: The Theory of Neuronal Group Selection.* New York: Basic Books. 1987.
10. D. David Bourland, Jr., Charles H. Morgan, and Karen L. Ruskin. "A Semantic Experiment: Searching for Undefined Terms." In Lee

Thayer, ed., *Communication: General Semantics Perspectives.* New York: Spartan Books. 1970.

11. Larry R. Squire, et al., "Activation of the Hippocampus in Normal Humans: A Functional Anatomical Study of Memory," *Proceedings of the National Academy of Science, U.S.A.* 89: 1837-1841. March 1992.

12. Alvin A. Goldberg. "Empirical and Experimental Research Possibilities in General Semantics." In Kenneth G. Johnson, ed., *Research Designs in General Semantics.* New York: Gordon & Breach. 1974.

PROLOGUE

"Doc, note: I dissent. A fast never prevents a fatness. I diet on cod."
— PENELOPE GILLIATT

EMORY MENEFEE ## E-PRIME OR E-CHOICE? *

M Y HIGH SCHOOL English teacher at Pampa, Texas, tried valiantly to teach me to avoid overusing the simpler tenses
of the verb "to be." Whenever I did this, she (and sometimes
I) thought it clarified my writing. I later discovered general
semantics and found that the situation was much more sinister: these little verbs (or their equivalent in other languages)
may have contributed to two millennia of intellectual sloth
and Aristotelian darkness. So perhaps it could be expected
that eventually there would be a movement to eradicate every form and use of "to be" from written and spoken English.

E-Prime is David Bourland's name for a version of English
minus all forms of the verb "to be," including "is," "am," "are,"
"was," "were," "be," and "been." In use, the verb appears
mainly as an auxiliary, or in sentences involving identity,
predication, existence, or location. Since identity and predication give rise to most problems blamed on the "to be" verbs
by general semanticists, some believe that their avoidance in
only those usages would suffice. However, E. W. Kellogg (1)

* This material first appeared in *Et cetera* Vol. 48, No. 2: 136-140. 1991.

and Kellogg and Bourland (2) stress that complete elimination of all forms of "to be" is the only satisfactory way to obtain maximal benefits. Some of these benefits were listed by Bourland (3), who stated that E-Prime (a) diminishes the ease of asking "meaninglessly" abstract questions such as "What is art?"; (b) makes it harder to frame internal and external "pigeonhole labeling" such as "I am a failure" and "She is Italian"; (c) eliminates use of "to be" forms in abbreviated explanation-dodging expressions such as "It is clear that..." and as a substitute for "equals" in verbal math; and (d) discourages the passive voice by forcing either identification or admitted ignorance of the role player. Claims are also made (1, 2) that E-Prime improves creativity, and that it helps in controlling semantic and signal reactions, especially when one speaks and thinks in it.

Probably not many people would object to these arguments. Nevertheless, I think we would be ill-advised to relinquish the full array of our language, flawed with "to be" and riddled with the passive though it is. Even though careless use of dynamite can kill, the explosive has not been banned; instead, people have chosen to learn its dangers and proper use. Rather than taking the axe to our rich language, let us learn (as we should have learned from our English teachers) how to use it optimally. This kind of optimum English I would call E-Choice (Note 1). Scientists are not often considered great writers, but they have evolved a way to write, in whatever language, that conveys necessary information with a minimum of ambiguity. In general, tentative conclusions and speculations are easy to recognize. In English, this style would be a form of E-Choice, exhibiting clarity and sometimes even gracefulness.

Before expressing structural opinions about E-Prime, I begin with a problem that it shares with many ideas proposed under the general semantics umbrella, namely that presumed benefits are rarely demonstrated except on an anecdotal level. Such demonstration, with even the crudest of quantification, would seem useful and perhaps even convincing when presenting E-Prime for acceptance to the large and varied world of English speakers. Enthusiasts (and I am one) tend to advocate general semantics for ameliorating a host of personal and interpersonal problems that are supposed to arise from our outmoded verbal baggage, with little or no evidence that they work. For a group that claims to be so strongly wedded to science, why don't we gather some hard data? (Note 2). Similarly, I agree with the premises of E-Prime given in the second paragraph, mainly because they seem reasonable, not because I have anything more than personal anecdotal experience to go on. I have convinced myself that general semantics has had a salutary effect in moderating my own behavior, but I know others knowledgeable in it who seem to have absorbed nothing — am I deluding myself? Where is our evidence? (Note 3).

Undesirable occurrences of "to be" appear to arise most often from abstraction mismatching, especially when a leading (subject) noun is equated to a noun of higher abstraction through an "is of identity," or when it is described by an adjectival construction of higher abstraction through an "is of predication." For example, in the sentence "John is a farmer," the word "farmer" is more abstract than "John," since the name presumably refers to a particular individual, whereas "farmer" represents a more general class. Hence, we are not unambiguously defining John by this construction. On the other hand, saying "That farmer's name is John" offers no problems of definition, once who "that farmer" is is understood. Similarly, "That painting is beautiful" predicates description in terms of a high-level abstraction, one that may or may not elicit sympathetic agreement. Recasting into "I think that painting is beautiful" equalizes the abstractions by reduction to internal dialogue, and is therefore not as subject to dispute. An alternative, should retention of an abstraction such as "beautiful" be desired, might be "Most would agree that this painting is beautiful."

I doubt that the above examples, and thousands like them, are likely to cause much confusion or disagreement. Such may not be the case with a statement like "Most blacks are untrustworthy, so I don't think we should approve this loan." This statement reflects an attitude that seems unlikely to depend much on the language chosen, or in particular on the "are." Rather, it involves "allness" and ethnocentric attitudes that could just as well have been expressed in E-Prime,

"Blacks have criminal tendencies, so..." Returning to the second paragraph of this article, it would seem naive and unjustified in the absence of contrary evidence to think that E-Prime could be of more than slight benefit in the "really big" problems that face modern overpopulated societies.

I do not wish to underplay the problems our antiquated language can create, but I do think the solutions are much more likely to be found in our learning to use (or, rather, not misuse) the language we have than in excising any particular parts of it in hopes of curing our communications-related ills. Part of the difficulty, if not most of it, lies in the nearly total ignorance of science, its methods, and its processes on the part of almost all the people of this earth. I say almost all because I doubt that more than a few million (this is purely a guess) might, from training or experience, have an accurate idea of what is involved in writing an acceptable scientific paper, designing an experiment, or describing and explaining a scientific procedure. In my experience as a practicing scientist, most people I know have little or no idea of the process of science, which makes them susceptible to whatever a media report or a self-styled "expert" may say. Aside from those ignorant of science merely through lack of training and interest, we sometimes see another group (often, unfortunately, associated with the arts), taking a pridefully ignorant anti-science position, based on the perceived "evils" science has wrought. Attempts at describing science in terms of a process to improve knowledge of our world, rather than the misuse sometimes made of technology by political and business interests, will often go unheard.

The language of science, including the verb "to be," has performed ably for a long time. The passive voice, deeply beloved by most scientific writers, persists in spite of generations of editorial assistants who have tried to discourage it (Note 4). Dogmatic statements are avoided by frequent use of "weasel words" such as "probably," "the data suggest," "in the author's opinion," etc. Scientists seldom use unqualified "is" verbs to equate a lower to a higher abstraction, just as they generally avoid highly abstract terms (e.g. "truth") altogether. Historically, however, such remarks have challenged the scientific community. For instance, taking an example from a recent E-Prime article by Wilson (4), I can assert that no contemporary physicist would utter absolutisms such as "The electron is a particle," or "The electron is a wave." However, such statements a century ago were part of a controversy that stimulated the most sweeping revolution ever seen in physics. It seems likely that Aristotelian thought stultified scholarship for 2000 years not because it codified the wrong definitions, but because a hundred generations of "thinkers" allowed themselves to remain so ignorant of the world around them that they would believe nearly anything. The situation is not much different today among those who choose to remain ignorant of science.

Although E-Prime can be a useful pedagogic tool to force extreme attention on the verb "to be," it seems quixotic to expect it to be widely accepted. E-Choice, by contrast, retains ordinary English, including "to be" in all its forms, but stresses the dangers of equating, by any construction, differing abstraction levels. Wider knowledge of science and its methods should help discourage the making and accepting of absolute statements and absurd abstractions, but the likelihood that many more people will gain such knowledge seems remote. It is a major aim of general semantics to encourage people to apply the language and thought processes of science to their own lives and problems; thus, even in the absence of extensive knowledge of science, a thorough understanding (and reduction to practice) of general semantics may circumvent language-originated problems and promote clearer thinking. We don't need to drastically alter the language, but we do need to maintain a watchful consciousness of our use and interpretation of it.

NOTES

1. As readers may surmise, the name E-Choice arose from the strained similarity between the term E-Prime and a USDA meat grade. I would hope it survives only in this article. After all, E-Choice is just English as we know it, expressed through a general semantics filter.

2. Bourland (3) counted the number of occurrences of sentences containing identity and predication uses of "to be" in various well-known documents, and attempted to show that on the basis of lower counts,

the U.S. Constitution has "great flexibility and power" compared to, say, the "rigid dogmatism" of Aristotle's *Politics*. This kind of quantification is probably specious, since one can find numerous examples of seminal scientific works that have very high identity and predication counts: Darwin's *Origin of Species*, and Watson and Crick's paper on DNA, to mention only two.

3. The kind of quantitative evidence needed to substantiate general semantics claims might involve at minimum the following of control and "treated" groups for a number of years, statistically sampling such indicators as divorce rate, drug abuse, job turnover, salary, criminal involvement, medical history, etc.

4. When I use the passive voice to say "The flask was heated to 100°C," I could hardly imagine any reader wanting to know who did the heating. In this way, the passive is a useful shorthand. In addition, certain nuances are unique to the passive and cannot quite be said otherwise (short of absurd circumlocutions): "I was born in 1929." Another usage difficult to restate in E-Prime includes progressive forms: "The motor is running."

REFERENCES

1. Kellogg, E.W., III, "Speaking in E-Prime," *Et cetera* 44(2):118-128 (1987).
2. Kellogg, E.W.,III and D.David Bourland, Jr., "Working with E-Prime: Some Practical Notes," *Et cetera* 47(4):376-392 (1990).
3. Bourland, D. David, Jr., "To Be or Not To Be: E-Prime as a Tool for Critical Thinking," *Et cetera* 46(3):202-211 (1989).
4. Wilson, Robert Anton, "Toward Understanding E-Prime," *Et cetera* 46(4):316-319 (1989).

"Able equalled I ere I dellauqe Elba."

— NAPOLEON PRIME*

SCHNAPPS RIDES AGAIN:

Reply to a Paper

D. David Bourland, Jr. **by Emory Menefee** †

T HE OTHER DAY, while suffering from the grippe, I muttered
that I felt sick as a dog.

Schnapps, the alert, over-achieving Dachshund (1, 2) replied, "How odd: I feel sick as a human." With ferocious
control I managed to keep from arguing the point, lest he
prove it by de-lunching.

Actually, the little fellow looked pretty good. When we
recently received our March, 1991, copy of *The Map* (monthly
newsletter for the San Francisco Chapter of the International
Society for General Semantics), we learned that the meeting
scheduled for 22 March would feature a paper on "Some Objections to E-Prime" by James French, and one on "E-Prime or
E-Choice" by Emory Menefee. Schnapps particularly wanted
to see what Emory did with his topic, since editor Bob Wanderer advertised it as "apparently an attempt to get to the
'meat' of the issue and find out what the 'beef' is [Wanderer's
verb]." Schnapps commented that he felt ready to handle
some of that meat and beef stuff.

---

* Since Menefee's paper began with a fine palindrome, we felt we should
provide one also. More or less.
† This material first appeared in *Et cetera* Vol. 48, No. 3: 292-295. 1991.

He had started training to get in shape for a good analysis on one or both of those papers. Of course he began by reviewing most of the literature on E-Prime. (3-8) Nonelementalistically, he also worked on the physical training side: The push-ups went very well — look, he only had two inches to go — but the sit-ups almost did him in. He has nagged me for some time to get him a Dachshund-sized Abdominizer similar to the one he saw advertised on Cable TV. Sounds like a special-order item to me.

Finally we received a copy of Menefee's paper. After pawing through it carefully, Schnapps sighed and then said, "Well, Bourland, it looks to me as if Menefee *has* you...dead to rights, whatever *that* 'means.' Never mind the facts that E-Prime (i) seriously reduces identification and predication constructions, and (ii) stops most of the elementalism fostered by the passive voice. (Note 1) And never mind the fact that (iii) by 'listening in E-Prime' (8) one may accomplish a beneficially delayed reaction. The basic fact remains: *E-Prime does not solve all language problems.* How remiss of you! At *your* age, how callow! Better that you just forget about the whole thing.

"And how could you ever have imagined that E-Prime might become widely accepted? You can tilt at windmills if you wish, but I refuse to gain enough weight to serve as a proper Sancho Panza. Somehow I don't recall your ever suggesting that, however.

"Who could quarrel with Menefee's clarion call for 'hard data' to demonstrate the actual effectiveness of general semantics? Of course, he may simply not have heard of a considerable amount of such material. (Note 2)

"Furthermore, you really should calm down, delay your reactions etc., concerning the material in Menefee's Note 2. He does not exactly qualify as a borderline dyslexic just because he couldn't follow your discussion of political documents. (7) Of *course* your material has nothing to do with seminal works in various sciences, but who cares? I, for one, think Menefee tried to run a welcome joke in there, mudslinging with 'specious' and invoking Darwin's great book in the same sentence.

"As Menefee so astutely points out in his final ringing paragraph, 'It is a major aim of general semantics to encourage people to apply the language and thought processes of science to their own lives and problems; thus, even in the absence of extensive knowledge of science, a thorough understanding (and reduction to practice) of general semantics may circumvent language-oriented problems and promote clearer thinking.' There you *have* it, in a nut shell. Wonder why it took Alfred Korzybski almost 900 pages to make that point? (9)

"It seems clear to me that some of you students of general semantics get lost messing about with the extensional devices (including E-Prime), training people in the mysteries of the Structural Differential, nattering about non-Aristotelian laws, multiordinality, undefined terms, and what not. People in — may I say it? — the *real* world just want Lieutenant Semantics: a little genuflection toward the map-territory analogy, and then one can sweep off to safer areas of talking about some aspect of science. As I have pointed out before, (2) if really pressed, we can discuss...not *non*-identity, but just a *little bit* of identity; not *non*-allness, but just a *little bit* of allness. Then, to round matters out, we could address the consequences not of *self*-reflexiveness, but *sort-of*-reflexiveness.

"Actually, I feel sorry for you, Bourland, knowing as I do that having stumbled around for over 40 years with E-Prime, which leaves all kinds of problems unsolved, you also did try to work on A-Choice, B-Choice, C-Choice, and D-Choice. Thanks to Menefee, we now know how close you came." (Note 3)

At that point Schnapps trotted off, his tail tracing a jaunty arc, humming to himself, "I've Got Friends in Low Places."

NOTES

1. See Menefee's Note 4: "When I use the passive voice to say 'The flask was heated to 100° C,' I could hardly imagine any reader wanting to know who did the heating." Bad timing, Menefee! Let us consider research in the field of genetics these days. If Dr. Margot O'Toole did

the heating, we might believe her. On the other hand, if Dr. Thereza Imanishi-Kari did it, we might *not* believe her, even if Nobel laureate David Baltimore confirmed her reading. See *Time* magazine for April 1, 1991, page 65. But of course such trivia really have nothing to do with the issue of the passive voice in science and elsewhere. The important matter concerns elementalism, almost always implicit in the passive voice, which makes it not only possible but even proper to suppress role-players and hence conceal, inadvertently or not, *who* did *what*.

2. In "E-Prime or E-Choice" we only find citations of material that appeared in *Et cetera*. As admirable as we regard that publication, occasionally one must also recognize the existence of another journal in the field: the *General Semantics Bulletin*. In addition, since 1935 we have had available the proceedings of various conferences, dissertations, monographs, etc., that have reported on the time-binding efforts of workers in the field of general semantics. A careful reading of the literature over the years will in fact show a considerable amount of "hard evidence" supporting the "salutary effects" general semantics has had on "moderating behavior." Menefee's call for more than anecdotal support for the "presumed benefits" provided by general semantics seems quite appropriate — if written in the 1940s. Specific comments on the role of general semantics in preventive psychiatry and as an adjunct to other psychotherapeutic procedures had received considerable attention by the end of the 1940s. Papers by Douglas G. Campbell (e.g., 10) and Korzybski himself (e.g., 11) provide outstanding examples. The most definitive paper confirming the utility of general semantics along these lines, in the writer's opinion, consists of Douglas M. Kelley's report of his treatment of neurotic soldiers during World War II. (12) For a random sample of other pertinent research, we refer Menefee and other interested parties to papers and monographs by Brown (13), Lauer (14), Leskow (15), Livingston (16), Moore (17), Ralph (18), and True (19). For a comprehensive run-down on one part of current research pertaining to general semantics, see Johnson's fine summary of graduate research. (20) To suggest, as Menefee does in his Note 3, that the "claims of general semantics" remain unsubstantiated merely documents the extensive educational efforts that await his pleasure.

3. Thank you, Victor Borge.

REFERENCES

1. D. David Bourland, Jr. "A Note on Paradogs," *Et cetera: A Review of General Semantics* 46(4): 322-323 (1989).
2. D. David Bourland, Jr. Correspondence, *Et cetera: A Review of General Semantics* 47(3): 283-285 (1990).
3. D. David Bourland, Jr. "A Linguistic Note: Writing in E-Prime," *General Semantics Bulletin* 32/33: 111-114 (1965/1966).
4. D. David Bourland, Jr. "The Semantics of a Non-Aristotelian Language," *General Semantics Bulletin* 35: 60-63 (1968).
5. D. David Bourland, Jr. "The Language of E-Prime," in Donald E. Washburn and Dennis R. Smith, eds., *Coping With Increasing Complexity*, pp. 88-104. New York: Gordon & Breach (1974).
6. E. W. Kellogg, III. "Speaking in E-Prime," *Et cetera: A Review of General Semantics* 44(2): 118-128 (1987).
7. D. David Bourland, Jr. "To Be or Not To Be: E-Prime as a Tool for Critical Thinking," in Kenneth G. Johnson, ed., *Thinking Creatically*, pp. 61-90. Englewood, N. J.: Institute of General Semantics (1991). A preliminary version of this paper appeared in *Et cetera: A Review of General Semantics* 46(3): 118-128 (1989).
8. E. W. Kellogg, III, and D. David Bourland, Jr. "Working With E-Prime: Some Practical Notes," *Et cetera: A Review of General Semantics* 47(4): 376-392 (1990).
9. Alfred Korzybski. *Science and Sanity: An Introduction to Non-Aristotelian Systems and General Semantics* (1933). Englewood, N. J.: Institute of General Semantics, Fourth Edition, 1958.
10. Douglas G. Campbell. "Neuropsychiatric Foundations and Clinical Applications of General Semantics," in M. Kendig, ed., *Papers from the Second American Congress on General Semantics*. Chicago: Institute of General Semantics (1943).
11. Alfred Korzybski. "A Veteran's Re-adjustment and Extensional Methods," *Et cetera: A Review of General Semantics* 3(2): 254-264 (1946).
12. Douglas M. Kelley. "The Use of General Semantics and Korzybskian Principles as an Extensional Method of Group Psychotherapy in Traumatic Neuroses," *Journal of Nervous and Mental Disease* 114(3) (1951).
13. Dona M. Brown. "The Use of General Semantics in Teaching Eighth Grade Language Skills," in M. Kendig, ed., *Papers from the Second*

American Congress on General Semantics. Chicago: Institute of General Semantics (1943).

14. Rachel M. Lauer. "Effects of a General Semantics Course Upon Some Fifth Grade Children," *General Semantics Bulletin* 30/31: 106-112 (1963/1964).

15. Sonia Leskow. "The Use of General Semantics in the Motivation of a Select Group of High School Students," *General Semantics Bulletin* 8/9: 81-86 (1952).

16. Howard F. Livingston. "The Effects of Instruction in General Semantics on the Reading of Poetry," in Lee Thayer, ed., *Communication: General Semantics Perspectives* pp. 123-126. New York: Spartan Books (1970).

17. Robert H. Moore. *Alienation in College Students: A Rational and Semantic Analysis*. Ph.D. dissertation. Tallahassee, Fl.: Walden University (1977).

18. Ruth S. Ralph. "The Effects of General Semantics on the Personality Adjustment of Elementary School Children," *Et cetera: A Review of General Semantics* 29(1) (1972). Abridged Ph.D. dissertation.

19. Sally Ralston True. "A Study of the Relation of General Semantics and Creativity," *General Semantics Bulletin* 30/31: 100-105 (1963/1964).

20. Kenneth G. Johnson. *Graduate Research in General Semantics*. Englewood, N. J.: Institute of General Semantics (1985).

REPLY₂ TO A PAPER

E. W. Kellogg III   ***BY EMORY MENEFEE*** *

To the Editor:

Like a dog of increasing notoriety, I too have a bone or two to pick with Emory Menefee, the author of "E-Prime or E-Choice?" (1) First, I felt a trifle annoyed that Dr. Menefee would write that "...Kellogg and Bourland stress that complete elimination of all forms of 'to be' *IS* the only satisfactory way to obtain maximal benefits" (emphasis mine). Obviously, E-Prime adepts such as ourselves would not hold such an absolutistic, "is of identity," and Aristotelian point of view! If Dr. Menefee's summary statement of our view in this regard exemplifies "E-Choice" in action by an accomplished general semanticist, I shudder to think what it might do in less competent hands. Compare this statement to one we've actually written: "Although a less extreme form of E-Prime that allows for an occasional use of 'is' would probably accomplish the same goals, we have yet to see anyone accomplish this." (2) And we still have yet to see anyone accomplish this. Although I agree with Dr. Menefee that it might seem quixotic to expect E-Prime to find wide acceptance, such an objection

---

* This paper first appeared in *Et cetera* Vol. 48, No. 3: 296-298. 1991.

13

misses the main point of E-Prime as a discipline — the salubrious effects that it can have on the writing, speaking, and "thinking" of the individual who uses it. Unlike Esperanto, E-Prime can actually facilitate and enrich the communicating process between the practitioner and the ordinary and unprepared English speaker. Once mastered, one can write and speak in E-Prime without making oneself noticeable in any way other than through clarity of expression. Briefly put, I do not see the future success of E-Prime as depending upon its wide acceptance, but upon its adoption by individuals who use it because of its practical value in their daily lives.

I too, like Dr. Menefee, would welcome a series of well controlled, well-funded, studies into the effects of general semantics training, including the effects of learning to write and speak in E-Prime. As Schnapps and Bourland have pointed out (3) numerous studies on the effects of general semantics training do exist. Unfortunately, one can characterize only a few of these studies as "well-controlled" by today's standards, and almost none of them as "well-funded"! The experimental investigation of general semantics principles and training procedures *per se* has proved of little interest in the past to the funding agencies and mainstream scientists capable of carrying out such work, and I doubt that this will change anytime soon.

However, rather than limiting ourselves to studies that specifically mention general semantics, let's take a more non-Aristotelian approach towards the problem of finding "hard data." Thousands of articles reporting on psychophysiological research appear yearly on subjects relevant to the concerns of general semantics in reputable scientific journals. In fact, many journals devote themselves exclusively to the reporting of scientific research into the mind-body-environment field. Terms such as mind-body, psychosomatic, psychoneuroimmunology, unknown or rarely used in Korzybski's time have gained acceptance in both the scientific and cultural milieu. I would guess that even general semanticists with a predilection for "hard data" will find much of interest there.

For example, although to my knowledge no one has yet investigated the effect of E-Prime *per se* on creativity, Dr.

Ellen Langer of Harvard reported (4) an enhancement of problem-solving ability when participants used objects defined conditionally instead of unconditionally: e.g. "this *could be* a pen" rather than "this *is* a pen." Obviously, such a study brings at least some experimental verification to Korzybski's warning concerning the "is of identity," and as such to the theory behind E-Prime as well. Until general semanticists (or perhaps a few of the future recipients of General Semantics Research Scholarships) have exhaustively searched the psychological and psychophysiological scientific literature, it seems premature to talk about the scarcity of hard data supporting the practices and principles of general semantics.

Finally, I heartily agree with Dr. Menefee's concluding statement, where he writes that "We don't need to drastically alter the language, but we do need to maintain a watchful consciousness of our use and interpretation of it." However, rather than "taking an axe"(!) to the English language as Menefee asserts, in my experience E-Prime simply brings about a little much needed pruning. Further, in achieving such a "watchful consciousness" I have found nothing as effective as the practice of E-Prime. In fact, I sometimes believe that the increased mindfulness of language that the effort of speaking, thinking, and listening in E-Prime brings may in the end prove more valuable to me than its more straightforward semantic benefits. In summary, after due consideration of the arguments presented in the article "E-Prime or E-Choice?," I choose E-Prime. And after due consideration of his article overall, I think Dr. Menefee should also.

E. W. KELLOGG III
ASHLAND, OREGON

REFERENCES

1. Emory Menefee, "E-Prime or E-Choice?," *Et cetera* 48(2): 136-140 (1990).
2. E. W. Kellogg III and D. David Bourland Jr., "Working with E Prime: Some Practical Notes," *Et cetera* 47(4): 376-392 (1990).
3. D. David Bourland, Jr., "Schnapps Rides Again: Reply to a Paper by Emory Menefee," *Et cetera* 48(3): 292-295 (1991).
4. E. Langer and A. Piper, "The Prevention of Mindlessness", *Journal of Personality and Social Psychology* 53:280-287 (1987), also recounted by Dr. Langer in her excellent book, *Mindfulness*, (New York: Addison-Wesley, 1989).

E-PRIME, E-CHOICE

Earl Hautala **AND CHOOSING** *

To the Editor:

Korzybski's epistemological system aimed at "consciousness of abstracting." He chose "science$_{1933}$" as his metaphysics. Clever fellow, Korzybski. Using science as his metaphysics allowed him to get on with the business of analyzing language without explaining the things he knew nothing about. He had only to point to what others could perceive and attach an appropriate label to it.

This form of epistemology could resolve differences in observation. Korzybski chose to analyze the traditional logic and syntax for the language(s) as the source of our difficulties in communication. Scientists had discovered the space-time continuum in which no two events occurred simultaneously. They had established a universe of energetic atoms where no item remained unchanged. The structure of the language demanded static things. People only think they can see static things because they fail to focus on the details made evident by scientific discovery.

A consciousness of abstracting requires the denial of identity, if one chooses to put into practice the postulates of Korzybskian metaphysics. That overturns Aristotelian logic, which demands static entities to keep the subjects of propositions in their proper place. At the most fundamental level Aristotelian logic confused propositions and logical functions.

* This material first appeared in *Et cetera* Vol. 48, No. 3: 298-299. 1991.

17

An observer standing in a pasture says: "That is a horse." The "that" refers to the physical thing and "horse" applies the label. Following Aristotle's lead he may then say: "That horse is that horse." Simplifying: "Horse is horse," "Have is Have," and finally by generalizing and abstracting "A is A."

Those trained in the use of E-Prime might say something like: "You can't say things like that." Obviously people can and do generate propositions that fall into the form of "A is A." Demanding or even suggesting that people change their speech patterns has quixotic overtones. Surely anyone who actively promotes the cause of E-Prime in daily discourse has something funny going on in his or her head. Perhaps we need to try a different approach. Would Korzybski have said, "When you say things like that (A is A) you fail to operate at a level which reflects consciousness of abstracting"?

The average person simply won't understand the statement. General semanticists, perhaps more aware of the pitfalls of ordinary communication, tend to say less. Those who choose to express some thought may do so by cloaking it in the jargon of general semantics. Those not familiar with the terminology find general semanticists clannish members of a group who speak a strange, secret language. Generalizing from these two examples, I would conclude that attempts to promote E-Prime may lead to undesired consequences.

E-Choice allows more latitude and promotes the spirit in which general semantics has carried on for years. We don't demand that everyone recognize general semantics, but for those individuals who have chosen to do so, it seems to have some benefits. E-Choice has at least one major drawback. People may not try hard enough to make E-Prime function. It requires daily effort to compose sentences in E-Prime. Like the learning of any foreign language, it takes a long time before the student begins to think in the language. E-Prime allows a student of general semantics to say certain things without using the jargon of general semantics and without losing sight of the goal, "consciousness of abstracting."

EARL HAUTALA
MARTINEZ, CALIFORNIA

EMORY MENEFEE'S REPLY TO
D. DAVID BOURLAND,
E. W. KELLOGG III,
EMORY MENEFEE # AND EARL HAUTALA *

G ENERAL SEMANTICS on the march! Perhaps we should extend Korzybski's five extensional devices to include David Bourland's: impersonally communicating in the name of
a dog. While framing the following remarks, I thought of
asking my daughter Andrea's cat, Mr. Itchy, to stand in for
me, but I expect he would just turn tail.

I appreciate E. W. Kellogg's thoughtful remarks, with
which I largely agree, though I must still assert that he and
Bourland have advocated complete elimination of all forms
of the verb "to be." In his and Bourland's article, we find:
"But why go to the extreme of trying to eliminate it [forms of
'to be'] totally? Because for better or worse, it looks as if only
an all-or-nothing approach to this problem works successful-
ly." (2)

Contrary to the implications in Bourland's remarks, I am
not hostile to E-Prime. Instead, I agree with the tenor of Earl
Hautala's remarks: Let them as wants it do it. My disagreement is primarily with the claims made for E-Prime. General
semantics needs an expanded role and membership for its
survival, and I believe that we can be more convincing if we
are fully accepted in academic and scholarly communities.

* This material first appeared in Et cetera Vol. 48, No. 3: 299-301. 1991.

19

One way to expedite this is by backing up our assertions with evidence presented in refereed journals. This might help counter such negative attitudes as recently expressed by Anderson, who characterized general semantics and general systems theory as "premature and intellectually lightweight." (1)

My lament about the lack of hard data regarding the efficacy of general semantics explicitly referred to long-term effects. There is no dearth of short-range evidence, though some may question procedures and analysis used to draw conclusions. Before-and-after test scores abound for students taking general semantics courses; other instances are given in Bourland's useful list of references. I confess to not having read or even seen all of these, but those I have examined appear to refer to short-range benefits, which I have no reason or evidence to dispute. I would, however, like to know what happened in later years to Kelley's soldiers, to Fleishman's street fighters, etc. In my view, general semantics needs to demonstrate some beneficial long-term alteration of behavior, or else we may deserve to be called "intellectually lightweight." For example, if a claim is made for increased creativity using E-Prime, then we need not only a measure for creativity but data to support the assertion; since creativity is unlikely to be defined from a one-shot affair, the data should probably extend for some years. Abundant accepted methodology exists for quantitatively assessing behavioral change.

Finally, referring to Bourland's Note 1, do I detect a trace of allness in this comment? Perhaps Aristotle had in mind the overwhelming majority of scrupulously honest scientists when he said that one swallow does not make a summer (nor, I might add, should it be expected to quench one's thirst).

REFERENCES

1. P. W. Anderson, "Is Complexity Physics? Is It Science? What Is It?," *Physics Today*, 44(7): 9-11 (1991).
2. E. W. Kellogg III and D. David Bourland, Jr., "Working with E-Prime: Some Practical Notes," *Et cetera* 46(4): 376-92 (Winter 1990).

Part One:

THE FIRST E-PRIME SYMPOSIUM

THE E-PRIME CONTROVERSY:
A Symposium

PREFACE

Attack on the Killer Be's

P HILOSOPHERS HAVE MADE a to-do over "to be" (and its cognate forms) long before such twentieth century un-Be-witchers as George Santayana, Bertrand Russell, I. A. Richards, and Alfred Korzybski began their campaigns against the Be-fuddlement of the human species. Raymond Gozzi informs us of an ancient "patron saint" of E-Prime, one Lycophron, a pupil of the rhetorician Gorgias (483?-376? B.C.E.), the antagonist of Plato's dialogue of the same name. According to Mr. Gozzi:

> Lycophron apparently grew tired of the endless Greek philosophizing about the existence of things we can only talk about, and became convinced that the verb "to be" misled people into positing the existence of non-existent verbal entities. As Gomperz [Theodore Gomperz, *Greek Thinkers*, Vol. 1. London: John Murray, 1901] put it, Lycophron felt that philosophers confused the use of "to be" as a copula and as [a predicator of] existence. His response was to avoid all use of "to be."

> Raymond Gozzi
> (Personal Communication)

"To be" continues to Be-devil the semantically sensitive. Their numbers have recently increased as a result of Cullen Murphy's *Atlantic Monthly* article (reprinted herein) and stories on National Public Radio, the Canadian Broadcasting Corporation, and elsewhere. As one might expect, some mistaken notions regarding E-Prime and general semantics appeared in the media melee. For example, Joel Achenbach, writing for the *Washington Post*, claimed that "there is an entire movement, many decades old, to eradicate 'to be' from the language. The movement, described in the *Atlantic Monthly*, is called 'general semantics,' and one of its tenets is that 'to be' is dangerous."

Kierkegaard, Sartre or Hamlet might indeed have claimed "that 'to be' is dangerous." But I haven't seen the list that includes the particular tenet Mr. Achenbach mentions, and I doubt if it would appear on any canonic semantic list in such a delightfully self-subverting form.

Perhaps E-Prime has had its fifteen minutes of fame and only a few grammarians, philosophers, and semanticists will maintain an interest in it. The verdict of E-Prime's severest critics may prevail, and historians will relegate E-Prime to a footnote referring to it as a cognitive-linguistic cul-de-sac. On the other hand, its advocates, whose writings indicate a profound knowledge of many hidden factors distorting human understanding, may indeed properly claim the attention of those seeking fruitful paths toward the realization of human potentialities.

The authors who participated in this issue's symposium certainly haven't answered all questions regarding the merits of E-Prime. However, with backgrounds in linguistics, physics, art, education, therapy, etc., they do offer us an intriguing intellectual excursion.

JEREMY KLEIN
EDITOR, *ET CETERA*

"TO BE" IN THEIR BONNETS

Cullen Murphy* *A Matter of Semantics* †

A FEW DAYS AGO I opened up a recent issue (Volume 48, Number 2) of *Et cetera*, the quarterly journal of the International Society for General Semantics, and within a few minutes of doing so got a bit of a surprise. The surprise came from an article by Emory Menefee, a former president of the ISGS, which bluntly calls into question attempts by many society members to promote something called E-Prime, a form of English that has for years ranked extremely high among the interests of the general semantics community. Advocates of E-Prime, for reasons that I'll come to, favor the elimination in English of every form of the verb "to be" — *be, been, is, am, are, was, were, 'm, 's, 're*, and all the rest. They not only promote E-Prime as a theoretical proposition but also try in daily life to erase *to be* and its inflections from everything they write. The most committed advocates use E-Prime even when they talk. Given all this, to see the E-Prime endeavor

* Cullen Murphy, the managing editor of *The Atlantic Monthly*, writes the weekly *Prince Valiant* cartoon. His father draws the strip.
† Reprinted from *The Atlantic Monthly*, February, 1992. Copyright © 1992, by The Atlantic Monthly Company. This article will appear in *Just Curious* a collection of essays by Cullen Murphy planned for publication by Houghton Mifflin Company as a Peter Davison Book in early 1995. Copyright © 1992 by Cullen Murphy. Included by permission of the author and the publisher.

25

criticized in an official organ — to see that endeavor, indeed, termed "quixotic" — naturally raised an eyebrow. When I queried the International Society for General Semantics about the matter, the executive director, Paul Dennithorne Johnston, assured me that the society never did, and does not now, regard E-Prime as tantamount to some sort of "party line." Well, fine. But it has strong support among the *nomenklatura*, and I do not expect them to hold their peace.

General semantics originated in the work of a Polish engineer, Alfred Korzybski, who first spelled out his ideas about language and other symbolic structures in 1933 in his book *Science and Sanity*. Korzybski had come to the United States in 1915 and eventually became a citizen. In 1938 he established the Institute of General Semantics in Chicago. The institute moved to Lime Rock, Connecticut, late in 1946. (The field has two journals. In 1943 a student of Korzybski's, the noted semanticist and one-term U.S. Senator S. I. Hayakawa, founded *Et cetera*, which currently has about 2,500 subscribers. Korzybski's associate M. Kendig founded the *General Semantics Bulletin* in 1950.) Explanations of general semantics can become pretty elaborate pretty fast, but the basic idea sounds simple enough. Most of us think of language as something that reflects reality or at least allows us to express our perceptions of reality. Without denying this, general semanticists believe that the very structure of language can influence or distort our perceptions, and they contend that a failure to observe the many ways in which language can do this results in an inability to apprehend the meaning not only of other people's words but of one's own words as well. This, of course, causes problems, the size of which can range from the most minor misunderstanding to complete metaphysical disarray, and the problems, naturally, spill over into the realm of behavior. Korzybski himself took a grave view of the actual and potential consequences of "semantic damage." Semanticists observe, tellingly, that the carnage of the First World War powerfully catalyzed Korzybski's thinking.

General semantics over the years has taken up a diverse array of subjects touching on language — for example, doublespeak, logic, newspaper headlines, nonverbal communication, objectivity, cultural relativism, euphemism, metaphor — but through it all the verb *to be* has remained a core of concern. That many people in the field, including Korzybski, would zero in on this verb strikes one, in retrospect, as entirely predictable; after all, philosophers had called attention to its problematic character at least as early as the seventeenth century, and their uneasiness had not let up by the twentieth. "The little word *is* has its tragedies," George Santayana wrote in 1923, in a passage that general semanticists quote frequently and fondly.

> It names and identifies different things with the greatest innocence; and yet no two are ever identical, and if therein lies the charm of wedding them and calling them one, therein, too, lies the danger. Whenever I use the word *is*, except in sheer tautology, I deeply misuse it; and when I discover my error, the world seems to fall asunder....

Santayana's complaint had to do with locutions like "Mary is a woman" and "Mary is cold," in which the verb *is* implies the tight coupling of equivalent things, whereas in fact in the first instance it joins nouns that have different levels of abstraction and in the second instance joins a noun to an adjective that neither completely nor permanently qualifies it. Transgressions like these may seem trivial, but in fact they pose fundamental problems of logic, and they greatly bother critical thinkers.

To these sins of the verb *to be* semanticists have added many others. For example, the verb makes possible the widespread use of the passive voice, conditioning us to accept detours around crucial issues of causality ("Mistakes were made"). It makes possible the raising of unanswerable, because hopelessly formulated, questions ("What is truth"?). It makes possible, too, the construction of a variety of phrases ("As is well known ...") that casually sweep reasoning under a rug. One also finds the verb *to be* pressed into service on behalf of stereotypical labeling ("Scotsmen are stingy") and overbroad existential generalization ("I'm just no good"). These issues aside, semanticists say, the verb *to be*, broadly speaking, imputes an Aristotelian neatness, rigidity, and permanence to the world around us and to the relationships among all the things in it — conditions that rarely have any basis in a dynamic reality.

Although Korzybski and others fashioned an indictment of *to be* relatively early in the history of general semantics, the idea of actually getting rid of the verb dates back only to the late 1940s, when it occurred to D. David Bourland, Jr., at that time a Korzybski fellow at Lime Rock. Bourland first used his writing system, which he called E-Prime (*E'*), in an article, "Introduction to a Structural Calculus: A Postulational Statement of Alfred Korzybski's Non-Aristotelian Linguistic System," that appeared without fanfare in the *General Semantics Bulletin* in 1952. (He derived the term "E-Prime" from the equation $E' = E - e$, where E represents standard English and e represents the inflected forms of *to be*.) Bourland would later recall that writing this article left him with "an intermittent, but severe, headache which lasted for about a week." Strange as it may seem, a piece of text in polished E-Prime does not necessarily alert readers to the E-Prime aspect of its character, and Bourland continued to use E-Prime, unnoticed by the outside world, in his work. Indeed, he deliberately took no steps to call wide attention to how he wrote, lest, as he also recalled, "I become regarded as some kind of nut." Eventually, though, a few close friends prevailed upon Bourland to go public, which in a manner of speaking he did, in 1965, with another article in the *General Semantics Bulletin*, this one titled "A Linguistic Note: Writing in E-Prime." Since then E-Prime in its written form has acquired several dozen practitioners within the general semantics community.

As for its oral form, those familiar with E-Prime point to an independent research scientist in Oregon named E. W. Kellogg III as perhaps America's most accomplished E-Prime speaker (the competition consists of three or four other people, including David Bourland), and I decided to give Kellogg a call. I expected to hear someone speaking in a slow and considered manner, as if picking his way uncertainly through a linguistic swamp, but he talked briskly and with what sounded like supreme self-confidence. Yes, he said, he halted a lot when he first started speaking E-Prime, in 1978, and a lot of sentences ended abruptly in the middle when he could see himself running into an *is*. At times he lapsed into a kind of pidgin E-Prime. The transition, in short, took some work. "I had to cope with all that backlog of '*is*-pattern' English," he explained. "And I had to do it in real time." But Kellogg got the hang of it stylistically after a year or so, and he now strives in his speech (as he and others also do in writing) to effect further refinements. These include ridding his vocabulary of instances of absolutism (for example, such words as *always* and *ever*, which imply immutability) and of many nouns made out of verbs (in particular those with a *-tion* ending, such as *visualization* and *procrastination*, which freeze ongoing processes into static events). Kellogg also hopes to reduce his reliance on *have*, which quite often can substitute for *is*, and on other crutches like *appear* and *seem*. "I aim at a more phenomenological ideal," he said. "I try to move towards a language that communicates the territory of my experience to myself and others as clearly and accurately as possible." As we spoke, Kellogg's voice at times gathered a certain momentum, clipped and commanding, comfortable in its fluency. As a salesman for E-Prime, he excelled.

Now back to Emory Menefee, who in his *Et cetera* article makes several arguments against E-Prime and in favor of what he calls E-Choice (a term that, as he good-naturedly acknowledges, "arose from the strained similarity between the term E-Prime and a USDA meat grade"). For one thing, Menefee notes, most general semanticists consider certain uses of *to be* unobjectionable — for example, as an auxiliary verb, or to convey the fact of existence, or to create metaphors. Why throw these uses out? (E-Prime advocates, in reply, make an argument for total abstinence similar to the ones heard with respect to smoking or drinking.) Moreover, Menefee goes on, most of the problems caused by the misuse of *to be* can occur in E-Prime as well, especially if a speaker hasn't internalized all the underlying logic involved; the bloody-minded human cortex can easily work its way around a little obstacle like the proscription of a few words. And in any event, Menefee observes, in the real world E-Prime can never hope to achieve a status other than its present one — as the plaything of a handful of enthusiasts. Menefee concedes, in the end, only that E-Prime may perhaps serve

usefully as a "pedagogic tool to force extreme attention on
the verb 'to be.'"

Anyone wishing to explore the E-Prime issue further can
turn to *Et cetera* itself and to a new collection of essays, titled
To Be or Not, published by the ISGS, in San Francisco. I myself, having seen the intensity that general semanticists can
bring to their work, have no intention of stepping cavalierly
into the maw of this debate. Volume 48, Number 3, of *Et cetera* will, I expect, feature bloody reprisals. And yet, having
used E-Prime for eight paragraphs now, I would venture to
pray that the parties involved could find common ground on
one point. Whether E-Prime deserves to become more or no
more than a pedagogic tool, surely we can all hope that it
might become *at least* a pedagogic tool. Almost all of us tend
to overuse *to be*. E-Prime shows how we overuse it. It forces
one relentlessly to confront sloppiness, laziness, fuzziness,
blandness, imprecision, simplistic generalization, and a half
dozen other all too frequent characteristics of casual prose.
As a self-administered exercise, this single restraint on style,
with all the discomfort that may ensue, offers more real insight in an afternoon than one can gain from a year's worth
of spoken precepts.

And the cost? In my case, a mere headache, severe but intermittent. I have reason to believe it will last about a week.

COMMENTS ON

Joseph L. Stewart* # TO BE OR NOT

MY FIRST ACQUAINTANCE with Dave Bourland goes back to 1949 when the two of us attended back-to-back seminar-workshops under Korzybski, just at the time Bourland was beginning to formulate what eventually became E-Prime. Dave's brain child may well represent the most significant new contribution to general semantics from Korzybski's time to the present. What a shame that he appears to have waited some 15 years before making his work on this known! This time gap becomes obvious when you check the dates of the various articles which make up this collection — from 1965 and 1968 to 1973 followed by a jump to 1987, with the bulk of the articles originally published from that time to the present.

This collection of generally well-written and germane articles serves the reader well in putting most, if not all, currently available papers written on this topic into a single volume. This also results in a great deal of redundancy. *To Be or Not's* (1) repetitions of basic general semantics tenets

---

* Joseph L. Stewart directs the Sensory Disabilities Program for the Indian Health Service in Albuquerque, New Mexico.

may cause the more sophisticated reader to flip through pages that contain new ideas or new interpretations. This would be most unfortunate since many of these restatements and reinterpretations present current and dynamic general semantics applications. Ruskin's paper on semantic problems in systems development serves as a particularly good example.

The many years of effort and the quality of these efforts throughout reflects the refinement necessary to bring a notion such as E-Prime to its present level. I feel that more research into the extensionality of historically durable and revered texts, alluded to briefly in the book, and additional E-Prime analyses along the lines of those presented on pp. 112-113 and Table 4 (p. 118) would have strengthened the overall quality. We need more research and analyses along similar lines.

Given the extent of linguistic bastardization passing as profundity these days, typified by the inundation of bureaucratic-style language, little gems such as the avoidance of "tion" in Ruth Ralph's paper (p. 9) add considerably to the overall volume. If I never hear another word such as "prioritization," for example, I can die a happy man. Ralph puts such usages into perspective in a very clever and readable manner without the hostility I seem to possess.

Not all the chapters provide equal provocation or pleasure but one of the shortest, the two-pager by Scott, merits special mention. Following the book's progression, the Kellogg and Bourland paper creates a nice transition into the more scholarly items which reaches its apex with "To Be Or Not To Be." Kellogg's writing throughout illustrates, to me, how a good idea can be improved upon and made more practical in everyday life.

Bourland's final essay on a non-Aristotelian paradigm for linguistics presents the most scholarly and thought-provoking issues in the book and necessarily requires the greatest amount of time in reading and understanding. While still contemporary, the 1973 date of this piece compels me to ask: "What has Dave done for us lately that demonstrates the depth of his scholarship as well as this does?"

While my contacts with Bourland over the past 40-plus years have been quite intermittent and relatively brief, I have continued to have a great deal of interest in watching the evolution of E-Prime. There is no doubt in my mind of the validity and value of the concept. This book, I hope, will make it better known and more broadly applied.

REFERENCE

1. *To Be or Not: An E-Prime Anthology*, edited by D. David Bourland, Jr. and Paul Dennithorne Johnston, San Francisco: International Society for General Semantics, 1991.

IS IS NOT IS IS NOT IS

WILLIAM DALLMANN* *And Other Thoughts On E-Prime*

I N A LETTER TO *Et cetera* I suggested a modification of E-Prime that I have used for several years: E-Prime$_{mod}$. (1) The **mod** version eliminates the **is** of identification (He is a general semanticist), the **is** of predication (She is beautiful), but retains **is** as an auxiliary (She is dancing), the **is** of existence (To be or not to be), and the denial of identity (The map is not the territory). D. David Bourland Jr., objected to this change from pure E-Prime. (2) Subsequently, others have discussed the pros and cons of E-Prime usage. (3,4)

I propose that we introduce the concept of non-identity to discuss non-identity itself in this context. For the sake of simplicity, let **is**$_1$ represent the **is** of both identity and predication. Let **is**$_2$ and **is**$_3$ represent auxiliary usage and existence respectively. Then **is**$_1$ is not **is**$_2$ and **is**$_2$ is not **is**$_3$. They mean different things; they are not the same word — a concept not unfamiliar to general semanticists.

As we continue to discuss the advantages and "proper" use of E-Prime, perhaps we would do well to remember the basic reason we want to use it in the first place. I conceive of it as a useful tool designed to increase our consciousness of abstracting — specifically, in this case, the perils of identifica-

* William Dallmann edits and publishes *The Intelligencer: A Journal Devoted to the Advancement of Uncommon Sense.*

tion, the pitfalls that entrap us when we confuse levels of abstraction. I think it possible the E-Prime$_{mod}$, which *differentiates* between the various meanings of **is**, may serve some of us even more effectively than pure E-Prime.

I thank David Bourland for his original article on E-Prime. (5) Over the years I have found the extensional devices suggested by Korzybski of greatest value, but they have not increased my awareness of non-identity to the degree that the frequent use of E-Prime has, whether in its pure form or modified. (I consider only practice at the "silent level," e.g., zazen, meditation, etc., more effective than E-Prime at increasing awareness of non-identity.)

In a thoughtful article, Emory Menefee has expressed his concern that we have not scientifically demonstrated the value of E-Prime. (6) I share that concern and would like to believe that one day some brilliant, dedicated person will devise an experiment in this regard that will yield unambiguous results. In the meantime, however, "science" understood in a broader sense can serve us. Wendell Johnson, who introduced me to general semantics through his book, *People in Quandaries*, wrote that "the children of science are from Missouri," and, as a scientifically oriented response to the authoritarian "voice of the Old Man," recommended the probe, "Let's see." (7) So let's see for ourselves the value of E-Prime or E-Prime$_{mod}$ by trying it, by **using** it for an extended period. Personal experience does carry weight; we need not discount it. Menefee makes the important point that we can make some use of the verb **to be** in an aware, responsible manner. (8)

When I first began to use E-Prime back in 1967 I experienced considerable difficulty. As I have said elsewhere, "When I first began to use it I became almost mute. In composing E-Prime sentences I had a feeling similar to that I had when attempting to pass through a mirror maze in a hurry; I would continually experience a shock as I bumped into 'is' just as if I bumped into glass." (9) Eventually, however, I gained some fluency and became highly aware of process in my world, of leaky margins between categories, of duality in the process of classifying, etc.

I think of the biblical narrative of the man, blind from birth, who gains his sight. To the skeptics who questioned him he replied, "...one thing I know, that though I was blind, now I see." (10) In a real sense this man speaks for me and, I suspect, for many others who have seriously experimented with E-Prime, in whatever form.

I cannot pretend that I have as much experience with psychedelics as has Robert Anton Wilson (11), but I have little reason to doubt him when he avers that "a revision of language structure... can alter the brain as dramatically as a psychedelic." (12) The terms "neuro-semantic" and "neuro-linguistic" suggest the relationship between the central nervous system and language structure. J. Samuel Bois, calling our attention to electro-chemical aspects of our make-up, reminded us that "the nervous system of a person who has taken LSD or submitted to electroshock treatment cannot be the same as it was before." (13) In this context he speaks of a "semantic jump," an irreversible revolution in our inner world of ideas and values.

I consistently use E-Prime$_{mod}$ in my writing. (Since April, 1990 I have published a minor journal, *The Intelligencer*, which may qualify as the first journal to use that style, (with the obvious exception of quoted material.) I do not, however, use that discipline in all of my speech, though I do so frequently. Yet I have noticed that when I do violate E-Prime an inner alarm bell rings, a red flag waves, and a voice cautions, "Watch it, man, you've just violated non-identity. Take care!" So I find that Bois' irreversibility factor applies; I cannot view the world as I did before I "ingested" the psychedelic E-Prime.

In a paragraph of uncommon sense, Wendell Johnson reminded us that:

> What is important in all this is not that we do indulge in self-projection or that *to be* is a "bad" word. There are no bad words; there are unfortunate ways of using any word....But the essential thing is *awareness* of projection. We need not always, by any means, express this awareness in so many words out loud or in writing. We can say, "It is a blue cur-

tain," or "It is art," and know quite clearly what we are doing. (14)

As for those who insist on using only pure E-Prime — if
they choose to do so (a la Menefee's "E-Choice" (15)), who
could possibly object?

NOTES AND REFERENCES

1. William Dallmann, "A Letter on E-Prime," *Et cetera* 47, No. 1 (1990): 77-78.
2. D. David Bourland, Jr., "E-Prime: The Debate Continues," *Et cetera* 47, No. 3 (1990): 283-284.
3. E. W. Kellogg III and D. David Bourland, Jr., "Working with E-Prime: Some Practical Notes," *Et cetera* 47, No. 4 (1990-1991).
4. Emory Menefee, "E-Prime or E-Choice?" *Et cetera* 48, No. 2 (1991).
5. D. David Bourland, Jr., "A Linguistic Note: Writing in E-Prime," *General Semantics Bulletin* 32-33 (1965-66): 111-14.
6. Menefee, op cit.
7. Wendell Johnson, *People in Quandaries* (New York: Harper and Row, 1946): 67.
8. Menefee, op cit.
9. William Dallmann, "E-Prime: A Practice for Awareness Engineers," *The Intelligencer*, 1, No. 10, (1990): 39.
10. John 9:25.
11. Robert Anton Wilson, *Cosmic Trigger* (New York: Pocket Books, 1977).
12. ——— , "Toward Understanding E-Prime," *Et cetera* 46, No. 4 (1989): 316.
13. J. Samuel Bois, *The Art of Awareness* (Dubuque: William C. Brown, 1966): 107.
14. Johnson, op cit, 64- 65.
15. Menefee, op cit.

METAPHOR AND E-PRIME:

Of the Subterranean "Is,"

Paradoxical Commands, and

RAYMOND GOZZI, JR.* **Tilted Abstraction Ladders**

WILL METAPHOR DISAPPEAR in E-Prime? Metaphor, after all, relies on the dreaded "is's" of identity and predication. Careless use of these "is's" has been warned against since the inception of general semantics, and E-Prime continues this valuable tradition.

But if we cannot use "is" in any variety, in our speech or writing, will this eliminate metaphor? On the surface level, some metaphorical statements will be inadmissible under the "strong" version of E-Prime advocated by Kellogg and Bourland. "Mike Tyson is an animal" would be an example of such a statement.

However, many metaphorical statements do not overtly use an "is" of identity or predication. But the "is" has not thereby disappeared — it has just gone underground. When we look below the surface structures of our language, we find metaphors and subterranean "is's" everywhere.

Take, for example, the simple act of naming, which may be the simplest metaphorical act, and which constitutes one core of our language.

* Associate Professor in the Department of TV-Radio at Ithaca College in New York State, Dr. Gozzi writes the "Metaphors in Action" feature appearing in *Et cetera*.

We speak of a computer "virus," or "worm," and we are saying that this piece of programming *is*, essentially, a virus in the world of computer networks, or *is* a worm burrowing through wires and software. We become so swept up in the metaphor that we label what happens as "infection," and design "vaccine" programs for defense.

Note, however, that the vile and despised "is" of identity or predication does not need to appear overtly in the metaphor. We can speak of computer "viruses" all day, in perfect E-Prime, yet the metaphorical use of the term will have imported a subterranean "is" of identity into all our uses.

Does E-Prime propose a hopeless task? Will it prove impossible to eliminate "is's" of identification and predication from our language?

This leads me to consider language as such. I will import the terms "ontology" and "epistemology" from philosophy to assist me. Ontology, as a field of study, ponders the nature of being. It is often contrasted with epistemology, which studies the nature of knowing.

Much of general semantics supplies, I believe, a contribution to epistemology — clearing up our ways of knowing so that we may function more humanely and effectively. It involves pointing to language itself as worthy of study, rather than the usual human trick of using language to point to something else as worthy of study. In this endeavor, E-Prime extends a long and useful tradition of clearing up the "noise" in our symbol systems.

However, when we consider the "ontology" of language itself, its very being, I believe we will be confronted at every turn with some variant of the "is" of identity, predication, existence, or location. Children ask, "What is this?" They are told, "It is a personal computer." The magical act of naming relies on the verb "to be" to establish a name — and then simply assumes the "is" of identity or predication every time we use the name. So with every name we will find a subterranean homesick "is."

If naming constitutes one of the primary acts of language, and if the assertion of the "is" of identity or predication constitutes the core of naming, then we will find the "is" of identity or predication underlying most of our surface structures, like a scaffolding which holds up a stage. We may dance and perform on the stage and pretend we don't know what's underneath, but without the underlying assertion of an "is," the whole thing collapses.

Korzybski was pointing out the dangers of these hidden "is's" which underlie language, I think, when he came up with his famous maxim "the map is not the territory."

This brilliant formulation relies on a metaphor: "language is a map, that which language describes is the landscape." Korzybski used two subterranean "is's" in the structure of his metaphor to attack other subterranean "is's."

In a way, the strategy of E-Prime is similar — using a heightened awareness of "is" to try to eliminate its use. There is something paradoxical about this — like being told not to think about a yellow personal computer. As soon as we remember what we are not supposed to think about, we are thinking about it. In E-Prime, in order not to use "is," we have to become constantly aware of it. Yet paradoxical commands can have great therapeutic value, and help shock us out of old, unhealthy habits.

So where does this leave us? I believe that when we look at the ontology of our language, its very being, we will find the foundations and underlying scaffolding rest heavily on the "is" of identity, predication, existence, and location. When we examine every name, we will find a subterranean "is." When we use metaphor, we become involved inextricably with assertions of "is."

The verb "to be," in fact, must be larger than anyone, except a few philosophers, suspects.

Viewed from the standpoint of this ontology, then, E-Prime is like Don Quixote tilting at windmills, or like sweeping "is" off the stage of language while ignoring the "is's" holding the whole stage up.

Yet from the standpoint of epistemology — helping us know better what we know, what we can know, what we do not really know — I think E-Prime is valuable. We certainly need to pay attention to the encompassing claims made by the little word "is": they can get us into a lot of trouble.

Even the paradoxical command: don't use the verb "to be," has great power. For it makes us think more about something we usually take for granted, and the bind it puts us in can make us search around for new ways of conceptualizing and writing.

I do not doubt that E-Prime will improve the writing of the general population should it be taught in writing classes. As an old abuser of the passive voice, I recognize a good strategy for better writing when I see one.

As far as future directions of E-Prime are concerned, I hope that Emory Menefee's suggestion about abstraction levels will be followed up — perhaps with graphics and illustrations. Menefee suggested that most of the undesirable uses of "is" occur when it links two terms on different levels of abstraction: we should not identify a specific person (John) with an abstract class (farmer), because this leads to stereotyping and inaccuracy.

The abstraction ladder has found its way into many textbooks, is easy to illustrate, and is a familiar general semantics concept. I would think that some good illustrations could be drawn which graphically demonstrate the use of "is" to link different levels of the abstraction ladder.

If E-Prime can help us level off the levels of abstraction in our sentences, as well as improve our writing and call attention to the dangers of the "is" of identification and predication, then I would say it has performed a valuable epistemological task. No matter if the underlying ontology of language is constructed out of the variations of the verb "to be": there is no escaping being.

REFERENCES

Kellogg, E. W., III, and Bourland, D. Jr. (1990-91). Working with E-Prime: Some Practical Notes. *Et cetera*, 47, (4), pp. 376-392.

Menefee, E. (1991). E-Prime or E-Choice? *Et cetera* 48, (2), pp. 136-140.

ROBIN T. LAKOFF* **NOT READY FOR PRIME TIME**

A T FIRST GLANCE, E-Prime seems an idea whose time has come. All too obviously, today's discourse is bogging down in illogic — some purposeful, especially in high places, some merely slothful but no less troublesome. Proponents of E-Prime attribute much of the murk to the ancient and tiny copulative verb, arguing that if we eliminate it, at least in its equative function, from the language, we will prevent a great deal of bad communication.

But simple solutions like this one too often prove simplistic, and I would argue that that is the case of E-Prime, on four grounds. In the first place, to the degree that adopting it inoculates the language against illogic, E-Prime does so indirectly — the gain in logic is not a direct result of the avoidance of *be*. Secondly, there are languages which make much less use of *be* than does English, but there is little reason to believe that their speakers thus achieve more logical communication. Thirdly, even if E-Prime were to produce the benefits claimed for it, its adoption would involve a radical change in the grammar of the language, one that would

* Robin Lakoff is Professor of Linguistics at the University of California, Berkeley. Her latest books are *Talking Power* (Basic Books, 1990) and *Father Knows Best* (Teachers College Press, 1992).

43

be extraordinarily hard to inculcate. Finally and perhaps most seriously, recasting sentences so that they do not contain *be* merely reorganizes their illogic rather than removing it. In this way, the avoidance of the copula encourages the reframing of questionable assertions as presuppositions — equally dubious but harder for hearers or readers to identify and examine.

Be, in the uses that E-Prime would proscribe, acts as an *equals* sign. If I write, "2 + 2 = 5," the fault in my proposition lies not in the "=," but in the reasoning process that caused me to produce the statement as a whole. The creator of the utterance bears the responsibility, not the creation. Suppose then I decide to avoid all future embarrassments of this kind by substituting // for =. That change will not improve my chances of reconciling my checkbook — only a better understanding of the principles of arithmetic will do that.

Perhaps, by being forced to substitute an unfamiliar sign for a familiar one, I will be induced to pay more attention to the process of addition than I normally would, and so get better results. But in this case, *any* substitution for the familiar formula will have similar effects: it is the compelling nature of novelty that creates logical thought rather than any particular change itself. The same is true when other syntactic constructions are substituted for *be* by users of E-Prime.

There is even some empirical evidence that removing *be* from a language, or at least making its occurrence less frequent than in English, has no discernible effect on the communicative logic of its speakers. Modern Russian does not use *be* in the present tense at all. Most of the ancient Indo-European languages (for instance, Latin, Greek, and Sanskrit) could optionally omit *be* to create "nominal" sentences. There is, needless to say, very little evidence indeed that speakers of these languages were any more logical than contemporary Americans.

While languages continually change in response to their own structural demands, human attempts to meddle with linguistic form have a doubtful track record. Occasionally attacks on one or another form have banished it outright or restricted it to marginal existence, as with *ain't*; but far more often, attempts to "improve" language by deliberate changes have met with abject failure and have sometimes led to worse situations than those they were designed to correct. Prescriptivists have been trying to get rid of the intransitive use of *lay* (replacing *lie*) for years, but *lay* keeps gaining new ground, with no consequent loss of clarity. Schoolteachers labored so tenaciously to rid the world of constructions like *Him and me are friends* that speakers of English have become terrified of the objective case in all compound pronoun constructions. The outcome? *This argument is between you and I* has become essentially Standard English — a triumph of linguistic insecurity. The linguist Robert A. Hall years ago wrote a book called *Leave Your Language Alone* — advice we should heed in this instance as elsewhere.

Finally, encouraging the replacement of *be* with other constructions will often have the effect of changing an illogical proposition from an assertion to a presupposition. Asserted matter in sentences is generally the new or most salient information — what a hearer or reader needs to know. Presuppositions express background information: what someone needs in order to make sense of the assertion or place it in a context. Compare the following sentences. In the first, the italicized matter is asserted; in the second, presupposed.

(1) *Michael Dukakis is President of the U.S.* and has dissolved the Internal Revenue Service.

(2) *U.S. President Michael Dukakis* today dissolved the Internal Revenue Service.

A hearer of (1) who is disturbed at the italicized matter is free to question it: it is accessible, syntactically and psychologically. By contrast, the same information is much more apt to slip by our notice in (2), since it is encoded in a form that we normally interpret as "old information," and pay it little heed. So it would not be strange to respond to (1), "WHO did you say was President?" But it might seem strange, or at least communicatively uncooperative, to do the same with (2). Slipping dubious matter into presupposed forms is one of the oldest, and sleaziest, tricks of the advertiser and the propagandist. The reformer must be wary of following in their footsteps.

Responsible analysts of language have as part of their job the tasks of explaining why and how language can be used to mystify and bamboozle and suggesting ways to avoid being victimized, and to use language to maximize reason, justice, and equality. E-Prime is a noble effort in those directions. It is valuable, too, in forcing people to think carefully about the consequences of their communicative choices. But I don't think it is likely to accomplish the laudable results it promises. It is true that language has been the bearer of vicious, destructive messages, and that these messages have often been believed and acted upon despite their irrationality. But language is only the messenger, not the message. To change the form of the language is like giving an evil message to a different messenger with the hope that when it is received, it will no longer have bad effects. To keep language from being illogical, its users must cease to think illogically. Or, at the very least, its users must become willing and able to do the hard work of determining the logic of the messages they receive, rather than hoping that language form itself will do that hard work for them.

TO BE OR NOT TO BE: AN EXPLORATION OF E-PRIME, COPULA DELETION AND FLAMING IN ELECTRONIC MAIL[†]

PHILIP A. THOMPSEN AND
DONG-KEUN AHN*

Abstract

T HE EFFICACY OF THE general semantics technique of E-Prime was explored in this study of copula deletion (omission of auxiliary verbs) and "flaming" (the fervent exchange of emotionally charged messages) in electronic mail. Copula deletion and flaming have been previously identified as characteristics of computer-mediated communication, while E-Prime is a general semantics technique that employs a deliberate alteration of language similar to copula deletion. If E-Prime can improve communication effectiveness and reduce misunderstandings, can copula deletion reduce the frequency of flaming in electronic mail? Or is the value of E-Prime to be found in the intent to alter linguistic habits,

* Philip A. Thompsen is Assistant Professor of Communication at William Jewell College in Liberty, Missouri. He currently is on leave as a Ph.D. candidate at The University of Utah in Salt Lake City. Mr. Thompsen's paper "Style in Public Speaking: A General Semantics Approach," co-authored with Tom H. Willett, appeared in *Et cetera*, Fall 1986. Mr. Dong-Keun Ahn is a graduate student in the Department of Communication at the University of Utah. In this paper, Mr. Ahn assisted with the data analysis.
† A paper presented to the Western States Communication Association 1992 Convention, Boise, Idaho. Due to space limitations, supporting statistical charts have been omitted.

rather than the alteration itself? To explore these questions, a computer program was developed that administered an interactive questionnaire to 214 users of an electronic mail system at a major university. Results showed that less than half of those surveyed were aware of either copula deletion or flaming in electronic mail. The most frequently cited motivation for copula deletion was the desire to write messages quickly. No statistically significant relationship was found between copula deletion and flaming in electronic mail, leading the authors to conclude that omission of the verb "to be" does not by itself convey the advantages of E-Prime.

Introduction

The application of computer technology for communication is becoming a significant area of study. In his overview of research on computer-mediated communication systems, Rice (1989) claimed that this area has received "increased attention" from a variety of disciplines, and he specifically notes the interest of scholars of communication, information science and management science. The need for understanding the influence of computers on how we communicate is expressed eloquently by Chesebro and Bonsall (1989):

> ...computerization is establishing an archetypal metaphor for human talk that is emerging as a controlling philosophy, if not ideology, in the United States. Technology and communication are now intimately interrelated. The terminologies, attitudes, and values utilized to describe a technology are increasingly becoming the foundation for characterizing and understanding human communication and therefore each person who finds that communication reflects and defines himself or herself. In other words, the computer revolution is now a personal issue, an issue that requires exploration, definition and analysis. (p.7)

Among those pursuing such "exploration, definition and analysis" are scholars of organizational communication (for example, Blackman and Clevenger, 1990; Compton, White and DeWine, 1991; Dunlap and Kling, 1991; Foulger, 1990;

Komsky, 1991; Papa and Papa, 1990; Rubinyi, 1989; Rice, 1987). One of the applications of computer-mediated communication (CMC) in organizations is the electronic mail system, in which people exchange mail messages using computer networks. Once found primarily in highly specialized and technical environments, electronic mail systems are becoming routine in many different kinds of organizations, as electronic mail gains acceptance as a communication medium. (See Komsky (1991) for a discussion of how "acceptance" has been defined by researchers, including conceptualizations of "routinization," "time since adoption," and "usage.") The computer industry has seized on the rapid implementation of electronic mail systems in business, with manufacturers emphasizing the benefits of electronic mail in marketing plans; as Schaefermeyer and Sewell (1988) point out, "computer-mediated communication has become the primary focus of the computer industry" (p.112).

The university, in particular, has been a site for rapid growth in the implementation of electronic mail systems. Because of the university's role as an "information processing organization," Komsky (1991) identified the university as "an exemplary setting for testing the efficacy and acceptance of electronic mail as a medium of communication" (p.310). Shamp (1991) noted that users at nearly three thousand universities throughout the world can now exchange electronic mail messages with each other. Through the rapid implementation of campus-wide computer networks, the interconnection of university electronic mail systems through networks such as Bitnet and Internet, and a growing recognition of the value of electronic mail for scholarly exchange, electronic mail is becoming an important form of communication in academic organizations.

Two qualities of computer-mediated communication messages that have been reported in the literature are "flaming" and copula deletion, and these two qualities represent the primary focus of our research. This research explored the extent of flaming in electronic mail, and attempted to identify some of the characteristics of those electronic mail users who have been exposed to flaming. We also explored the extent of and motivation for copula deletion in electronic mail messages. And by comparing the extent of flaming and copula deletion, we sought to test one of the premises of the general semantics technique of E-Prime, a technique for increasing awareness of abstraction through the deliberate deletion of the verb "to be."

A General Semantics Approach

This study was primarily exploratory in nature. Copula deletion and flaming are two characteristics of electronic mail that seem to warrant further exploration. But some readers may wonder why copula deletion and flaming would be explored together in one study. On the surface, they seem to be two disparate phenomena of electronic mail. What's the reason for combining the two in this study? On what basis do we suspect a possible relationship between them? The motivation for investigating both is derived from the theoretical foundations provided by the system of general semantics, and the general semantics technique of E-Prime in particular.

Although general semanticists disagree on how to describe their area of inquiry, a few definitions might be illustrative for the reader unfamiliar with this multidisciplinary approach to understanding human symbolic behavior. In a recent issue of *Et cetera: A Review of General Semantics*, Robert Wanderer (1991) provides a compendium of nearly eighty different definitions of general semantics, including:

- General semantics is the science and art of understanding and of being understood. (William Pemberton)
- General semantics is a linguistic self-control which teaches how symbols are related to experience so as to make it less likely that we take too seriously the absurd or dangerous nonsense that, within every culture, passes for philosophy, wisdom and political argument. (Aldous Huxley)
- General semantics is simply the name we give to all those inquiries which take as their starting point the pre-eminence of symbols and structure in human communica-

tion, and which are dominated by the paradigm of communication as environment. (Neil Postman)

Alfred Korzybski is acknowledged as the founder of general semantics, and two of his books, *Manhood Of Humanity* and
Science and Sanity are generally considered the seminal works
in the field. Although both books were published more than
half a century ago (the first in 1921, the second in 1933), the
discipline he founded remains a vibrant area of academic inquiry. Johnson (1991) notes that when *Science and Sanity* was
published, it was seen by some as:

> a formidable tome published privately by a largely un-
> known author — an independent scholar who lacked the
> "proper" academic credentials. It didn't fit the categories
> revered in academia — not quite philosophy, or linguistics,
> or psychology, or logic, or neurology, or mathematics — yet
> borrowing from all of these and more...Somehow it inspired
> many popularizations, over a hundred and fifty doctoral
> dissertations, and two scholarly journals, as well as many
> college and university courses, international conferences,
> and seminars. (p.59)

Korzybski outlined an area of scientific inquiry (what Johnson calls "an open-ended linguistic system for finding answers") that has attracted the interest of a number of scholars
of communication. (Note 1)

Korzybski was particularly interested in the process of abstracting that is inherent in human communication. This
idea is often summarized by the phrase, "the map is not the
territory," which is to say the language we use to describe
reality (the map) can sometimes be confused with reality itself (the territory). Korzybski argued that humans can take
abstracting for granted, a condition sometimes referred to as
the "semantic reaction of identification," contributing to misunderstanding and dysfunctional communication. He developed a system for giving people a greater awareness of the
process of abstraction, a system that included linguistic tools
he called "extensional devices." By using these linguistic
modifications, people could develop a greater awareness of

the limitations of language, and a greater appreciation for the potential communication difficulties that can arise when one takes abstraction for granted.

One of the potential trouble spots in the English language, what Bourland (1968) called the "supreme irritant," is the verb "to be." Korzybski (1933) cautioned against the "is of identity"; he claimed that "the little word 'to be' appears... responsible for many human semantic difficulties" (p.399). Bourland (1965-66) suggested these difficulties might be overcome through the use of a subset of the English language, called "E-Prime," which omitted all forms of the verb "to be." Wilson (1989) claimed that "E-Prime provides a straight-forward training technique for acquiring...a 'semantic hygiene' against the most prevalent forms of logical error, emotional distortion, and 'demonological thinking' " (p.316). Kellogg and Bourland (1990-91) assert that E-Prime "encourages, even forces, the user to write, speak and think more clearly and accurately" (p.377).

As one might imagine, using E-Prime involves quite a bit of conscious effort. It often requires recasting sentences to de-emphasize the traditional subject-predicate form. Because E-Prime greatly reduces the passive voice, the speaker or writer finds it difficult to conceal the humans involved in an assertion; Bourland (1968) claims that "E-Prime tends to invite attention to the agents involved in information transactions" (p.60). But perhaps most important, E-Prime encourages users to qualify their assertions, to transform identification sentences such as "this is good" into such less imposing constructions as "this seems good to me."

While the general semantics technique of E-Prime requires deliberate effort, copula deletion in electronic mail appears to be a "naturally" occurring form of "to be" omission. Must deletion of the copula be deliberate to have therapeutic value, or is copula deletion alone sufficient to have an effect? There have been many claims, but little evidence, that this is the case. Kellogg and Bourland (1990-91) argue that intention is critical:

> While the discipline of E-Prime aims at reducing dishonesty and prejudice (prejudging) in our communications, the

technique of E-Prime does in no way guarantee such a result. We have found that while E-Prime can facilitate honest communication, that as in any other language, the intention of the individual involved plays the predominant controlling role. (p.382)

They add that some languages (such as Russian and Hebrew) often use "simple juxtaposition for identity and predication structures," resulting in sentences that literally translated into English would appear as "I farmer," an example they provide that is quite similar to the sentences employing copula deletion in electronic mail. They conclude that the absence of "to be" alone "does not necessarily confer any advantages to it" (p.379). Yet they cite no specific research that supports this claim.

An electronic mail system therefore seems to provide a unique opportunity to test the assertion that simple copula deletion, without deliberate intent, by itself has no general semantics value. We reasoned that flaming could be used as a dependent measure for such a test, for it has been viewed as a dysfunctional characteristic of computer-mediated communication. For example, Kiesler, et al. (1984) note that administrators of electronic bulletin boards often monitor for flaming, "manually screening messages every few days to weed out those in bad taste" (p.1130). If the deletion of the copula in electronic mail did provide some of the benefits of using E-Prime, this might be revealed in a reduction of the frequency of exposure to incidents of flaming. On the other hand, if simple copula deletion in electronic mail does not seem to influence the frequency of exposure to flaming, this would support Kellogg and Bourland's claim. We turn now to a discussion of our specific research questions.

Investigating Copula Deletion, Flaming, and E-Prime: Our Research Questions

Copula Deletion. One of the characteristics of computer-mediated communication messages reported in the literature is the omission of nonessential linguistic elements. In their examination of the syntactic and stylistic features of text transmitted through computer networks, Ferrara, et al. (1991) noted the frequent omission of finite forms of the copula (an auxiliary or "linking" verb, most often the verb "to be"). For example, when composing an electronic mail message, one might write "The lecture boring today, but the discussion good" instead of "The lecture was boring today, but the discussion was good." They found the copula missing in 27% of the dialogues included in their study (p.20). This observation, along with other instances of linguistic abridgement, contributed to a characterization of computer-mediated written discourse as a "reduced register" (p.21).

Although Ferrara, et al. noted the omission of the copula in electronic mail, they did not assess the extent that users were aware of this phenomenon. We posed the question:

RQ (Research Question) 1a: To what extent are users of electronic mail aware of copula deletion?

We asked our respondents whether or not they were aware of copula deletion in electronic mail. If they reported that they had noticed it, we also asked them to estimate the extent of copula deletion in the messages they read, as well as the messages they send to other electronic mail users.

Ferrara, et al. suggested that future research should explore the motivations for deleting the copula. Our study, therefore, attempted an initial assessment of the motivations for copula deletion in electronic mail messages. Thus:

RQ1b: What do users report as the reasons for copula deletion?

We presented respondents with a list of five possible reasons for copula deletion, and asked them to select which (if any) seemed the most likely reason for copula deletion.

As an additional exploration into the nature of copula deletion in electronic mail, we attempted to identify some of the characteristics of those who notice copula deletion.

RQ1c: Are there characteristics that can significantly distinguish those electronic mail users who report an awareness of copula deletion from those who don't?

We asked respondents about the amount of time they spend working with the computer, the type of computer they use most often, the number of electronic mail messages they typically receive each day, whether they subscribe to electronic mail "discussion lists," and if they do subscribe, the approximate percentage of their electronic mail they receive that is sent by discussion lists. From the responses to these questions, as well as demographic questions asking the respondent's age, sex, and academic position, we attempted to create a profile of the electronic mail user who is aware of copula deletion.

Flaming. Another characteristic of electronic mail, commonly called "flaming," we define as "the heated exchange of messages expressing hostility or defensiveness toward others on the computer network." (Note 2) Baron (1984) found the frequency of flaming in computer conferencing "most striking" (p.130). In their study of electronic mail users in a large office equipment firm, Sproull and Kiesler (1986) reported that their respondents experienced flaming in electronic mail messages an average of 33 times a month (p.1508). Both of these studies suggest "flaming" is a widespread phenomenon in computer-mediated communication systems.

Is flaming also a frequent occurrence among users of electronic mail in a university setting? In exploring this question, we first considered the more fundamental issue of the extent of awareness of flaming among the users of electronic mail we surveyed. Thus:

RQ2a: To what extent are users of electronic mail aware of flaming?

We asked respondents whether or not they were aware of the term "flaming." If they weren't, we provided the above definition, and asked them if they had ever been exposed to an incident of flaming. We then sought to assess the frequency of exposure to flaming:

RQ2b: How often do users of electronic mail experience incidents of flaming?

We asked our respondents to estimate the number of incidents of flaming they had experienced in the past year.

We also explored the characteristics of electronic mail users who are exposed to flaming. Sproull and Kiesler (1986) suggested that flaming is an example of "uninhibited behavior" that may be due to the relative paucity of "reminders of the presence of other people and of social norms" in electronic mail (p.1501). We reasoned that some of the characteristics of electronic mail users we explored (see RQ1c above) might provide us with clues to the kinds of electronic mail users exposed to flaming. Thus:

RQ2c: Are there characteristics that can discriminate between those who are exposed to flaming and those who are not?

Using the responses to our questions of computer usage and electronic mail habits, as well as our demographic questions, we attempted to create a profile of electronic mail users who have been exposed to flaming.

E-Prime. The presence of both copula deletion and flaming in electronic mail seems to provide an opportunity to test the general semantics technique of E-Prime, and in particular, the efficacy of deleting the verb "to be" as a linguistic alteration. We explored whether or not omission of the verb "to be" by itself offers any of the benefits of E-Prime, as reflected in the frequency of exposure to flaming. Thus:

RQ3:   Is there a relationship between copula deletion and flaming in electronic mail?

We compared our respondents' estimates of copula deletion with their estimated frequency of exposure to flaming. If a negative correlation was found (that is, if greater copula deletion was associated with fewer incidents of flaming) this would seem to indicate that there may be value in deleting the verb "to be," regardless of one's intent. On the other hand, if no correlation was found, this would provide evidence in support of the claim of Kellogg and Bourland (1990-91) that deletion of the verb "to be" by itself does not necessarily provide any advantages.

Procedures

The Sample. Subjects for this study consisted of those who voluntarily responded to an invitation to participate in the research project. An electronic mail message was sent to all users of the electronic mail system provided by the computer center at a major research university, inviting them to take a short survey on electronic mail usage. Although messages were initially sent to a total of 1,233 electronic mail addresses provided by the director of the computer center, 184 were returned as undeliverable mail (primarily rejected by the mail system as having invalid electronic mail addresses), resulting in a pool of 1,049 electronic mail users. Three weeks after the initial messages were sent, a follow-up message was sent to those who had yet to take the survey. A total of 214 responses were received, resulting in a response rate of 20.4%. Men (79.4%, n=170) outnumbered women (20.6%, n=44) in our sample, which included 82 students, 64 faculty members, and 68 respondents in staff or other non-academic positions. Ages of our respondents ranged from 20 to 68, with an average age of 35.66 years (SD=10.18).

The Questionnaire. A computer program was created for the purpose of administering the questionnaire. This program was written using the "command procedure" language of the VMS operating system on a Digital Equipment VAX computer. Ten questions were asked of all respondents, and up to nine additional questions were asked depending on responses to three "screening" questions. (For example, if a person responded that he or she had not been exposed to flaming, the question asking for an estimate of the frequency of flaming was not asked.) Five of the questions were copula deletion items, five questions related to flaming, and five measured electronic mail and computer usage habits. There also were three demographic questions (sex, age and academic position) and one question asked if the participant would be willing to take electronically-administered surveys of this nature in the future. Two of the questions were open-ended (one question on copula deletion and one on flaming), seeking from the respondent extended narrative answers; the remaining questions were closed-ended, "forced-choice" items.

Data Analysis. Responses to the questionnaires were sent to one of the authors of this study in the form of three electronic mail messages. One of these messages contained the numeric data from the closed-ended questions, the other two messages contained the narrative data from the open-ended questions. The Statistical Package for the Social Sciences (SPSS) was used for data analysis of the quantitative data; the primary statistics used were frequencies and t-tests. An analysis of data from the open-ended questions was not reported in this paper, but the results of a content analysis of this data is being prepared for a future paper.

Results

RQ1a: To what extent are users of electronic mail aware of copula deletion?

We presented our respondents with a description of copula deletion, and asked them if they had noticed it in the electronic mail messages they had read. A slight majority of our respondents (54.7%, n=117) stated that they were not aware of copula deletion in electronic mail messages, over a third (37.4%, n=80) reported they had noticed it, with the remainder stating they didn't know for sure (7.9%, n=17). It would seem that most of our respondents had not noticed copula deletion, but it should be pointed out that this is a measure of awareness, and not a direct measure of the amount of copula deletion.

We obtained such a measure, although indirectly, by asking those who were aware of copula deletion to estimate the percentage of messages they had read (and sent) that contained instances of copula deletion. Our data suggest that copula deletion, when it is perceived by electronic mail users, is not seen as a frequently occurring phenomenon. Over half (57.5%) of our respondents estimated that copula deletion occurred in no more than 20% of the messages they read. Our respondents noticed copula deletion more in the messages they read than in the messages they sent; almost three-fourths (72.6%) estimated that they employed copula deletion in no more than 20% of the messages they sent. These figures are similar to the finding of Ferrara, et al. (1991) of copula deletion in 27% of the messages in their sample.

RQ1b: What do users report as the reasons for copula deletion?

If respondents stated that they were aware of copula deletion in their electronic mail messages, we asked them to assess the reasons for copula deletion. We presented respondents with five possible reasons for copula deletion, and asked them which, if any, of these reasons seemed the most plausible. The majority (67.5%) of the respondents attributed copula deletion to the motive "in order to write quickly." One out of eight respondents felt copula deletion was motivated by a desire to make messages sound more conversational. Since much of the E-Prime literature suggests that the verb "to be" is an unnecessary part of the English language, we included in our question the response "because these words aren't needed"; however, this motivation was selected by the smallest number of respondents in our study. This suggests that although copula deletion and E-Prime may share the semantic reduction of omitting forms of the verb "to be," they seem to have dissimilar motivations.

RQ1c: Are there characteristics that can significantly distinguish those electronic mail users who report an awareness of copula deletion from those who don't?

Using t-tests, we compared those who were aware of copula deletion with those who weren't across five independent variables. Only the variable "age" showed a significant difference ($p=0.028$), indicating that those who were aware of copula deletion tended to be younger. The variable "number of E-mail messages received each day," approached a significant difference level ($p=0.069$). Although those respondents aware of copula deletion reported being exposed to a higher average number of flaming incidents during the previous year, the difference was not statistically significant ($p=0.241$).

RQ2a: To what extent are users of electronic mail aware of flaming?

Slightly more than half (52.8%, n=113) of our respondents were aware of flaming. Of the remainder, 43% (n=92) reported that they were not aware of flaming, and 4.2% (n=9) said they didn't know. We asked those respondents who said they were aware of flaming to provide a definition for it. Upon close examination of these definitions, we found 19 that clearly described the term flaming outside of the electronic mail context (most of these defined flaming as "homosexual" or "on fire"). Removing these cases reduced the number of those who were aware of flaming (as related to electronic mail) to 94 (43.9%). It was unclear, however, if these respondents provided definitions of flaming outside of the electronic mail context because of a lack of awareness of flaming as a characteristic of electronic mail; it could be that some of these respondents knew of flaming as a term related to electronic mail, but chose to define it in other terms.

In any case, we have greater confidence in the question that inquired about actual exposure to flaming. After providing our definition of flaming ("the fervent exchange of messages, often personally attacking and/or expressing defensiveness, on computer communication networks"), we asked respondents whether they had ever been exposed to an incident of flaming. Well over half (58.4, n=125) reported that they had not been exposed to flaming, while 38.8% (n=83) reported that they had, and 2.8% (n=6) said they didn't know.

RQ2b: How often do users of electronic mail experience incidents of flaming?

We asked those who had been exposed to flaming to estimate the number of incidents of flaming they had experienced in the past year. A little more than a fourth (27.7%) reported that they had experienced at least 25 flaming incidents, and about a third (31.3%) reported experiencing less than 5 flaming incidents.

RQ2c: Are there characteristics that can discriminate between those who are exposed to flaming, and those who are not?

As we had done with the copula deletion awareness measure, we used t-tests to compare those who were exposed to flaming with those who weren't. Of the six independent variables tested, two variables showed a highly significant difference: time per week with the computer ($p < 0.0005$), and the number of E-mail messages received per day ($p < 0.0005$). This suggests that those exposed to flaming spend more time working on the computer and received more electronic mail messages. Those exposed to flaming tended to receive a higher percentage of E-mail from discussion lists, although this difference only approached a significant level ($p = 0.076$). Although age was a significant predictor of copula deletion awareness, it was not a significant predictor of flaming exposure (p=0.229). Neither were the copula deletion variables significant predictors of flaming exposure.

RQ3: Is there a relationship between copula deletion and flaming?

No significant difference was found between the variable "awareness of copula deletion" and the frequency of flaming measure, and no significant differences were found between the variable "exposure to flaming" and the two copula deletion interval measures. As an additional test for a possible relationship, we conducted t-tests between the variable "awareness of flaming" and the set of independent variables. Again, no significant differences were found with the two copula deletion measures. These tests did reveal significant differences with three of the independent variables: time per week with the computer, number of E-mail messages per day, and percent of mail from discussion lists. Thus, those who were aware of flaming tended to spend more time with the computer, receive more electronic mail, and receive a higher percentage of that mail from discussion lists. However, neither awareness of flaming nor exposure to flaming were significantly related to frequency of copula deletion in electronic mail messages.

Discussion

This study was an exploration into copula deletion and flaming in electronic mail. Our research sought to provide a quantitative description of the phenomenon of copula deletion in electronic mail, including an assessment of the level of awareness of copula deletion among electronic mail users, their estimates of the extent of copula deletion, and the reasons they think it happens. Our study also sought a better understanding of flaming: the level of awareness of flaming among electronic mail users, and the extent they have been exposed to it. We also wanted to find out which of our measures could be used to characterize those aware of copula deletion, and those exposed to flaming. And the presence of both of these phenomena provided a unique opportunity to test the efficacy of the general semantics technique of E-

Prime: specifically, to investigate whether the crucial aspect of E-Prime is the deletion of the verb "to be" or the intent of the user of E-Prime to alter linguistic habits.

The results of our study show that most of the electronic mail users in our sample were unaware of copula deletion and unexposed to flaming. This may be due to different levels of observance and sophistication among our respondents, but it may also indicate that copula deletion and flaming are not as widespread in electronic mail in a university setting as they may be in other settings. Copula deletion may be less frequent in an academic setting because of a greater stigma attached to nonstandard English usage. Perhaps flaming is more common in non-academic settings where the average user may be younger and more likely to use electronic mail for socialization.

There was a segment of our sample, however, that did show high levels of awareness of and exposure to flaming. Those users who subscribed to discussion lists were much more likely to be exposed to flaming, and the higher the percentage of mail from discussion lists, the greater the frequency of exposure to flaming. Sproull and Kiesler (1986) noted that flaming may be related to the lack of "reminders of the presence of other people" (p.1501); it may be that flaming is more likely to occur in mail from discussion lists because the reader attributes the discussion list as the source of the message, rather than the actual sender of the message. Discussion lists also provide the opportunity to send and receive messages from previously unknown individuals, which could lead to a more impersonal, more computer-like image of the electronic mail "partner," a phenomenon Shamp (1989, 1991) has referred to as "mechanomorphism."

We suspected that there might be a relationship between flaming and discussion lists, so we included an item in our survey that asked respondents whether flaming was more likely on discussion lists than in "personal" electronic mail messages. Over two-thirds (67.5%, n=56) of our respondents said that flaming was much more likely to occur on discussion lists, and an additional 14.5% (n=12) said this was somewhat more likely. It seems clear to us, then, that discussion lists are a major source of flaming incidents, at least in academic settings.

We found no significant relationships between any of the copula deletion and flaming measures. We interpret this lack of relationship as support for the claim of Kellogg and Bourland (1990-91) that the intent of the user of E-Prime, rather than simple copula deletion, is the source of the efficacy of E-Prime. Copula deletion by itself does not seem to produce a reduction in exposure to flaming. What remains to be tested is whether training in E-Prime can lead to reduced exposure to flaming. While the efficacy of E-Prime as a general semantics technique has been documented elsewhere (see for example, Elkind, 1976), it is not clear whether the value of E-Prime would be influenced by communication situations where copula deletion is already present to some extent. In other words, would the presence of copula deletion in electronic mail have any influence on the benefits of deleting the verb "to be" by E-Prime users? This is an issue we feel deserves additional research.

NOTES

1. Johnson himself is an Emeritus Professor of Mass Communication at the University of Wisconsin-Milwaukee; other communication scholars who have contributed to the general semantics literature include Elwood Murray, Joseph A. DeVito, Neil Postman and Lee Thayer.

2. Although we have provided a definition of flaming, there are a number of other definitions in the literature. Baron (1984) included in her description of flaming the characteristics of "speaking incessantly, hurling insults, [and] using profanity" (p.130). According to *The Hacker's Dictionary*, (Steele et al., 1983) flaming means "to speak rabidly or incessantly on an uninteresting topic or with a patently ridiculous attitude." Kiesler et al. (1984) define flaming as "the practice of expressing oneself more strongly on the computer than one would in other communication settings" (p.1130).

3. Since some questions were not asked of all respondents, the reported N in some tables may not equal the total number of respondents (N=214).

REFERENCES

Baron, N. S. (1984). Computer-Mediated Communication as a Force in Language Change. *Visible Language*, 18(2), pp.118-141.

Blackman, B. I., & Theodore Clevenger, J. (1990). The Promises, Possibilities and Pragmatics of Using Pictograph Surrogates in On-Line Messaging: Implications for Managing the Adoption of Computer-Mediated Communication Technology. Paper presented to the 76th Annual Meeting of the Speech Communication Association Chicago, Illinois.

Bourland, D. D., Jr. (1965/1966). A Linguistic Note: Writing in E-Prime. *General Semantics Bulletin*, 32-33, p.113.

Bourland, D. D., Jr. (1968). The Semantics of a Non-Aristotelian Language. *General Semantics Bulletin*, 35, pp.60-63.

Chesebro, J. W., & Bonsall, D. G. (1989). *Computer-Mediated Communication: Human Relationships in a Computerized World*. Tuscaloosa, Ala.: The University of Alabama Press.

Compton, D. C., White, K., & DeWine, S. (1991). Techno-Sense: Making Sense of Computer-Mediated Communication Systems. *Journal of Business Communication*, 28(1), pp.23-43.

Dunlop, C., & Kling, R. (Ed.). (1991). *Computerization and Controversy: Value Conflicts and Social Choices*. Academic Press.

Elkind, S. A. (1976) *To Be or Not To Be: An Investigation of Linguistic Relativity by Altering the Language of Encounter Group Members in a Manner Suggested by General Semantics*. Ph.D. dissertation, California School of Professional Psychology.

Ferrara, K., Brunner, H., & Whittemore, G. (1991). Interactive Written Discourse as an Emergent Register. *Written Communication*, 8(1), pp.8-34.

Foulger, D. A. (1990) *Medium as Process: The Structure, Use, and Practice of Computer Conferencing on IBM's IBMPC Computer Conferencing Facility*. Ph.D. dissertation, Temple University.

Johnson, K. G. (1991). Relevant? *Et cetera: A Review of General Semantics*, 48(1), pp.59-61.

Kellogg, E. W., III and D. D. Bourland, Jr. (1990-91). Working With E-Prime: Some Practical Notes. *Et cetera: A Review of General Semantics*, 47(4), pp.376-392.

Kiesler, S., Siegel, J., & McGuire, T. W. (1984). Social Psychological Aspects of Computer-Mediated Communication. *American Psychologist*, 39(10), pp.1123-1134.

Komsky, S. H. (1991). A Profile of Users of Electronic Mail in a University: Frequent Versus Occasional Users. *Management Communication Quarterly*, 4(3), pp.310-340.

Korzybski, A. (1921). *Manhood of Humanity: The Art and Science of Human Engineering*. New York: Dutton.

Korzybski, A. (1933). *Science and Sanity*. Lakeville, Conn.: International Non-Aristotelian Library.

Papa, M. J., & Papa, W. H. (1990). Perceptual and Communicative Indices of Employee Performance with New Technology. *Western Journal of Speech Communication*, pp.54 (1), 21-40.

Rice, R. E. (1987). Computer-Mediated Communication and Organizational Innovation. *Journal of Communication*, 37(4), pp.65-94.

Rice, R. E. (1989). Issues and Concepts in Research on Computer-Mediated Communication Systems. In J. A. Anderson (Ed.), *Communication Yearbook* 12 (pp.436-476). Newbury Park, CA: Sage Publications, Inc.

Rubinyi, R. M. (1989). Computers and Community: The Organizational Impact. *Journal of Communication*, 39(3), pp.110-123.

Schaefermeyer, M. J., & Edward H. Sewell, J. (1988). Communicating by Electronic Mail. *American Behavioral Scientist*, 32(2), pp.112-123.

Shamp, S. A. (1989) *Mechanomorphism and Perceptions of Computer Communication Partners*. Doctoral dissertation, The University of Utah.

Shamp, S. A. (1991) *Mechanomorphism in Perception of Computer Communication Partners*. In press.

Sproull, L., & Kiesler, S. (1986). Reducing Social Context Cues: Electronic Mail in Organizational Communication. *Management Science*, 32(11), pp.1492-1512.

Steele, G., Woods, D., Finkel, R., Crispin, M., Stallman, R., & Goodfellow, G. (1983). *The Hacker's Dictionary*. New York: Harper and Row.

Wanderer, R. (1991). General Semantics: A Compendium of Definitions. *Et cetera: A Review of General Semantics*, 48(1), pp.31-43.

Wilson, R. A. (1989). Toward Understanding E-Prime. *Et cetera: A Review of General Semantics*, 46, pp.316-319.

GENERAL SEMANTICISTS

Earl Hautala* *AND E-PRIME*

W E SEEM TO HAVE the ingredients for a dispute among some individuals who believe that they subscribe to the illuminating formulations of general semantics. Do we have a tempest in a teapot or do we have something more sinister?

The proponents of one position would prefer the use of E-Prime by all those who would call themselves "general semanticists." Another group of proponents would allow communicants to choose their verbiage without fear of ostracism. As with any choice between alternatives, it seems reasonable to survey the consequences, before doing anything irreversible.

For those who can understand the intent of E-Prime, it has some potential benefits. The exclusive use of E-Prime will curtail the generation of overt identities as in:

"John is a Martian."

You may fill in any other noun in place of Martian.

It tends to reduce a speaker's ability to slip in groundless authoritarian statements:

* Earl Hautala, President of the International Society for General Semantics, lives in the San Francisco Bay Area.

"Mary is beautiful."

You may fill in any other adjective in place of beautiful.

Thinking about the scope of human communication I find that we can still categorize (abstract) without using "is."

"John, that Martian over there, hangs around other Martians" or "Mary, the good looking one, just became a member of the board."

In point of fact, the exclusive use of E-Prime does not hamper expression. Anyone can fly the banner of E-Prime and still attach abstract labels to either extended objects or substantives. The exclusive use of E-Prime will not end prejudice, greed, or dishonesty. If E-Prime will not serve as a panacea for all the problems of communication, we could still look to it for some benefits.

We might find additional consequences in requiring E-Prime of those who would call themselves "general semanticists." I have heard people referred to as "semanticists," but I don't think that I have seen any professionals given the exclusive title of "general semanticist." Given the requirement, that everyone who would hold the title of "general semanticist," must pass the E-Prime test, we might end up with an organization with 5 members, more or less. That does not strike me as a potential benefit.

I have contended for quite some time, that the literature of general semantics escapes the understanding of a great many people who might benefit from its formulations. When asked about *Science and Sanity*, Einstein supposedly said, "That crazy book?", which may say something about the difficulty of getting into the subject matter. From a personal perspective, I would recommend against adding additional prescriptions with respect to an already difficult subject. General semantics has to do with the study of communication explored from a foundation in modern physics. I don't expect to see the older Aristotelian perspective and the prehistoric grammatical structure of the Indo-European languages melt before the formulations of general semantics in the next few decades, let alone this week.

The mental exercise of attempting to think, write or speak in E-Prime does the job. It increases our awareness of the words we use, even in our unspoken thoughts. In the modern vernacular, it "raises our consciousness" of the problems of categorizing, or if you prefer, abstracting. Look, right there, before your very eyes, Korzybski's own wording of the goal of general semantics,

"consciousness of abstracting."

A little study of generally accepted history suggests a surer path to success for general semantics. Ideas have strange consequences. Some of them lead to extinction. Any group which promotes life-long celibacy must eventually disappear. So what happens if we continue to promote "consciousness of abstracting." Maybe we can begin to understand the full implications of speaking in the "deity mode." That in turn, could lead to an examination and re-evaluation of our ideas, thoughts, and maybe even our assumptions. That gets right down to the root of the problem. If you have to re-think your assumptions, you own the responsibility for those things (those process-events) which you can control. I suggest that the study of general semantics can lead to increased self-responsibility. The process takes time.

Let's stay within the bounds of choice and self-responsibility. Eventually those who study general semantics will choose for themselves, how and when E-Prime will serve them best.

Andrea Johnson* **OH TO BE A WRITER**

"In order to write factually, you have to tell it like it is."

*"If a thought is about you, and it is written by you,
then you write: 'I am.' "*

S O RESPOND MY students when asked to identify helpful writing paradigms. After listing these handy homilies, they confidently move to review their next writing assignment: a one page autobiography. Several brows furrow, and one student asks, "What do you mean, 'write this paper in E-Prime'?" "Ahh," I reply. "Good question."

Dr. Kenneth G. Johnson introduced me to E-Prime, the writings of D. David Bourland, Jr., and not coincidentally the E-Prime autobiography assignment, when I studied general semantics as a graduate student at the University of Wisconsin-Milwaukee. Bourland, a student of Korzybski,

* Associate Professor Andrea Johnson teaches general semantics and communication courses at Alverno College, Milwaukee, Wisconsin.

coined the term E-Prime to signify English minus the verb "to be" — *is, am, are, were, was, be, being, been.* Bourland suggests that writing and speaking without using any forms of the verb "to be" can assist the user in attaining a kind of vigorous clarity. More importantly, he notes that E-Prime functions as an additional extensional device as it provides a means for making more accurate mappings.

I offer this background information, along with a copy of Bourland's article, "To Be or Not To Be: E-Prime as a Tool for Critical Thinking," printed in *Et cetera* 46, no. 3, to my students. (1) Now, disarmed of their writing caveats and looking decidedly concerned, they take their assignments home.

The following week, before discussing their work, I ask the students to evaluate the exercise and then write their responses to the assignment.

1. Relate your experience in writing your autobiography in E-Prime. What proved most difficult? Easiest?

2. Bourland suggests that writing in E-Prime keeps you honest because you focus on the territory (what you do) rather than map (what you say you are.) After writing this autobiography, what do you think?

3. What if you could have used *to be* verbs in this exercise. Would the picture of you seem different if you had said "I am" or "I was"?

4. Will you use E-Prime in the future?

And what did they think, feel, believe, sense, learn, identify, observe?

"It forced me to pay more attention to what I wanted to say. It's easy to say 'I am a mother,' but what does that really mean?"

"I might develop my work more if I had to fully explain myself. I know I should do this anyway, but if I write in E-Prime, I couldn't get around it."

"E-Prime forces you to follow some of the rules of general semantics — you become more conscious of maps and your extensional world."

"After writing this paper, I think of myself as having more confidence and strength. I made a clearer map of me and how I see the territory. I feel like I learned a lot about myself."

"The most difficult part was getting out of the habit of labeling myself as 'being' something. If I can eliminate some labeling, it will be easier for a reader to understand what I mean."

"Without E-Prime, I would have made more absolute statements about what are essentially self-perceptions."

"Even while writing this response, I've noticed how many times I've used 'to be' — it gets annoying."

"I don't think I would have sounded as creative if I had used 'to be' verbs. 'To be' verbs do not really describe anything accurately or interestingly. This assignment has made me more aware of how often I use 'to be' and the effect it has on my writing. I will try to cut down."

At the end of the semester, when asked to evaluate the most helpful or valuable assignments in class, many students named the E-Prime autobiography. Several noticed that they had learned how to talk more positively about themselves. Some suggested that using E-Prime helped clarify the meanings of intensional and extensional orientations for them. Others observed an improvement in their ability to write from a clearer analytical perspective.

One student said she liked the E-Prime exercise best because she had always wanted to be a writer and now, she happily proclaimed, "I am a writer!". A student who knew how to listen in E-Prime tactfully advised, "Maryanne, you probably learned how to write better." Yep.

NOTE

1. Bourland's article also appears in *To Be or Not: An E-Prime Anthology*, edited by D. David Bourland, Jr., and Paul Dennithorne Johnston, available from the International Society for General Semantics. In slightly expanded form it appears as a chapter in K. G. Johnson's *Thinking Creatically*, also available from the International Society for General Semantics.

THE NO NO BEEN Catalog

Sophisticated Products for the discriminating semanticist

The Is-inator
Unique patented blending action separates the "to be" verbs (is, am, was, were, be, been) by centrifugal force. (Not guaranteed to eliminate contractions.) Replaceable blades. 110 volt AC only. Cat. # 421. $45.95

The Swiss Army Structural Differential
Check your levels of abstracting in the field. Parabola blade. Perception level blade. Fido blade. Assorted label blades. Cat. # 4536. $95.95

The Honey Maker
Don't waste those *be's* you eliminated when you took up E-Prime. Put them in our patented E-Prime Honey Maker and get delicious prime quality honey in virtually no time at all. Contains saccharin. Cat. # 4423. $407.95

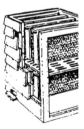

The Restorator
Restores lost "is's" to emaciated verbiage, turning it into USDA prime choice prose. Cat. # 2B. $29.95

The Index Gun.
Just point and shoot. The Index Gun applies index numbers to anything in its sights. Now you really can tell the difference between Fido$_1$, Fido$_2$, and Fido$_{12}$, members of the class "Mamma Fido's litter" in your garage. Cat. # 124757883748392019384 746389810394738292365 74834. $46.81

The Wrist Radio Communicator
How often have you had the feeling that your meaning of a word differs drastically from that of the other party? Our communicator eliminates the apparent disparity of meaning between you and your communicatee, thus perpetuating the illusion that you both mean the same thing. Cat. # @!$#%*&#@. $1.95

The GS Field Glasses
Use these *before* you process your abstracting with our Swiss Army Structural Differential. Our patented filters pick out only your abstractions, leaving the rest of the universe for somebody else to deal with. Cat. # 00. 195.95

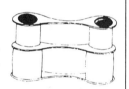

The Hyphenator
This-handy-tool-puts-hyphens-between-every-word-you-say-thus-providing-a-map-that-reflects-the-interconnectedness-of-all-things-whew. Cat. # 1-3-4. $4-9.9-5

The Bit-Map
Our new digitized bit-map puts the bits and pieces of your territory where you want them, on a flat piece of paper where they will hold still long enough for you to understand what happened. Of course by then it has already happened. Annual upgrades for a nominal fee. Cat. # 1234. Price subject to change without notice.

Fido₁
Essential for giving examples of indexing. Low maintenance. Folds away for storage. Capacity, 2 fifths of a gallon. Dog. # 34. $345.98 Without cask: $3.50 With scooper: $1,000.00

The Non-Identification Bracelet
Hardened steel will break even the strongest engraving tool, thus making it impossible to put your social security number, telephone number, emergency medical info number, or anything else on this particularly ugly piece of human adornment. Catalog number unavailable. $.99

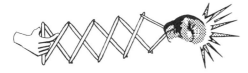

The Extensional Device
Stops your getting lost in high abstractions. Cat. # KO2342. $101.95

The Ultimate Abstractor
With this patented GS tool, you can't ignore *consciousness of abstracting*. Add 20% for Nitrous Oxide. Recognized as a legitimate expense by most insurance companies. Ear plugs optional. Cat. # 999. $79.99

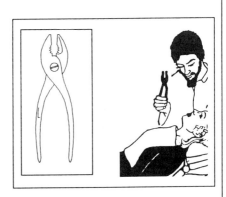

The Generic Symbol
Many symbols have severe limitations. Conventionally, a particular symbol has finite meanings. As a result, people can hold you accountable for something you said. Solve this sticky problem with the generic symbol, which can mean anything you want it to mean. The ultimate ambiguity. Cat. # ?!? (Politicians: ask about bulk discount.) $9.99.

The Knee-Jerk Antidote
Those knee-jerk reactions can hurt! Avoid the pain with our patented elixir. Also cures boils, bunions, bankruptcy, and the blues. 150 Proof. Non I.D. required for those over 21. Cat. # XXXXX. $19.95 per pint.

The Extension Ladder
Combination extensional device and abstraction ladder helps you clean up those hard-to-reach abstractions. Wastebasket included. Warning! Liable to collapse without notice. Catalog number unavailable because we don't want to get involved with petty details. Price: We'll let you know.

The Intensional Device
Blocks out external interference so you can live entirely in your own symbolic world. (Do not use this device until you have paid for it!) Cat. #, Price: You decide.

Computer Dating Service
Semanticists recommend dating. Our patented computer watches everything you do and puts a date on it. Not for the paranoid. Cat. $\#_{1992}$ 1254. $Price_{1992}$ $40.95

THE TOP TEN ARGUMENTS

James D. French*　*AGAINST E-PRIME*

Argument #10:

T HE CLAIM THAT E-Prime has an inherent, beneficial effect on
a person's writing ability seems highly questionable, considering that E-Prime deliberately eliminates a whole class of
statements from the language, resulting in fewer alternatives.
The English writer can use *all* of the statements available to
the E-Prime writer, *plus* a whole class of statements containing the verb "to be." The greater variety of available wordings should make the English writer's efforts *more* interesting
to read, not less. (Any bad writing that occurs because of the
over-use of the verb "to be" — a common failing — can be
more easily overcome by simply *cutting back* on one's use of
"to be," rather than resorting to E-Prime.)

---

* James D. French, a computer programmer at the University of California,
Berkeley, has had papers on general semantics and logic published in several
journals, including *The Journal of Symbolic Logic*.

Argument #9:

Even if E-Prime should improve one's writing, that is not a reason to promote it as a general semantics practice. The class of items that we might call "effective writing techniques," fall outside the subject matter of general semantics, and so any incidental benefits are as irrelevant to general semantics as they would be to any other discipline. Imagine if you will that E-Prime improved the writing of students and professors in the physics department of some university. Would we then consider E-Prime to be an element of physics?

Argument #8:

The harmful effects that may result from the use of the is-of-identity and the is-of-predication are often ameliorated by the context, and so the need to eliminate all such statements from our language is not as great as the advocates of E-Prime apparently assume. It is one thing to say, "The rose is red" in a flat statement of "fact"; it is quite another to say, "The rose is red *to me*." If in response to the question, "What does John Jones do for a living?" I answer, "He's a professor," there seems to be little that a general semanticist should quarrel with, given that the response is occurring within the context of asking what the man does for a living, a context that greatly affects the meaning of the answer.

Argument #7:

The range of perfectly acceptable "to be" statements covers a vast expanse, and includes asymmetrical relations, e.g., "Mt. McKinley is higher in elevation than Mt. Shasta"; negation, "The map is not the territory"; location, "Oakland is on the west coast"; auxiliary, "It is raining," "I am going to the store," etc.; and possibly many other unidentified forms, e.g., "I am aware of that." These forms must be sacrificed when adopting E-Prime, at considerable cost for no proven benefit.

Argument #6:

Eliminating "to be" from the English language may have little effect on eliminating *identity* from the language. A statement such as, "The practice of E-Prime is silly," has a telltale form, and can be easily recognized by general semanticists as having the structure of identity (or predication). Yet, a statement of apparently equal identification, "The silly practice of E-Prime continues," can be made in E-Prime without the verb "to be." The latter form may even hold more dangers. Since the E-Prime statement assumes an identity rather than asserting it, our ability to recognize it as a problem is hampered. That does not favor the adoption of E-Prime.

Argument #5:

Identity-in-the-language is not the same thing as the far more important *identity-in-reaction* (identification), and the two should not be confused. A whole system, called general semantics, was developed to cut the link between identity-in-the-language and identity-in-reaction. Through the practice of *silence on the objective levels,* adopting a self-reflexive attitude, e.g., "as I see it," "it seems to me," et cetera, and by the use of quotation marks — "It 'is' a great day," — and so on, the link can be cut. Korzybski claimed that persons properly trained in general semantics could use any language and not be led astray. (It should be noted that one of the training techniques of general semantics is to reword is-of-identity and is-of-predication statements, e.g., "That man is a fool" becomes "I evaluate that man as a fool." This technique existed long before E-Prime was thought of, and differs from it in that, although the technique is encouraged, there is no absolute requirement to use it in all circumstances or to extend it to statements that actually do not violate the principles of the discipline.)

Argument #4:

The advocates of E-Prime assume that it is far easier to eliminate the verb "to be" from the English language than it is to eliminate just the is-of-identity and the is-of-predication; they also apparently feel that serious efforts have been made to do the latter and that the attempts have failed. Neither assumption seems supported by the available facts. I doubt that more than a handful of people have seriously tried to train themselves to distinguish between the different uses of the verb "to be." Who has, for example, gone over his or her writings, checking the sentences that contain the verb "to be" as an auxiliary verb (for example, "I am going to the store"), and underlining other sentences that use "to be" to express identity or predication? Although it might take months to easily (automatically) distinguish between appropriate and inappropriate uses of the verb "to be," it takes months or years to learn E-Prime. The Spanish language, regarded as one of the easiest to learn, has two verbs for "to be"; one is used to indicate permanence, and the other, temporary states. Spanish-speaking people apparently have no trouble making such distinctions. For many people, it might actually be easier to distinguish between different uses of the verb "to be" than to eliminate "to be" entirely from the language.

Argument #3:

There may be considerable benefits to humankind in the use of the verb "to be" that the formulations of general semantics do not take into consideration. We know that one of the best languages for time-binding is mathematics, a language that relies heavily on the notion of equivalence and equality. "$Y = Z$" seems quite similar in form to "John Jones is that professor." Mathematicians do not ascribe content to their languages, however, whereas English speakers frequently confuse language and "reality." For the purposes of time-binding and progress, it may be better to keep "to be" in the language — but cut the link between identity-in-the-language and identification-in-our-reactions (by training ourselves in general semantics) — rather than to take a meat-axe to the verb "to be."

Argument #2:

The phrase "the natural order of evaluation," as a general semantics formulation, refers to the process of moving from lower orders of abstraction to higher; from, for example, the notions of test-taking, attending classes, and reading text-books, to the generalized notion of "student." A civilization advances when it can move from the idea of individual trees to that of "forest." Korzybski claimed that the capacity to pro-duce higher and higher abstractions leads to a general con-sciousness of abstracting, which he described as "the very key to further human evolution." (*Science and Sanity*, 3rd ed., p.xxi) E-Prime tends to make the expression of higher orders of abstraction more difficult; instead of describing someone as a student, for example, the E-Prime speaker is more likely to say, "She attends classes at the university," or some such thing. That sort of forced return to lower orders of abstrac-tion may have drawbacks that the advocates of E-Prime have not examined. It would seem more in line with the time-binding of the human race, to leave the individual free to choose the appropriate order of abstraction in the given case, rather than to erect a structure that forces him or her to lower orders. Of course, many individuals do neglect the lower orders of abstraction in their talking and reacting, but train-ing in general semantics may be a better prescription for that malady than E-Prime.

Argument #1:

E-Prime makes no distinction between statements that cross the principles of general semantics and statements that do not. A statement such as, "I am going to the store," vio-lates no formulation of general semantics, yet E-Prime pro-hibits it. That clearly places E-Prime outside the interrelated set of principles and practices that constitute the discipline.

The first question we should ask of a principle or practice of general semantics is whether or not it fits the facts (and the other formulations of the system), not whether or not it is expedient. The map-territory paradigm, the verifiable premises of the discipline, the deliberately limited nature of Korzybski's formulations, all suggest that we should not allow a practice that lacks consistency with the other tenets of general semantics into the system. In my opinion, E-Prime goes way beyond the borders of what a discipline with scientific aspirations should tolerate.

POETRY AND E-PRIME:

Risa Kaparo* *Some Preliminary Thoughts*

P OETRY DISTINGUISHES ITSELF from other writing in several important ways. Perhaps we feel this distinction most significantly in the power poetry has to not only evoke new meaning responses within us, but to vivify our awareness of the immediate. To this end, a writer must create space in which readers can extend their attention and differentiate the creative edge of their sensing-feeling-knowing by creating a suspension of the usual movement of thought, assumptions, values, purposes so that greater subtleties of meaning — the paradoxes, ambiguities, uncertainties, etc., — can unfold in an entirely new coherence.

To the extent that the writer finds expression of his or her own self-sensing awareness on the page, he or she invites the reader into the "as it happens" flowering of experience. Language paradoxically can have the power to silence. The

* Risa Kaparo, Ph.D., as founder of Inquiry, a non-profit institute, and as a partner in Learners Unlimited, has developed and facilitated seminars and workshops for educators and health practitioners from the perspective of learning, as an organismic, self-organizing process. Her writing has appeared in national and international magazines and journals. Her poem "Waste," written in E-Prime, follows this article.

85

poem provides an environment in which the reader can enter a first person, subjective awareness of the "here/now," the fluctuations of feelings and sensations, needs and desires, imagination and intuition. In this way, the writing creates a context in which the reader can extend his or her awareness, just like walking in a garden might nourish within awareness a growing range of sensitivities that enrich a vital, felt-sense of aliveness.

As writers, we need to disenthrall ourselves from the "it is so ness" of thought and the authoritarian voice of hierarchical writing because it perpetuates the tendency to take what we read "on faith" as truth or fact. Our organismic functioning can serve as a "semsorium" (1) where we can sense meaning N-dimensionally, as it unfolds in the flow of experiencing. When we read something, the very act of reading can arrest the mechanical, assumptive activities of thought for a moment and suspend us in a fuller movement of attention. In these critical moments, the old structures of consciousness may re-organize into new orders of meaning, and we find renewal.

Writing in E-Prime (English without the use of the verb "to be" in any conjugational form) has proven very effective in bringing awareness to certain aspects of the fragmentation of thought. In addition, in doing away with the "is" of identity and predication, the ongoing challenge of writing or speaking in E-Prime, may prove most valuable in de-automating our use of language, allowing for a different quality of attention to arise.

As Ernest Fenollosa points out: "The moment we use the copula, the moment we express subjective inclusions, poetry evaporates. The more concretely and vividly we express the interactions of things the better the poetry. We need in poetry thousands of active words, each doing its utmost to show forth the motive and vital forces. We can not exhibit the wealth of nature by mere summation, by the piling of sentences. Poetic thought works by suggestion, crowding maximum meaning into the single phrase, pregnant, charged, and luminous from within." (2)

Fenollosa drives this point home by suggesting English has "...only one real working verb, to-wit, the quasi-verb 'is' ...all other verbs...(transform) into particles and gerunds." This weakening of language results in a logic which fragments our experience into rigid classifications of "things" (i.e., "to run" practically becomes a case of "running." Instead of thinking directly, "the man runs," our logician makes two subjective equations, namely: "The individual in question is contained under the class 'man'; and the class 'man' is contained under the class of 'running things.' ").

Thus, eliminating the copula "is" or the negative copula "is not" enables us to move into a way of organizing meaning outside of the usual classificatory ordering that reifies "thingness." For example, it calls into question the continuity over time we attribute to the subject "I," which tends to elicit a sense of separateness from all that the "I" participates in. Perhaps of even greater significance, the influence of language in constellating a more or less static, semi-independent, semi-permanent object of the "self" orients attention toward a third person perspective — an inferential perspective that tends to dissociate thought from the process of experiencing.

In contrast, an active, descriptive mode of languaging encourages a phenomenological self-sensing awareness through which we can learn into subtler levels of differentiation and extend ourselves into a more creative mode of responsiveness and participation. We can liken this awakening to what occurs when a dreamer shifts into lucid dreaming and consciously participates in the unfolding of the dream. Poetry can provide an environment where a reader awakens to the movement of his or her most immediate felt-sense of meaning — opening new realms of possibility for creative participation in life.

NOTES

1. A word coined by the learning theorist, David Boulton (1992).
2. Ernest Fenollosa (1853-1908), a collector, curator and critic of Chinese and Japanese art. From an essay "The Chinese Written Character as a Medium for Poetry," first published in 1920 in *Instigations of Ezra Pound*.

Waste

She probably had no family or will — a ward of the state —
one of the nameless. Still she arrived basically intact
except for the feet and head
which went to the dental and podiatry schools.
Someone helps me lift her from the shelf and
roll her out of the refrigerated room.
I lean in for the first cut but withdraw my scalpel, having neglected
to secure the wheels and stop. Pulling the mask
from my mouth and nose, I touch one palm of the rubber glove against the other
and for a moment close my eyes —
needing to find some way
of respect.

Taking a deep breath, I press the blade through several layers
of skin and subcutaneous tissue, cutting along the sternum.
Then since nothing else will do
I break into her flesh with my fingernails and peel back the sheaths
of fascia. Her left breast
falls into my hand
still embedded in its husk of skin.

As the cadaver warms, the air grows heavier with formaldehyde.
I cut into the abdomen and feel nausea.
The stench of adipose tissue — reeking more lurid than muscle, skin, bone.
I look around the stainless steel and formica room
wishing for plants that metabolize the chemical.
I imagine the time when earth lay covered in green, the plants
smothering in their own waste. This
before the advent
of a new class *mammalia*
that could live off that oxygen.

In winter when the earth lay creatively fallow, Rudolf Steiner
blended manure with rotting compost
potentialized the mixture
homeopathically
and buried it in antlers
to draw power from the stars.

He never used human feces
to fertilize soil for our consumption
because
he felt we've already abstracted what we need from our food
the way a cow takes substance to fatten on
and leaves the stuff of human intelligence untouched.
So I think of our waste

and wonder what we leave behind
that could nourish another.
I wonder most about meaning,
whether we could learn to live off our own waste.
I think of my mother's dying still to come.

I cut through the sternum with a power saw, dig my hands
between the ribs and pull as hard as I can.
Membranes tear into strands that gleam like water webs.
And the colors — teals and lilacs, even after the formaldehyde
or maybe because of it, I do not know.
I lift the fine lace of her lungs on the tips of two fingers and blow
gently, the way children do with dandelions. I watch them
float on my breath.

Risa Kaparo

Ralph Kenyon* **E-PRIME: The Spirit and the Letter**

E VER SINCE I FIRST READ about E-Prime, I have made an analogy employing the familiar distinction between the letter of
the law and its spirit. I make a similar distinction in the use
(and misuse) of E-Prime. One can use E-Prime by conform-
ing to the letter of its prescription — do not use any form of
the verb 'to be' — while committing all manner of identifications, which E-Prime ostensibly aims to eliminate. It is also
possible for one to sprinkle one's formulations liberally with
various forms of 'to be' while scrupulously avoiding identification.

In my interpretation or understanding, one uses E-Prime in
order to make clear who makes what judgements. E-Prime
says "say who says so." E-Prime sentences should reveal who
makes what judgements, not conceal them. "Take responsibility for your judgements; state them openly."

* Ralph Kenyon has an extensive background in physics, engineering, and
mathematics. Currently, he is completing work on his Ph.D. in philosophy at
the University of Massachusetts Amherst. He also writes software for
PolyMorphic Systems microcomputers and edits PolyLetter, a computer-users
group newsletter.

Applying the "Letter/Spirit" distinction

Let me apply the "Letter/Spirit" distinction in the analysis of one statement put forth as an example of E-Prime. Elaine Johnson presents the following sentence as an example of one of her high school student's new-found ability to write in E-Prime.

"I found the movie more rewarding than the novel." (1)

While some might evaluate this sentence as a good example of E-Prime, I do not think it satisfies the spirit of E-Prime very well. When one finds something, one usually finds it in some *place* — in this case, in a different category of (more) rewarding things than the category of rewarding things in which one found the novel. Moreover, the sentence treats "rewarding" as some characteristic of the novel that one can discover or *find*. I think that even the choice of the adjective 'rewarding,' which directly modifies 'movie' and implicitly modifies 'novel' misleads readers in the direction of attending to objects and properties of objects.

Consider, for a moment, the sentence that the above sentence rather obviously derives from:

The movie *was* more rewarding than the novel (*was*).

This sentence asserts the existence of a relation between two things. I certainly disapprove of the above sentence more than I disapprove of the following one:

I found the movie *to be* more rewarding than (*I found*) the novel (*to be*).

This sentence at least includes explicit reference to a speaker (I), and paraphrases to E-Prime readily, by simply making the verb 'to be' implicit by omission.

I found the movie more rewarding than the novel.

Still, the term 'finds' externalizes one's attention to "what one finds"; one generally "finds" a thing. I offer the term 'evaluate' as better indicating the judgement involved.

I *evaluate* the movie *as* more rewarding than the novel.

But even this still suggests a comparative judgement about properties of objects.

Let's get "rewarding" back into direct personal experience and acknowledge more explicitly what we usually mean by "*being* rewarded" — we *like* how we feel about it. Would you consider the following paraphrase too direct and simple?

I liked the movie better than I liked the novel.

This sentence most directly presents my understanding of the spirit of E-Prime. The speaker (I) takes direct responsibility with an active verb ('like') and presents his/her own comparative judgement (better).

But we must all walk before we can run and crawl before we can walk. So, I suppose the offered sentence makes a step in the right direction. The above analysis shows a sequence of paraphrases, on a simple theme, going from "not-very-E-Prime-like-at-all" to "very-E-Prime-like".

Abusing E-Prime

I perceive some people as "abusing" rather than using E-Prime. One can perform simple substitutions on sentences to replace the verb 'to be' with a direct substitute while not eliminating the identification at all. Such substitutions constitute, in my opinion, mere baby-steps in the right direction. But when someone claims that they "use" E-Prime, as if it were an "all or none" (two-valued) choice, I get annoyed, especially if I see them just making what I call "euphemistic" simple substitutions for 'to be.' "Exists as" indeed, I say! One can abuse E-Prime because one can eliminate the verb 'to be' without eliminating identification. I say that it is equally pos-

sible to eliminate identification without eliminating all forms
of the verb 'to be.'

Identification without 'to be'

The syntactic device of a complement (objective or nominative) does the job quite well. Here are some examples.
"John, the commie, did so-and-so." "She went to see Murphy,
the butcher." The verbs 'qualifies as' and 'exists as' have been
used in some general semantics writings as direct substitutes
for 'is'. 'Exists as' is a particularly obvious example, in view of
the fact that one of the meanings of the verb 'to be' is "to exist", and when something "exists" as something else, it is taking the place of that other thing. Of course one can "identify"
the verb 'identify' as the most obvious identification not using
the verb 'to be.'

'To be' avoiding identification

One can be using the verb 'to be' while avoiding identification. The auxiliary form, such as 'is' in 'is using,' or in 'is running' does not identify the subject with any thing or category.
If we avoid using 'to be' as a linking verb connecting a predicate nominative or a predicate adjective with a subject, we
will avoid identifying the subject with the nominative or the
adjective. "The color is green," or "That room is the bath-
room" are among the example sentences to be avoided.

Desirable identification

There are times when identification is desirable. How
happy would you be with someone who refuses to give you
the conventional name for something? Inquire of someone
their given name. You thereby ask for the symbol by which
to "identify" him or her. How do you teach kids the names of
things without implicit or explicit identification? Names are,
after all, the means by which we communicate the "identity"

of things or people. "Who is the speaker?" or "Who speaks?" asks for something other than the sensory experiences that the asker already has.

I have pontificated enough concerning my view that E-Prime is not always desirable and that it can be misused. In general, I favor the spirit of E-Prime. I'd like to see it used more often, but with careful attention to the *spirit* of E-Prime (as I understand it).

NOTES AND REFERENCES

1. Elaine C. Johnson, "Discovering E-Prime," in *To Be or Not: An E-Prime Anthology*, edited by D. David Bourland, Jr. and Paul Dennithorne Johnston, International Society for General Semantics, San Francisco, 1991, p. 6.
2. The use of quotation marks in this article conforms to the convention that is standard in the academic writings of philosophy, linguistics and mathematics. Single quotes (') are used to indicate that the word or phrase itself is being discussed. Double quotes (") are used when quoting text and as the extensional device to indicate that the word or phrase may be being used in a non-standard sense (scare quotes).
3. The idea for this paper occurred to me a number of years ago. It was finally written on March 31, 1992, and was first published in *ETC*. Vol. 49, No. 2, Summer 1992, pp. 185-188.

THE WORD "E-PRIME"

Robert Wanderer* **IS NOT THE THING**

E-Prime presents a dilemma to the general semantics-oriented person seeking to represent the stuff *Out There* more accurately.

I believe it merits our praise for eliminating false-to-fact constructions such as the *Is of Identity* and the *Is of Predication*, near-meaningless phraseology such as "it is known that...," and passive forms which fail to fix responsibility for the action they attempt to describe.

But I'm left with several nagging questions: Must we also lose the "acceptable" constructions using "to be"? Does making the big effort to ban "to be" lead us to overlook other problems? And can we gain the advantages without loss of accuracy and occasionally awkward constructions which substitute for the unacceptable language?

On the first question, E-Primeologists say yes: They find it more consistent and practical to eliminate all forms of "to be" rather than try to differentiate between the OK and the not-OK forms. On the second question, we cannot fairly blame E-Prime for not doing what it doesn't claim to do. In *To Be or*

* Robert Wanderer writes the "Illustrating General Semantics" feature for *Et cetera*. He also edits *The Map*, the newsletter of the San Francisco Chapter of I.S.G.S.

Not, Kellogg and Bourland call E-Prime a "practical starting point in the development of a non-Aristotelian language" (p.37), which seems to suggest that other reforms may come later. But I'm still uncomfortable with the awkward substitutes; I wonder if the cure is worse than the alleged disease.

My name is Robert Wanderer. That sentence uses a "semantically acceptable" form of "is," but E-Prime rejects all forms of "to be." E-Primeophiles suggest I eliminate that "is" by saying such things as "People call me Robert Wanderer" or "At my birth, my parents decided to name me Robert Wanderer." But I find these convolutions not only longer and less clear, but somewhat inaccurate: Is my name Robert Wanderer just because the majority of my friends say so, and am I using that name only because of a decision my parents made many years ago?

Similarly, I find Kellogg's suggestion that we change "What is your name?" to "What do you call yourself?" (p.97) as somewhere between quaint and ludicrous, with a possibility of insulting.

Kellogg translates "This food is good" to "This food tastes good" (p. 96). I see "I think this food tastes good" as still better, but I would rank "I think this food is good" as better than his "This food tastes good," since I consider affixing responsibility more important than eliminating "to be."

Bourland offers a translation of a passage from Machiavelli's *The Prince*, changing the first sentence from "Everyone admits how praiseworthy it is in a prince to keep faith..." to "Every one admits that praiseworthy princes should keep faith..." (pp.112-113). I consider the use of "should" as much of a problem in its own way as the use of "is," and we would need a longer and more involved translation to assign responsibility.

I see Bourland at his weakest when he attempts to deal with Korzybski's "Whatever you say a thing is, well, it is not; for the word is not the thing" (p. 111). As he points out, the statement had considerable shock value. Bourland's offer to explain Korzybski's dictum by using the Structural Differential I consider both a cop-out and not understandable to many people; and his translation "One must differentiate carefully between structures on the Object Level ("perceived

reality") and related structures on the Symbolic Level" as losing not only the shock value but the elegant simplicity of the
original.

Let me try to state my difference with the Bourland/Kel-
logg point of view. We probably agree on aiming for a clearer, more accurate representation of the *Out There* in the
words we use to deal with it. We probably agree on eliminating the "bad" forms of "is." But they seek to eliminate all
forms of "to be" even when the result strikes me as inaccurate
or weird or even just plain dumb. I gather I put more emphasis than they do on cutting back use of "shoulds" and other ways we fail to take responsibility; or perhaps they agree
but see this as a possible future development. Also, I wonder
if the debate over "to be" might tend to lead people in the
general population to regard general semantics and E-Prime
as too "far out" for consideration.

Certainly we can regard E-Prime as a useful teaching technique to improve writing and thinking and as a way of alerting students to the problems of language (while keeping in
mind the central goal of accuracy and clarity). While I have
generally tried to avoid "to be's" in this piece, I reserve the
right to steer clear of the awkward extremes of E-Prime. As
someone once said, the word *is* not the thing.

THERESA PARKINSON* **_BEYOND E-PRIME_**

W HILE READING _To Be Or Not: An E-Prime Anthology_ I gained the impression that the writers, despite their scholarly efforts, fail to see and address a key issue. Both Paul Johnston, in his introduction (p. xiii), and David Bourland, in: "To Be or Not To Be: E-Prime as a Tool for Critical Thinking" (p. 117), refer to Korzybski's remark distinguishing between the successful results of engineering and scientific activity and the fruitless and sad results of political activity. And, of course, the classic explanation for this state of affairs follows: the engineer and the scientist use a language that has a structure similar to that of the objects they deal with, whereas "the politicians normally employ a language of archaic structure that uses static terminology in describing dynamic human socioeconomic issues," etc. Hence, according to Korzybski and the proponents of E-Prime, we must needs seek a remedy in the restructuring of language.

However uncommon, "common sense" should immediately alert us to the fact that in the solution which he presents, Korzybski himself introduces error by making a false identification, the very sort of identification he decries so intensely in most of his writings. What applies to physical nature does not necessarily apply to human nature. The workings of the former manifest strict, unalterable laws: a ball thrown into the air does not debate as to whether it will descend or not;

* Theresa Parkinson recently obtained her Ph.D. from McGill University, Montreal. Currently, she pursues musical studies in piano performance at the Southern California Conservatory of Music in Sun Valley.

gravity pulls it down. Man can, by choice, propel himself into space and remain there almost indefinitely, or he can create artificial anti-gravity states, because of the formidable potential in his creative mind. Similarly, man can choose between following a reasonable course of action and an unreasonable one, depending on what suits his good or evil intentions and purposes. Contrary to Korzybski's opinion, morality and reason do not necessarily walk hand in hand. As Paul Valéry, the French poet and thinker, in parodying Pascal's famous epigram (1) so well worded it: "The heart has its reasons, which reason only knows too well!" (2)

Ironically, this freedom of choice, which inanimate physical nature does not possess (animals, too, have freedom of choice to some measure, whence the proverbial: "You can lead a horse to water but you cannot make it drink!"), and which Korzybski fails to take into account in his Theory of Time-Binding, likewise determines the success and failure of E-Prime.

I do not deny that E-Prime, as an intellectual exercise, can yield benefits. Nor does E-Prime necessarily prohibit metaphors, poetic expression, literary endeavor, the passive mode, as Allen Read seemed to fear, and as Paul Johnston cleverly demonstrated in his short story "Labels." However, we agree that "one can reflect his bigotry in E-Prime; one can make invalid (or worse, partially valid) statements in E-Prime; and one can make cynical, self-serving statements in E-Prime", (3) that one can even in E-Prime maintain assumptions, identifications, notions of permanence, gross generalizations, etc. Likely a Daltonian would view Serina's "gold-red" (4) hair, and Bramble's "olive green" (5) shirt differently, but these are minor assumptions. More alarming, though, Joseph Goebbels' remark would hardly have seemed less ignominious had he phrased it in E-Prime: "The Jew, a waste product, must needs undergo extermination!" (6) What a choice example of E-Prime the following Biblical passage offers: "The fool hath said in his heart: 'There is no God.' " (Psalms 14:1)!

If, then, "the *technique* of E-Prime does in no way guarantee... reducing dishonesty and prejudice (prejudging) in our communications," (7) if "E-Prime does not cure or resolve all

linguistic and behavioral problems," (8) if "the intention of the individual involved plays the predominant controlling role," (9) if the present writer can write this little critique of E-Prime in E-Prime, what can David Bourland mean when he states that "E-Prime provides a simple discipline that does work"? (10)
    I quote Robert Wilson:

> The Sapir-Whorf-Korzybski Hypothesis holds that a change in language can alter our perception of the cosmos. A revision of language structure, in particular, can alter the brain as dramatically as a psychedelic. In our metaphor, if we change the software, the computer operates in a new way. (11)

    Omitting the fact that von Neumann and Brillouin find the comparisons established between the brain and the computer of limited and dubious value, (12) let us assume that the usage of E-Prime can effect changes in perception of the world and changes in behavior. At this point I wish to thank Emory Menefee for noting that, after all, the proof of the pudding lies in the tasting, and, hence, for asking, "why don't we gather some hard data?... Where is our evidence?" (13) Why do we not look to "divorce rate, drug abuse, job turnover, salary, criminal involvement, medical history, etc." (14) among the users of E-Prime to ascertain the effectiveness of this discipline?
    E-Prime situates itself on the abstract level of language, the level of the labels. Unfortunately, wars, such as the recent Gulf War brought on by such men as Saddam Hussein, occur not on an abstract but on a too-real objective level. Children do not need words to sense neglect or abuse by parents or adults. Lovers hardly restrict themselves to precision in verbal communication when exchanging caresses. Language constitutes only a part of human communication.
    Restructuring verbal communication, in order to improve its clarity and accuracy and to implement changes of perception in the user, falls into the area of treating the symptoms without curing the illness. One can liken abolishing the verb "to be" from the English language to banning all knives, even

from the kitchen, because these instruments have killed people!

Seriously, unless the discipline of E-Prime touches the illness that plagues mankind, unless it teaches men to choose to maintain amiable relations among themselves and to earnestly concentrate on all the means that such a choice would entail, then it can only remain an intellectual game, the pastime of mandarins, or of computer programmers!

NOTES

1. Pascal, *"Le coeur a ses raisons que la raison ne connaît pas."* "The heart has its reasons which reason does not know."
2. Paul Valéry, " *'Le coeur a ses raisons...que la raison ne connaît pas.'* Elle ne les connaît que trop." (*Cahiers*, XXIX, p. 747)
3. D. David Bourland, Jr., "To Be or Not To Be: E-Prime as a Tool for Critical Thinking," *To Be or Not: An E-Prime Anthology*, San Francisco: International Society for General Semantics, 1991, p. 108.
4. Paul Dennithorne Johnston, "Labels," *To Be or Not: An E-Prime Anthology*, op. cit., p. 133.
5. Ibid., p. 131.
6. D. David Bourland, Jr., op. cit., p. 110.
7. E. W. Kellogg III and David Bourland, Jr., "Working With E-Prime: Some Practical Notes," *To Be or Not: An E-Prime Anthology*, op. cit., p.44.
8. Ibid., p. 44.
9. Ibid., p. 44.
10. D. David Bourland, Jr., op. cit., p. 106.
11. Robert Anton Wilson, "Toward Understanding E-Prime," *To Be or Not: An E-Prime Anthology*, op. cit., p. 24.
12. See John von Neumann, "The Language of the Brain Not the Language of Mathematics", in *The Computer and the Brain*, New Haven: Yale University Press, 1958, p. 80, and L. Brillouin, "Thermodynamics and Information Theory," in *American Scientist*, vol. 38 (1950), pp. 598, 599.
13. Emory Menefee, "E-Prime or E-Choice," *Et cetera: A Review of General Semantics*, vol. 48, no. 2 (Summer 1991), p. 137.
14. Ibid., p. 140.

There are no bad words; there are
unfortunate ways of using any word.

— *Wendell Johnson*

'S WORD PLAY AT THE

Emory Menefee* # GRAMMAR REFORM SCHOOL

T HE IDEA OF reforming languages to weed out undesired
spelling, grammar, and whatnot has preoccupied small
coteries of well-meaning people for years. Unfortunately for
the proponents, language users seem to adopt changes only
slowly, if at all, through a poorly understood process of
evolution and diffusion, even if these changes seem eminent-
ly reasonable. E-Prime (E') has been suggested as a "new paradigm" for English (1), as it surely would be if generally
adopted, since it requires eliminating *all* forms of the verb "to
be" from written and spoken English. However, I suspect
(and hope) that this purist language will also see limited acceptance, and that those interested in obtaining the benefits
claimed for E-Prime will follow the less stringent suggestions
advocated by general semanticists for over 50 years.

For reasons that may become clear, I have dubbed as "E-
Choice" ordinary English in which people have become

---

* Dr. Menefee, a resident of Richmond, California, divides much of his time
between general semantics and research in physical chemistry (mostly polymer
physics and hair growth).

acutely conscious of their use and interpretation of "to be" verbs and other linguistic snags, eliminating those occurrences that might be called pernicious (2,3). Most serious students of general semantics have become conscious in this way, and sharply limit their indiscriminate use of "to be" verbs. I believe that most English speakers can learn to use the language in this more effective way, particularly if they know and apply the basic ideas of general semantics, coupled with some awareness of the principles of scientific investigation. Although the claims of general semantics need more testing, an abundance of individual testimony supports the idea that application of its principles can facilitate trouble-free discourse in ordinary English. On the other hand, E-Prime demands a major change in grammatical usage to fulfill dubious claims of nearly automatic benefits. Incidentally, I wish to assert here that I am impressed by the efforts of those who wish to write, speak, think, or whatever, in E-Prime. However, I object to and doubt many of the unfounded claims made about its benefits, and would especially dislike efforts to impose it editorially on others. E-Primers claim so much for this language (4) that I must amplify my opinion of it as unnecessary, awkward, and even antithetic to the ideas of general semantics. In succeeding paragraphs, I deal with increasingly "serious" criticisms, beginning with simple difficulties in making particular statements, and ending with a critique of the premise that one can substitute a mechanical device for the process of understanding.

Say What?

Clearly, one cannot say things the same way in E-Prime as in ordinary English or E-Choice, because one does not have the same words available. Nevertheless, I think that E-Primers strongly believe that E-Prime not only can convey the same meaning, but in a "better" way, especially if one avoids translating from ordinary English and writes or speaks solely E-Prime. However, here are a few phrases out of a countless number that seem to have no exact E-Prime counterparts:

Is it raining now?

It was the best of times, it was ... [and other "it was" or "it is" expressions].

The motor is running [and other progressive forms].

My name is Jack.

The doors are locked.

The flask was kept at room temperature during the polymerization.

The velocity of light in free space is constant.

The last expression perhaps needs comment. One can more properly say, "Within the requirements of special relativity, the velocity of light in free space is constant." But circumlocutions that say the velocity "appears" or "remains" constant seem to imply experiment, whereas the relativistic requirement is inflexible (until disproved).

These examples are cited merely to demonstrate that E-Prime is indeed a language different from ordinary English, with the unusual characteristic that some meanings are hard or impossible to translate into it, but not from it. Obviously, *anything* said in E-Prime can be said in E-Choice.

World Without Is

How would people fare in a culture in which everybody was reared from birth to speak E-Prime? We know the kinds of problems our ordinary English have caused us. Many people kill over insults, delight in deceiving one another, believe in pseudo-science over conventional science, elect politicians on the basis of lies and videotape, etc. In a World Without Is, one might expect such problems to vanish. But would they? Or rather, why should they? One can frame idiocy and deception in E-Prime quite easily, if it suits a purpose, and merely listening to an "is-less" language can hardly confer any remarkable ability in critical thinking. The so-called "is of identity" and "is of predication" forms can and do trap the unwary into believing some assertions are more definite or "real" than the abstractions warrant, but learning to eliminate or ignore these usages is a principal aim of general semantics, regardless of the verbal structures used.

The leading exemplars of written and of spoken E-Prime, E. W. Kellogg III and D. David Bourland, Jr., call the use of "is" the "deity mode," with the implication that those who use it set themselves up as supreme, god-like authorities about the nature of things (4). It is difficult for me to find in a statement such as "I'm sure that bird is an egret" a god-like pronouncement. There are occasions when the use of "is" in identity and predication seems pernicious and should be avoided, though I suspect that nearly all of its occurrences are benign. Purist E-Prime dogma has it otherwise, with the belief that nearly all occurrences of the verb "to be" in "is of identity" and "is of predication" modes are pernicious. These usages are supposed to encourage thinking about the world as containing static, independent objects, instead of ever-changing kinetically interacting processes that gain much of their "reality" from our perception — roughly the way physics currently looks at matter (ironically enough, a view disseminated by scientists in papers and talks abundantly containing "to be" verbs and the passive voice). According to E-prime dogma (5), various major ills of society can be blamed on the Aristotelian attitude encouraged by the use of "to be" verbs, including environmental problems and our sluggishness in responding to them — presumably because we who use ordinary English believe the world will always stay the same. If I could even halfway convince myself that our global problems could seriously be blamed on a verb, I would most certainly hie to the nearest stump to advocate purist E-Prime. However, as with other E-Prime claims, this one is presented with no evidence. Nevertheless, perhaps I shall add the impending destruction of the world to the list of evils caused by "to be," along with 2000 years of intellectual sloth and Aristotelian darkness (2).

The Pernicious Is

The three "laws of thought" are usually given as "laws" of (a) identity, (b) contradiction, and (c) the excluded middle. These give rise to what is currently called "crisp" logic, as opposed to "fuzzy." Like Galilean mechanics, crisp logic is often all that is called for, and certainly simpler. It gives rise to "yes or no" voting, "guilty or not guilty" judgments, the ability to call the bird an egret instead of something else at the same time, etc. Even though crisp logic has many drawbacks and traps, the alternative of implementing fuzzy logical rules in all cases seems formidable. It is crisp logic, however, that has engendered the idea of E-Prime, since the verb forms "to be" lend themselves to "exact" statements. How did this come to be?

Interestingly enough, Aristotle does not cite the "law of identity," at least in my reading of him (McKeon edition). He does make such remarks as "what is, is," etc., but most of his effort went into the other two "laws." Leibnitz is supposed to be the first to state the law of identity as "A=A." Frankly, I have never had much trouble with this one. I am quite aware that in our space-time frame A now is not the same thing as A ten seconds ago. At the event (particle) level the "law" may be presumed always false, but at some higher levels of labeled abstraction, I can believe it. The tree I look at today is, to an adequate approximation in my mind, the same tree I saw yesterday. Life is made somewhat more bearable to me by accepting this kind of identity. Even in my is-ridden world, I have no difficulty recognizing changing situations, which are mostly all too obtrusive.

For some reason, the idea of an "is of identity" usage came to be centered not on "A=A" but on "A=B" statements, at least in the minds of the founders of general semantics. In other words, "Jack is an idiot" is considered an "is of identity," not "Jack is Jack" or "An idiot is an idiot." So, perhaps some of our confusion arose by this naming. If the various usages of "is" had been more carefully described, perhaps the task of general semantics could have been slightly easier. Instead of lumping everything into "is" of identity and predication, we might have various kinds of "is" of assertion, such as

Is of opinion: That painting is beautiful; Jack is an idiot.

Is of description: The pencil is green.

Is of approximation: The density of lead is 11.3 g/cc.

Is of labeling: My name is Jack.

Is of fact: Hoover was the 31st President of the U.S..

Is of equality: 1+1 is 2; The velocity of light is constant.

etc.

The purpose of this exercise is not seriously to propose a different "is of" for every possible usage, but to suggest that we *can* remain aware of the abstractions in our discourse, and realize that there is no such thing as exactness, but only assertions that have precision ranging from zero to very high. The assertions given above range from vague to precise. All, however, are subject to question at some level, depending on how the elements are defined. Such problems are implicit in any form of English, whether it be ordinary English or E-Prime.

In the second paragraph I alluded to the value of knowing the principles of scientific *investigation* rather than the principles of science. Given the present low esteem that early-grade science training suffers in the United States, one could hardly expect more than a smattering of education in the facts or principles of science. However, its methods are easily explained and grasped, and could fit into almost any curriculum. One general idea is this: whenever we investigate some part of our world and attempt a predictive explanation for it, we are apt to be proved wrong, although what we say may serve our needs adequately for the time being. Hence, our pronouncements about the sensed world should be said in a way that leaves the question of an "ultimate" explanation open. These assertive pronouncements can, if necessary, be "fuzzified" through hedge words and phrases: "I think," "the information suggests," "probably," "in my opinion," etc. Instead of rephrasing in E-Prime, we thus have the option of using an E-Choice version of an "is of identity" or "is of predication" expression: "I think Jack is an idiot." Incidentally, E-Prime constructions may also require hedging (e.g., "I think he looks ugly" for "He looks ugly.")

The semantic "safety" of our discourse bears some proportionality to our consciousness of the abstractions we use, where consciousness here means some degree of awareness of the words we use, their role as abstractions, and how they may be received and interpreted (or misinterpreted). A major aim of general semantics is to train oneself to be so conscious of abstracting that awareness of it is ever-present. In this condition of internalization, I think that one can use and interpret any grammar, including "to be" usages or otherwise, without risk. E-Prime, through its "simple" rule of elimination of all "to be" verbs, provides a mechanical way to replace internalized consciousness. Over-reliance on this device will therefore represent a failure of consciousness of abstracting, and hence a failure of general semantics, since consciousness of abstracting goes far beyond the use of "to be" words. Still, E-Prime may have considerable pedagogic value. In the way that parsing by diagram may clarify grammatical structure, proscribing "to be" verbs in written and oral exercises may help students learn to avoid unnecessary reliance on these forms.

To summarize, E-Prime may be described as a semantically limited subset of English, which calls extreme attention to the confusion of abstraction that can be generated by some usages of "to be" verbs. E-Prime no doubt has pedagogic value in forcefully calling attention to the abstraction confusion caused by some "to be" usages, and to an over-dependence on "to be" verbs. However, its presumed benefits seem to be fully realizable through the use of ordinary English under conditions of internalized consciousness of abstraction, a course that involves little alteration of the structure of English.

Acknowledgement: I thank E. W. Kellogg III for written and oral communication on this topic, and Jeremy Klein for helpful discussion during preparation of this manuscript.

REFERENCES AND NOTE

1. Bourland, D. David, Jr., "A Non-Aristotelian Paradigm for Linguistics," in *To Be or Not: An E-Prime Anthology*, D. David Bourland, Jr. and Paul Dennithorne Johnston, eds. International Society for General Semantics, San Francisco, 1991, p. 135.
2. Menefee, Emory, "E-Prime or E-Choice," *Et cetera,* 48 No. 2 (1991) 136-140.
3. William Dallmann has suggested [*Et cetera*, 47 No. 1 (1990) 77-78 and in an article in the present issue] a modified E-Prime that he calls E-Prime$_{mod}$. This version eliminates "to be" in identity and predication, but retains it as an auxiliary and for the description of existence or non-identity.
4. Kellogg, E. W., III, and D. David Bourland, Jr., in *To Be or Not: An E-Prime Anthology*, D. David Bourland, Jr. and Paul Dennithorne Johnston, eds. International Society for General Semantics, San Francisco, 1991, p. 45.
5. ibid, p. 37.

Responses

D. David Bourland, Jr., the inventor of
E-Prime, and E. W. Kellogg III, a leading
E-Prime theorist and advocate, respond to
criticisms raised in the preceding pages.

THE GOOD, THE BAD, AND THE UGLY:

Comments on the

E. W. Kellogg III*   *E-Prime Symposium*

Since the publication of Cullen Murphy's article " 'To Be' in Their Bonnets" in the February, 1992, issue of *The Atlantic* magazine, the idea of E-Prime (English without the verb "to be") has aroused the curiosity and interest of people across the United States. (1) This interest grew further when Robert Siegle of National Public Radio's "All Things Considered" interviewed me as one of the few who speak fluently in E-Prime. Although the NPR broadcast provided neither a phone number or address, the International Society for General Semantics received hundreds of calls from people wanting to order the book *To Be or Not: An E-Prime Anthology*. (2)

From the response, it looks as if E-Prime has more widespread appeal than anyone expected. Although E-Prime has aroused controversy since Dave Bourland went public with the idea in 1965, only recently has it surfaced in such a way

* Dr. E. W. Kellogg III presently serves as the Vice-President of Publications of ISGS. Currently, he has an E-Prime workbook underway. The workbook will comprise a sort of short course (about 10 classroom sessions) aimed at high school English classes that will allow students (and teachers) to experiment with E-Prime.

as to make it virtually impossible for the general semantics community at large to ignore. I feel delighted that the editor of *Et cetera*, Jeremy Klein, has given me the opportunity to preview and comment upon the papers included in this special E-Prime symposium issue.

Those familiar with my articles (3, 4) know that I have made a long-term commitment to training myself in a more "mindful," non-Aristotelian and phenomenological orientation by changing the way I use language. In spite of my enthusiasm for E-Prime as an experimental discipline, its use does entail certain difficulties. In his article "The Word 'E-Prime' Is Not the Thing," veteran general semanticist Robert Wanderer grabs the bull by the tail and faces the situation. (5) He asks the following questions, among others: "Must we lose the acceptable constructions using 'to be'? Does making the big effort to ban 'to be' lead us to overlook other problems? And can we gain the advantages without loss of accuracy and occasionally awkward constructions which substitute for the unacceptable language?"

Although anyone seriously interested in E-Prime will need to consider these important questions for themselves, I will take this opportunity to answer them from my own point of view. Must one eliminate the use of every form of "to be" in order to reap the benefits of the discipline? William Dallmann, in his "Is Is Not Is Is Not Is And Other Thoughts On E-Prime," proposes E-Prime$_{mod}$, a form of E-Prime that disallows the use of "to be" in its identity and predication modes *only*. (6) In its written form at least, Dallmann's variant succeeds in allowing the user to more clearly communicate with others, while eliminating "to be" in its most pernicious usages.

Must one use 100% E-Prime to reap any of the benefits? Certainly not. Any reduction in the use of "to be" can prove beneficial, and I applaud the efforts of anyone who moves in this direction. An all-or-nothing attitude can sabotage the learning of E-Prime by the beginner, and even after achieving a certain level of skill an individual may not choose to go "all the way". (3, 4) However "weaker" forms of E-Prime can no longer take advantage of the relatively simple rule (no use of *any* forms of "to be") that allowed me to make changes in my language use in "real time" — while speaking or thinking. This has brought about such deep-seated changes in the way that I process information that I even dream in E-Prime. For advanced practitioners who want to reap the *maximum* benefit, and to learn to habitually *think* in E-Prime, I recommend that they adhere to the rule of complete elimination of "to be," because at this point in time (1992) only this extreme form of the discipline has succeeded in achieving such a result.

Moving on to Wanderer's second question, does making the big effort to ban "to be" lead us to overlook other problems? To this I can answer with a fairly definitive "no." Although beginners may need to make a "big effort," as with any other learned skill the effort required decreases markedly with practice. This has allowed me to focus and implement further refinements in my use of language, such as Alan Walker Read's deletion of absolutisms (words such as always, never, all, none etc.), or Korzybski's extensional devices. (7, 8) Although eliminating "to be" makes a practical starting point towards a more non-Aristotelian language, it only begins a process which seems to have no end.

E-Prime as a discipline does not begin and end with the elimination of "to be." The rule provides the focus, but the intention of the practitioner plays an even more important part. I myself aim at a phenomenologically ideal language (E-Prime$_p$), that represents and communicates the territory of my experience both to myself and others as clearly and accurately as possible. In this regard it makes sense to differentiate between the "spirit" and the "letter" of the law, and I can at least agree with Ralph Kenyon when he draws attention to this distinction. (9) Philip Thompsen and Dong-Kuen Ahn's interesting paper on "flaming" provides tentative (*very* tentative) support for the idea that when E-Prime "works," the intention of the individual does play a predominant controlling role. (10)

However, it seems a mistake to tackle this particular issue with an either/or attitude. After reading *Science and Sanity*, and a plethora of other general semantics books, I labored with the best of intentions to incorporate the insights of general semantics into my life. Months of energetic efforts on

my part led to very little progress. My discovery of E-Prime
in 1977 changed this situation radically by providing me with
a practical focus and a guiding principle through which I
could coordinate my efforts. In my experience, E-Prime as a
discipline requires both the spirit and the letter of the law to
succeed. In theory we can separate the two; but in practice
they make an integrated whole.

Arriving at last at Wanderer's third question: "...can we gain
the advantages [of E-Prime] without loss of accuracy and occasionally awkward constructions which substitute for the
unacceptable language?" Before answering this question, let
me point out that such "awkward constructions" occur almost
exclusively in spoken E-Prime translations of colloquial expressions of the "Who are you?" and "How are you?" ilk. In
practice, and in the context of a living conversation, I usually
come up with suitable alternatives. On the phone I will ask
"May I speak with Paul?" instead of "Is Paul there?" Although
it may require a bit of creative effort, I've found that such
"awkward constructions" decrease markedly as one's skill in
speaking in E-Prime increases.

The discipline of E-Prime confers many advantages to the
practitioner, and certainly other methods exist to achieve at
least some of them. In achieving a "consciousness of abstracting" E-Prime works extraordinarily well. I find myself often
reminded of Ellen Langer's work at Harvard as I go about my
daily tasks, and now believe that the "side effect" of increased
"mindfulness" may in the end prove as important as its more
straightforward linguistic benefits. (11) However, at least in
this respect, other methods, from the phenomenological
epoché to zen meditation, may achieve an effect comparable
to that of E-Prime.

However, E-Prime does more than increase "consciousness
of abstracting" in its users, it also changes the way in which
they structure language. To paraphrase McLuhan, "the medium conveys its own message," and it seems almost axiom-
atic among general semanticists that the *structure* of a
language can profoundly influence the mental processes and
behavior of the individuals who use it.

I contend that in the majority of its occurrences in the "is of
identity" and "is of predication" modes the verb "to be"

appears in pernicious usages, because it encourages "false to facts" habits of thought through which we see a world made up of unchanging independent objects. In contrast, science (1992) describes the world as a conglomeration of ongoing interdependent processes in which our perception as individuals plays a not inconsiderable part. In this respect, one must at least eliminate "to be" in its identity and predication modes in order to achieve an improved congruency between the map of language and the territory of experience. In my judgement, nothing else can do the same job.

A number of the participants in this symposium issue argue that even if one overtly removes "to be" from English, that it still "exists" through implication in certain sentence structures. For example, in his article "Metaphor and E-Prime" Raymond Gozzi, Jr. talks about the subterranean "is" of identity or predication. (12) Do such covert forms of "to be" exist and do they play a role even in the overtly "is-free" language of E-Prime?

Although I consider this an important question, it appears based on a number of false assumptions. For example, Gozzi contends that the "act of naming relies on the verb 'to be' to establish a name — and then simply assumes the 'is' of identity or predication every time we use the name." Really? When someone asks me "Who are you?" and I reply "Ed" must this necessarily mean "(I am) Ed" instead of the E-Prime alternative "(I label myself) Ed"? The naming function does not require "to be" overtly or covertly, and if a child asks me "What is this?" while looking at my computer, I will more than likely point at the object in question and say "We call this a computer."

I assume that because Gozzi thinks in "is" English, he made assumptions about the *necessary* participation of the "subterranean is" in "naming" and "metaphor" that appear invalid upon closer examination. The subterranean "is" of identity or predication may exist, but it seems clear that their existence depends upon the intention of the individual, and not upon a hypothetical property of the "underlying ontology of language."

Similarly, the unconscious reintroduction of forms of "to be" by individuals who read articles written *about* E-Prime can seriously hamper their understanding *of* E-Prime. No matter how carefully I may say or write something in E-Prime, I have discovered to my annoyance that even intelligent individuals often retranslated my statements into some sort of absolutistic "is" equivalent, and then responded to what they think I said, but didn't! For example, in his article "E-Prime or E-Choice" Emory Menefee wrote that "...Kellogg and Bourland stress that complete elimination of all forms of "to be" IS the only satisfactory way to attain satisfactory benefits" (emphasis mine). (13) Obviously, we do not hold such a position, and I would hope that readers at least of this article will make a conscious effort to respond to what they see written, and not to some "is" English translation of it.

I found the reintroduction of "is" effect in full flower in James French's article "The Top Ten Arguments Against E-Prime." (14) In this article Mr. French fabricates clay pigeons of his own design and then shoots them down. As someone who knows the subject from the "inside-out," I found his arguments of little merit. For the most part he simply presented his subjective opinions as objective facts. He also neatly avoided considering one of the most important arguments in favor of E-Prime — that individuals who actually give E-Prime a fair try usually find something of value in it. Experience does count for something, and if you tell carpenters that a hammer will not drive nails they will not take you seriously. Unfortunately, although I cannot take Mr. French's comments seriously myself, they may discourage others from trying E-Prime for themselves and making a judgement based upon their own experience.

Some Final Words

Readers of this special issue of *Et cetera* may have noticed that most of the participants of this symposium at least agree on the usefulness of E-Prime as a tool for the teaching of general semantics. In a more widespread application, I hope that short courses in E-Prime will eventually find increased use in high school and college English classes. In this format, E-Prime can provide a practical and entertaining way of helping students gain awareness of how they overuse and abuse the verb "to be," and of the opportunities offered by other verb choices and sentence structures. So far, a number of English teachers have established that E-Prime can work effectively in this regard, and it seems reasonable to predict that ever larger groups of students will find themselves exposed to E-Prime, and to general semantics, in this way. (15-17)

E-Prime as a discipline involves a number of limitations that most English speakers would find onerous, and I certainly would not expect it to hold any more appeal to the majority of English-speaking people than a low-fat vegetarian diet would to the same group. Only recently has research conclusively demonstrated that such a diet confers long-term health benefits, and despite the hard evidence in its favor, it has only begun to gain in popularity. (18) Perhaps a hundred years from now empirical scientific research will show that E-Prime confers mental health benefits among those who practice it. Time will tell.

As one of the few committed to E-Prime in both its written and spoken form, it seems obvious that I have found the benefits well worth the time and effort involved. E-Prime plays an integral role in my life, and it has significantly enhanced it in too many ways to mention here. Those who do not find E-Prime to their taste, like Mr. French, may well cry "Where's the BEef!" opting for a "richer" linguistic diet, regardless of the potential cost to their mental health. (Note to Emory Menefee: a good pun never dies, and a bad pun never, ever, dies.) Fortunately, the future success of E-Prime may not depend upon its wide acceptance, but upon its adoption by individuals who use it because of its practical value in their daily lives. If the articles in this special symposium issue of *Et cetera* have intrigued you, I suggest that you experiment with E-Prime and judge its value for yourself.

NOTES AND REFERENCES

1. Murphy, Cullen, " 'To Be' In Their Bonnets," *The Atlantic Monthly*, February, 1992, 18-24.
2. *To Be or Not: An E-Prime Anthology*, ed. by D. David Bourland, Jr., and Paul D. Johnston (San Francisco: International Society for General

Semantics, 1991). Articles referenced here and reprinted in this anthology indicated with a #.

3. E. W. Kellogg III, "Speaking in E-Prime: An Experimental Method for Integrating General Semantics into Daily Life," *Et cetera* 44, no. 2 (Summer 1987) 118-128 #.

4. E. W. Kellogg III and D. David Bourland, Jr., "Working with E Prime: Some Practical Notes," *Et cetera* 47, no. 4 (Winter 1990-91) 376-392 #.

5. Robert Wanderer, "The Word 'E-Prime' Is Not the Thing," *Et cetera* 49, no. 2 (Summer 1992).

6. William Dallmann, "Is Is Not Is Is Not Is And Other Thoughts on E-Prime," *Et cetera* 49, no. 2 (Summer 1992).

7. Allen Walker Read, "Language Revision by Deletion of Absolutisms," *Et cetera* 42, no. 1 (Spring 1985) 7-12.

8. Alfred Korzybski, *Science and Sanity* (Lakeville, Conn.: International Non-Aristotelian Library and Publishing Company, 1933). 4th ed. 1958.

9. Ralph Kenyon, "E-Prime: The Spirit and the Letter," *Et cetera* 49, no. 2 (Summer 1992).

10. Philip A. Thompsen and Dong-Keun Ahn, "To Be or Not To Be: An Exploration of E-Prime, Copula Deletion and Flaming in Electronic Mail," *Et cetera* 49, no. 2 (Summer 1992).

11. Ellen J. Langer, *Mindfulness* (New York: Addison-Wesley, 1989).

12. Raymond Gozzi, Jr., "Metaphor and E-Prime: Of the Subterranean 'Is' Paradoxical Commands and Tilted Abstraction Ladders," *Et cetera* 49, no. 2 (Summer 1992).

13. Emory Menefee, "E-Prime or E-Choice," *Et cetera* 48, no. 2 (1991) 136-140.

14. James D. French, "The Top Ten Arguments Against E-Prime," *Et cetera* 49, no. 2 (Summer 1992).

15. Ruth S. Ralph, "Getting Rid of the *To Be* Crutch," in *Classroom Exercises in General Semantics*, ed. by Mary Morain (San Francisco: International Society for General Semantics, 1980) #.

16. Elaine C. Johnson, "Discovering E-Prime," *Et cetera* 45, no. 2 (Summer 1988) 181-183 #.

17. Andrea Johnson, "Oh To Be a Writer," *Et cetera* 49, no. 2 (Summer 1992).

18. See John Robbins, *Diet for a New America*, (Walpole, NH: Stillpoint Publishing, 1987) for a summary of scientific research on this topic.

D. David Bourland, Jr.*   *E-PRIME AND UN-SANITY*

1. Introduction

I WANT TO EXPRESS my appreciation to Jeremy Klein, Paul Johnston, and the Board of Directors of the International Society for General Semantics for seeing fit to devote this issue of *Et cetera* largely to discussions of E-Prime. The dozen or so papers provide interesting insights into the semantic reactions of people who have concern for these matters. On the other hand, as I read some of the papers I started wondering, "Whatever happened to the peer review committee?" In the early 1980s, while serving as The American Legion Commander for the Department of Panama Canal (which encompasses the countries of Central America), I came to know the fine U. S. Ambassador to Panama, the Hon. Ambler Moss. Once, he told me of a strange experience he had during a Communist-sponsored riot which featured a horde of people throwing rocks and ink bottles at the U. S. Embassy, screaming his name and suggesting that he go elsewhere. I

* D. David Bourland, Jr. a retired Associate Professor of Linguistics, has written on general semantics topics for many years. In 1965 he invented E-Prime.

123

had a somewhat similar feeling while reading some of the contributions to this issue, particularly Dr. Theresa Parkinson's offering.

Table I gives an "Agony Matrix" that summarizes my opinion of the problems ten contributors exhibited in their papers. I have no real quarrel with the positions described by Dallmann (save as noted in Section 2.b), Hautala, Johnson, Stewart, or Thompsen/Ahn. They stated their view in usually admirable ways. Following the material of Table I, I will comment more or less at length on Problems 2 ("Nervously Clinging to Various Uses of 'to be' ") and 4 ("Unclear on the Purposes of E-Prime"), plus the papers by French, Gozzi, and Parkinson. But first, allow me to give a few brief comments on other, minor matters. I congratulate Earl Hautala, Andrea Johnson, and Dr. Theresa Parkinson for writing their contributions in E-Prime. I hope that they each continue to exercise their E-Prime abilities.

Earl Hautala offered a quotation attributed to Einstein that snarled at *Science and Sanity*. I doubt that Einstein said, "That crazy book?" I would like to know the supposed source of that quote. We all know that a huge number of apocryphal anecdotes cluster about that great scientist.

Wanderer stated, "I see Bourland at his weakest when he attempts to deal with Korzybski's "Whatever you say a thing is, well, it is *not*; for the word is not the thing." Odd. I always have regarded myself at my weakest when attempting to squat with 210 kilos (= 464 lbs.) despite age, heart problems, iatrogenic arthritis of the knee, and tendonitis. If Bob Wanderer likes the cited slogan, fine. However, I reject his characterizing reference to the Structural Differential as a "cop-out." Do we want simply to amaze the unwashed, or to try to train people in better evaluations?

2. Two Outstanding Problems with Understanding E-Prime

When a large proportion of so distinguished a group of (supposedly) general semantics cognoscenti have difficulty with certain aspects of E-Prime, it certainly gives me pause. Although both matters have received extensive treatment in various places, let us do them all over again.

TABLE I
AGONY MATRIX

PROBLEMS

AUTHOR	1	2	3	4	5
Dallmann		x			x
French	x	x	x	x	
Gozzi	x	x	x	x	
Hautala					
Johnson					
Kenyon	x	x		x	
Parkinson			x	x	x
Stewart	x				
Thompsen	x				
Wanderer	x	x		x	

Problems:
1 = Paper not written in E-Prime

2 = Nervously clinging to various uses of "to be"

3 = Redefinition of general semantics, Korzybski's position

4 = Unclear on the purposes of E-Prime

5 = Confusing title

TABLE II
FRAGMENT OF A GENERATIVE GRAMMAR OF ENGLISH

1. S->(T) (Loc) NP + VP

2. NP->
   (Det) $\left\{ \begin{array}{l} S \\ N\ (AP) \\ Pro \end{array} \right\}$

3. VP-> (Modal) (Asp) Tense (Intens) V

4. V-> $\left\{ \begin{array}{l} V_1 \text{ [intrans]} \quad \text{(Prep P)} \\ V_2 \text{ [trans]} + NP \\ V_3 \text{ [linking]} \left\{ \begin{array}{l} NP \\ AP \end{array} \right\} \\ \\ V_4 \text{ [to be]} \left\{ \begin{array}{l} \emptyset \\ NP \\ AP \\ VP \end{array} \right\} \end{array} \right\}$

.
.
.

Where
S = Sentence
T = Time expression (e.g., today)
Loc = Location (e.g., in Peoria)
NP = Noun Phrase
VP = Verb Phrase
Det = Determiner
N = Noun
Pro = Pronoun

Prep P = Prepositional Phrase
AP = Adjective Phrase
Modal = might, could, ...
Asp = Aspect
Tense = ± Present
Intens = Intensifier
Parentheses = optional selection
Curly brackets = "select one"

a. *Uses of "to be"*
The Oxford English Dictionary (in both editions) notes five uses of "to be":
I. *Absolutely*, including to exist or occur in the world of fact (as they put it); II. *Where* or *how* (location); III. *Copula* with adjective, substantive, or adjective phrase; IV. *Auxiliary* with participles and infinitives, which includes most of the passive voice; and V. *Phraseological Combinations* which covers "to be about to," and other, mainly archaic, constructions.

All the writers listed in Table I, except Dr. Parkinson, seem to understand the epistemological reasons for avoiding Uses III and IV. As a reminder I cite the basic recruiting call for E-Prime:

> The subject-predicate form, the "is" of identity, and the elementalism of the Aristotelian system are perhaps the main semantic factors in need of revision, as they are found to be the foundation of insufficiency of this system and represent the mechanism of semantic disturbances, making general adjustment and sanity impossible. (1, p. 371)

Material written by such leading exponents of general semantics as Korzybski himself, Wendell Johnson, J. S. Bois, and Allen Walker Read all employed Uses III and IV of "to be," even while inveighing against Use III. In my experience, only those shifting to E-Prime have managed to avoid Uses III and IV, *at the price of giving up Uses I, II, and V.* I submit that when we write about serious matters we rarely, if ever, need Uses I, II, and V.

Speaking brings other problems, for we obviously do not just speak about weighty subjects. At first I tried to speak mainly in E-Prime, but to allow myself the standard social formulas that require Uses I and II: "I am David Bourland," "Today is Saturday," "Where is the book?" etc., with the intent of trying to keep from sounding like a nut case. Then, as I continued to have trouble with spoken fluency in E-Prime, I eventually came to suspect that the difficulty came from my "Social Is-iness." Upon stopping *any* use of "to be," I became gradually more fluent in spoken E-Prime. I admit that I sometimes still use odd constructions, but ever more rarely.

The parallel between the adverse effect of Social Is-iness and the effect of Social Drinking on struggling alcoholics seems inescapable.

To sum up, if *you* can stop employing Uses III and IV while allowing yourself I, II, and V, go ahead. I doubt that you can, for reasons of neural Darwinism, as extensively studied and reported by Edelman. (2, 3, 4)

b. Purposes of E-Prime

By (i) removing the forms of "to be" from the lexicon and, perhaps more importantly (ii) deleting the verb "to be" from the grammar, we produce a subset of English. This subset has the properties of the complete elimination of the "is" of identity and "is" of predication, plus making the passive voice rather awkward. These amount to significant contributions, but obviously do not solve *all* the problems of identification, confusion in orders of abstraction, etc. In addition, E-Prime removes the most frequently used static verb in English, a verb that can only give a snap-shot description of the flow of events in a dynamic world. This constitutes, for me at least, the fatal flaw in Dr. Dallmann's E-Prime$_{mod}$.

3. Reply to French

In his Arguments 10 and 9 French seems annoyed that anyone would find writing in a subset of English somehow an improvement over using the whole set. I suppose he cannot understand that the verb "to be" can seduce us into undesirable patterns of speech and writing. Too bad. This amounts to a mere matter of opinion. He can pursue it, if he wishes, with people who teach writing — Elaine Johnson, Dr. Ruth Ralph, Andrea Johnson — or, for that matter, with Cullen Murphy of *The Atlantic Monthly* or free-lance writer Debra Ryll. I suspect that the French paper might have had a higher quality had he written it in E-Prime.

Arguments 8 and 7 discuss trivial examples of "How to Live with Use III" (in the case of 8), and "But I Need These Acceptable Statements" (in the case of 7). Check the comments on static verbs above.

With regard to Arguments 6 and 5, French evidently does not understand that huge amounts of identity statements do in fact involve "to be," with deleterious effects on humans. Dr. Albert Ellis has provided us with extensive support — clinical support, mind you — along these lines. See his Korzybski Memorial Address, delivered last November, or references (5) and (6).

Argument 4 refers to French's unhappiness with assertions (not just assumptions) that one can more easily eliminate "to be" from the language than avoid the "is" of identity and "is" of predication otherwise. These assertions have the support of the testimony and experience of various general semanticists. Incidentally, French would do better to confine himself to the semantic problems of his native language, rather than speculating about the problems of Spanish-speakers.

Concerning Argument 3, may I remind French that "=" translates, in English, to "equals." As I have mentioned before, I suspect that teachers who drill very young students to say "4 plus 2 *is* 6" set up a potential problem for some of them when they reach fractions. After all, even the slowest student can see that "2/4" *is not* "1/2." Of *course*, mathematical hot-shots like French and Bourland had no trouble along those lines, but what of the others?

The basis of Argument 2 consists of "E-Prime tends to make the expression of higher orders of abstraction more difficult." Although, when writing in E-Prime, one does tend to *start out* with the usually less-judgmental lower orders of abstraction, E-Prime simply does not impede the time-binding activities involved in constructing higher order abstractions. See the last paper in reference (7) for a reasonable example ("A Non-Aristotelian Paradigm for Linguistics").

I have, from the beginning, seen E-Prime as a potential addition to Korzybski's extensional devices. Experience over the years, by me and a number of others, as given in reference (7), confirms that view. In his supposed Argument 1, French demonstrates the shallowness of his opinions on E-Prime, despite the illusion of depth on the surface. "The first question we should ask of a principle or practice of general semantics is whether or not it fits the facts and the other formulations of the system, not whether or not it is expedient," said French. Well, check the quotation given above in Section 2 from page 371 of *Science and Sanity*, French. What word or words there do you not understand? And where did you get that nonsense about "expedient"?

4. Reply to Gozzi

Why should metaphor disappear in E-Prime? My copy of Webster's Unabridged Dictionary explains that term in the following way: "A figure of speech denoting by a word or phrase usually one kind of object or idea in place of another to suggest a likeness or analogy between them (as in *the ship plows the sea* or in *a volley of oaths*)..." Neither the definition nor the examples involve what Prof. Gozzi facetiously calls "the dreaded 'is's' of identity and predication." On the surface level. Of course, lacking a precise definition of any other level or levels, we can only address ourselves rationally to the surface level. It seems unfortunate to me that Prof. Gozzi turned to philosophy, rather than to linguistics, in defense of his theory (actually, more of an assertion than a theory) concerning the inevitability of the verb "to be" in underlying ("subterranean") structures of language. I say unfortunate, for little remains today of the once-proud field of ontology outside of phenomenology. My colleague, Dr. E. W. Kellogg, III, may enjoy debating this issue and the interactions of E-Prime and phenomenology.

A properly trained child, if you will pardon the near-oxymoron, would ask, "What do we call this?" And then Mommy or Daddy would reply, "(We call it) a personal computer," with no magic involved. Sorry, Prof. Gozzi: "with every name we will find a subterranean homesick 'is' " only as a consequence of Aristotelian assumptions from philosophy or, for that matter, linguistics. Assumptions always false to facts.

E-Prime involves more than just fiddling with the lexicon. It also has powerful syntactic consequences. A discussion of this point requires the careful statement of what one *means* by English syntax. Table II contains a beginning fragment of a generative grammar of English, inspired by reference (8), to illustrate where and how the verb "to be" enters the picture, and what remains when we make the E-Prime choice.

Table II shows explicitly a part of what some linguists consider the basis for a "deep structure." When we remove "to be," (V_4 in Table II), we have pruned a high-level rule that reverberates throughout the language. To a certain extent the linking verbs can fill many of the roles played by "to be" in standard English — and improve the quality of the resulting statements at that. Some of the linking verbs (particularly "to seem" and "to appear") tend to become overworked in one's early days with E-Prime. Unfortunately, they can preserve in large part the "to be" sentence pattern. Consider these examples:

(1) Jack is a jerk.
(2) Jack seems (like) a jerk.
(3) Jack acts like a jerk.
(4) I have seen Jack act like a jerk on three occasions.

While I would prefer (2) to (1), as having become less pompous and allowing for some degree of error on the part of the speaker, only (4) really tells us something potentially useful about the speaker-Jack interaction.

I certainly agree with Prof. Gozzi that naming consists of "one of the primary acts of language," but the "is" of identity or predication does not function as the "core of naming." One cannot deny that theories exist that proclaim such a circumstance, but those theories have little to do with the world as described by the physics of this century. A whole field exists that has bearing on these important issues. We call it "general semantics." Prof. Gozzi, please see reference (1).

We hear from Prof. Gozzi that, "The verb 'to be,' in fact, must be larger than anyone, except a few philosophers, suspects." On the contrary, this verb portrays a static relationship that has no place in the semantic reactions of people trying to come to grips with a dynamic, ever-changing world. And those alleged "few philosophers" should probably seek counselling and not operate any heavy machinery.

I would like to thank Prof. Gozzi for reminding me of the rightful place the "abstraction ladder" has in the theory I call "Lieutenant Semantics." See references (9) and (10). I will certainly make use of this insight in the future. Prof. Gozzi would do better, in my opinion, to proceed from focussing on what he calls Korzybski's "maxim" of the map-territory relation to a study of the non-Aristotelian premises and their consequences. I also suggest that he hop off the "abstraction ladder" and study the Structural Differential carefully. (1, p. 386ff).

I regret that I no longer teach a course in general semantics. I did so for almost ten years, using reference (11) as the text. For you active teachers out there, Prof. Gozzi has presented you with a great exam quotation in his closing remark: "No matter if the underlying ontology of the language is constructed out of the variations of the verb 'to be': there is no escaping being." Have the students comment on *that* statement from a non-Aristotelian point of view!

5. Reply to Parkinson

I feel sure that Paul Johnston joins me in thanking Dr. Parkinson for lumping us together in the same state of ignorance as Korzybski in her first three paragraphs. How could I hope that she would understand E-Prime, when she has expended so much energy making up nonsense and attributing it to Korzybski? Item: (when summarizing Korzybski's alleged false identifications comparing bridges, treaties, etc.) "What applies to physical nature does not necessarily apply to human nature." Whoever said it did? Certainly not Korzybski. Nor I, for that matter. Item: "Contrary to Korzybski's opinion, morality and reason do not necessarily walk hand in hand." Whoever said they did? Certainly not Korzybski. Nor I, for that matter. Given that Dr. Parkinson does not understand time-binding and has no hesitancy in accusing Korzybski of ridiculous positions he did not espouse, why should anyone expect her to understand E-Prime? Yes, she used it in her paper, and did so very well. She probably also uses her TV: does she understand how the electrons do what they do in it? I call her understanding of E-Prime into question due to the following surprising statement: "What a choice example of E-Prime the following Biblical passage offers: 'The fool hath said in his heart: "There is no God." ' (Psalms 14:1)." In my heart I say: that does not give much of an example of E-Prime (see Section 2.b if necessary).

Dr. Parkinson further shows a certain amount of reading incapacity when she says:

If, then, "the *technique* of E-Prime does in no way guaran-tee...reducing dishonesty and prejudice (prejudging) in our communications," if "E-Prime does not cure or resolve all linguistic and behavioral problems," if "the intention of the individual involved plays the predominant role," if the pres-ent writer can write this little critique of E-Prime in E-Prime, what can David Bourland mean when he states that "E-Prime provides a simple discipline that does work"? (See Parkinson's paper for references cited.)

If you check that last statement, attributed to me, you will find that it refers to "Piecemeal attempts to avoid the undesir-able uses of 'to be' (that) simply have not worked." (7, p. 106) In this paper I have called them Use III. Do you deny that E-Prime prevents problems with Use III, Parkinson?

If the reader has not already done so, I invite him or her to review Dr. Parkinson's last three paragraphs. Rarely does one encounter such a parade of tired cliches that whine over the distance between activities on the objective level and those on the symbolic level. I fail to see, however, how Dr. Parkinson could have omitted comparing E-Prime to re-arranging the deck chairs just before the *Titanic* went down. In closing, let me say that perhaps the most amusing aspect of Dr. Parkinson's paper consists of its title. She certainly never got *to* E-Prime; how could she possibly think that her temper tantrum had anything to do with "*Beyond* E-Prime"?

REFERENCES

1. Korzybski, Alfred. *Science and Sanity: An Introduction to Non-Aristotelian Systems and General Semantics.* Lakeville, Conn.: International Non-Aristotelian Library Publishing Co. 1933. Fourth edition, 1958.
2. Edelman, G. M. "Group Selection as the Basis for Higher Brain Function," in F. O. Schmitt, F. G. Worden, and S. G. Dennis (eds.), *The Organization of the Cerebral Cortex: Proceedings of a Neurosciences Research Program Colloquium,* pp. 535-563. Cambridge, Mass.: MIT Press. 1981.
3. Edelman, G. M. "Neural Darwinism: Population Thinking and Higher Brain Function," M. Shaftto (ed.), *How We Know: Nobel Conference XX,* pp.1-30. San Francisco: Harper & Row. 1985.
4. Edelman, G. M. *Neural Darwinism: The Theory of Neuronal Selection.* New York: Basic Books. 1987.
5. Ellis, Albert. *How to Live with a Neurotic.* North Hollywood: Wilshire Book Co. Second edition, 1975.
6. Ellis, Albert. *Sex and the Liberated Man.* Secaucus, N. J. : Lyle Stuart. 1976. (Second edition of *Sex and the Single Man.*)
7. Bourland, D. David, Jr., and Paul Dennithorne Johnston (eds.) *To Be or Not: An E-Prime Anthology,* San Francisco: International Society for General Semantics. 1991.
8. Chomsky, Noam. *Syntactic Structures.* The Hague: Mouton. 1967.
9. Bourland, D. David, Jr. "Reply to Dallmann," *Et cetera: A Review of General Semantics.* 47: 283-285. 1990.
10. Bourland, D. David, Jr. "Reply to Menefee," *Et cetera: A Review of General Semantics* 48: 292-295. 1991.
11. Korzybski, Alfred. *Selections from Science and Sanity.* Lakeville, Conn.: International Non-Aristotelian Library Publishing Co. 1948. Eighth printing, 1976.

Part Two:

THE SECOND E-PRIME SYMPOSIUM

E-PRIME SYMPOSIUM II

Preface

W ELCOME TO *ETC.*'s second symposium on E-Prime — not, one hopes, more of the same — but, rather, a second drinking party (in Plato's original sense), featuring a quite different array of discursive libations, bracers, and chasers.

Some readers seem to have misunderstood the aims of the first symposium. Its participants did not endeavor to produce a simple verdict on E-Prime: a Yea or Nay; thumbs up or thumbs down. Instead, that symposium continued this journal's tradition of investigating the potentials of *purposive linguistic revision* by focusing on the particular methodology of E-Prime. Certainly E-Prime merits extended examination, if only by virtue of the controversy it has engendered within (and recently outside of) general semantics circles.

Several questions seem to underlie much of the analysis in both symposia: (1) Does E-Prime enlarge and advance the discipline of general semantics? (2) Does E-Prime violate certain "canons" of general semantics? (The relation of general semantics to the canons of contemporary science and logic deserves, certainly, its own symposium.)

We may not have resolved these issues definitively in these symposia, but we have made a start — "Well thou hast begun" (Herrick).

JK

137

DO AWAY WITH "TO BE" —

E. W. KELLOGG III* *There, Pupils, Lies the Answer* †

D OES THE ENGLISH LANGUAGE really need the verb *to be* or does its use involve more liabilities than benefits? For the past several hundred years, philosophers, scholars, and English teachers have warned against the abuse of the verb (basically *am, are, is, was, were, be* and *been*).

More pragmatically, English teachers continue to tell students: "Vary your verb choices! Use the active voice! Release trapped verbs! Say who did what to whom!" These pretty much boil down to one simple rule: "Avoid the verb to be!" But in the past even those who warned against the verb continued using it themselves.

In 1965, D. David Bourland, Jr., now a retired professor of linguistics, made the audacious suggestion that we could give up the use of *to be* altogether, and that this modification of English (labeled by him "English-Prime" or "E-Prime") might even improve the language. At first, Bourland's idea may sound odd and impractical, but over the past 25 years

* E. W. Kellogg III currently serves as Vice-President of Publications of ISGS.

†Copyright © 1992 E. W. Kellogg, III. First published in *Newsday*, September 16, 1992.

numerous articles, books, and even dissertations have confirmed E-Prime's usefulness.

Some advocates consider E-Prime a more descriptive form of English that tends to bring the user back to the "level of first-person experience." It eliminates the overdefining of situations that confuse one aspect of an experience with a much more complex totality. This occurs mainly in sentences using the "is of identity" ("John *is* a jerk") and the "is of predication" ("The apple *is* red"). Writing can improve with E-Prime because users must often replace the passive voice ("It was done") with the more informative active voice ("Russell did it"). It also encourages the use of verbs other than *to be* by eliminating sentence structures of the X *is* Y form ("Elaine *is* a teacher") and using subject-verb-object structures instead ("Elaine teaches English").

The verb *to be* encourages the "Deity mode" of speech, as seen frequently in political speeches and in statements such as "This *is* the truth." Even the most uninformed can use this mode to transform their opinions magically into godlike pronouncements on the objective nature of things. E-Prime minimizes such presumption, and users must often take overt responsibility for their opinions. For example, "The Northlight is a good restaurant" might become "I enjoy eating at the Northlight restaurant." The unrecognized assumptions that *to be* often introduces can also impair perceptivity and even creativity. For example, compare "The man is drunk" to "The man acts drunk" or "There is no solution to this problem" to "No one has solved this problem yet."

Does E-Prime have any disadvantages? Well, practitioners lose *to be* as an auxiliary verb, to indicate existence and to create metaphors. Although some critics would say that such losses reduce the viability of E-Prime as an independent language, most at least appreciate its effectiveness in the short term as a pedagogic tool. So far, some English teachers have established that courses in E-Prime can provide a practical and entertaining way of helping students gain awareness of how they overuse and abuse the verb *to be,* and of the opportunities offered by other verb choices and sentence structures.

E-Prime involves a number of limitations that many would find onerous, and one would no more expect it to appeal to the majority of English-speaking people than a low-fat vegetarian diet would to the same group. The controversy over E-Prime has just begun, and the summer [1992] issue of *ETC: A Review of General Semantics* presents many of the pros and cons of the issue. Although practitioners of E-Prime advocate the complete elimination of *to be*, they assert than any reduction in the use of the verb can have beneficial effects. The future success of the movement for such reduction may not depend upon its wide acceptance, but upon its adoption by individuals who use it because of its practical value.

DeWitt Scott, an editor for the San Francisco Examiner, wrote that "removing the supreme irritant, *to be*, forces me to express myself in straightforward statements and come out of the clouds." Robert Ian Scott, a professor of English at the University of Saskatchewan, minimized his use of *to be* to such an extent in his textbook *The Specific Writer* that less than five percent of the sentences use the verb. The February, 1992, issue of *The Atlantic Monthly* magazine brought the idea of E-Prime to the attention of a broad audience in an article called " 'To Be' in Their Bonnets."

George Santayana put it this way in *Skepticism and Animal Faith*: "Whenever I use the word *is*, except in sheer tautology, I deeply misuse it; and when I discover my error, the world seems to fall asunder and the members of my family no longer know one another."

Stuart A. Mayper* **E-PRIME AND E-PLUS**

E-PRIME AROSE as a bold stratagem, a straightforward attack on a pervasive problem of English — the way the ubiquitous verb "to be" tempts us into identities. Korzybski tells us we should avoid identities at 'all' costs, and E-Prime accomplishes that by forbidding *any* use of this verb. The resulting restriction of language does force us to think about its structure rather than rattle on in habitual patterns; it reveals some hidden assumptions; it toughens (though sometimes lengthens) our sentences.

But it presents a classic example of throwing out the baby with the bathwater. The verb "to be" has many useful functions in English, other than sowing confusion; it contributes greatly to the language's subtlety and flexibility. E-Prime has not yet provided satisfactory substitutes.

As an auxiliary verb, "to be" puts other verbs into the progressive mode ("I am walking", "I was running"). That focuses on the instant present, distinguished from the more

---

* Stuart Mayper, Emeritus Professor of Chemistry at the University of Bridgeport (CT), is editor of the *General Semantics Bulletin* and a Trustee of the Institute of General Semantics.

timeless mode of the simple verb ("I walk ten blocks every day," "I often ran three miles in my younger days").

The auxiliary "to be" also forms the passive voice, allowing one to emphasize the object of an action without having to specify a subject. We know that authors, especially scientists, may abuse the passive, but one can also use it skillfully to give situations a terser "realism." "The car was run off the road" has more impact than what E-Prime would permit: "The car ran off the road," or "Something or someone ran the car off the road."

Korzybski noted two other uses of "to be": to indicate predication and existence as well as identity. He observed: "The fact that four semantically entirely different words should have one sound and spelling appears as a genuine tragedy of the race; the more so since the discrimination between their uses is not always easy." (1)

To assuage this tragedy I proposed (initially with tongue in cheek, but now I begin to take it seriously) that instead of amputating the verb, we apply constructive surgery: designate the manifold forms of "to be" to clarify its various functions, assign them on the basis of these semantical distinctions rather than those of person and number. (2)

With a nod acknowledging Dave Bourland as my preceder and inspirator, I termed my resulting enriched language *E-Plus*. Its rules follow:

I Assign **be** (past, **been**) in all persons for *predication* or as an *auxiliary* verb — normally succeeded by an adjective (including a present or past participle).

"The apple be red"; "I been hungry; the apple be eaten."

II Assign **am** in all persons for *existence*. (Past tense: shall we invent a new word, **wam**?) This allows E-Plus to make a distinction resembling that which Spanish makes between "ser" and "estar": "estoy borracho" = "I be drunk" (right now); "soy borracho" = "I **am** drunk" ("I exist drunk") — what Bourland gave as an example of a "durative" difference.

III Assign **is** (past, **was**) for *identity*. Yes, we need to speak in identities, if only to make crisp denials: "The word *is not* the thing; the map *is not* the territory." But I also can cite some poetic positives: "Bess, you is my woman now," and Pogo's "We have met the enemy and they is us."

IV The usual examples given for the "is of identity," such as "The apple is a fruit; John is a farmer" turn out to not quite fit. To quote reference (2): "No alert user of English would conclude from 'The apple is a fruit and the orange is a fruit' that an apple is identical to an orange. The 'is'es quoted do not assert identity, a symmetrical relation; they assert a nonsymmetrical one we can call *class membership*." The two items connected by such an "is" differ in order of abstraction. I proposed for this very common relation that we use **are** (past, **were**): "The apple are a fruit; John are a farmer." Or more comfortably in the plural, "Apples are fruits; John and William are farmers" — but "John and William is not each other."

E-Prime, it turns out, are a very powerful training device (I switched in my writing here from E-Prime to E-Plus.). I suggested to Bourland that we might try giving students alternate assignments in E-Prime and E-Plus; whether that would result in greater power or utter insanity remains to be seen.

One other point: I note that some of the illustrative quotations in Rules I and III above sound just like "Black English." This been not intentional, but it makes me wonder; could it am that the distinctions I be trying to make here are reflections of some structural aspects of African languages? Has our new Indo-European linguistic sophistication been anticipated?

REFERENCES

1. Korzybski, A. (1933) *Science and Sanity: An Introduction to Non-Aristotelian Systems and General Semantics.* Lakeville, CT: The International Non-Aristotelian Library Publishing Co. (now part of the I.G.S., Englewood, NJ). 4th edition, 1958. p. 750 (Supplement III: A Non-Aristotelian System and its Necessity for Rigour in Mathematics and Physics.)
2. Editorial — "Reforming the Language," *General Semantics Bulletin* # 55 21-3 (1990).

AN AUTO-INTERVIEW ON

Russell Joyner* # THE NEED FOR E-PRIME

Q. THIS STRIKES ME as a bit of a conceit. Why do you insist on interviewing yourself — do you fear, from other interviewers, embarrassing questions, questions revealing lack of knowledge, unclear thinking or other symptoms of incompetence to discuss E-Prime?

A. Yes, the possibility of embarrassing questions has occurred to me. Although I claim no expertise for discussing E-Prime, I might feel insecure facing some other questioner. But much more important than any feeling of uneasiness, I need time to search for thoughtful answers to questions of substance. Many of the television interviews I have seen demand immediate, knee-jerk responses to unanticipated questions. This seems counterproductive to me — unless the program seeks to reveal what the interviewee will say *without thinking*. So I only want to deal with questions I have had some time to consider.

Q. E-Prime — English without any form of the verb "to be," — seems a vast subject when you realize that it touches

* Past Editor of *ETC.* and former Executive Director of ISGS, Russell Joyner lives in San Francisco.

on so many instances of thought, of expression and on so many situations in human affairs: the linguistic habits we speakers of English have developed since infancy, linguistic habits connected with learned behavioral responses to the world as well as to internal stimuli. Do you feel comfortable trying to delve into such a highly abstract subject, a subject so sweeping it practically begs for self-destroying generalizations?

A. No. The enormity of it numbs my mind. Attempts to draw even a small sample from a population of contexts that includes "am," "is," "are," "was," "were," "being," etc., overwhelm me. I suggest that we try to reduce the subject to a more manageable scope for this brief interview by focusing attention on a few uses of "is" and closely related matters.

Q. Agreed. You say that you want to learn to write in E-Prime. You want to give up writing all statements of the type "A is B," where either A or B can refer to *anything*, from real or imaginary words, numbers, or other symbols to real or imaginary objects, events, or processes?

A. Yes.

Q. You want to give up statements like "That woman is Ms. Quick, my next-door neighbor."; "Fred Williams is a Vice President."; "His teacher is Nadia Komiska." These statements rank among the most verbally economical ways of expressing the naming relationship that we have in the language. We use "is" statements very often in communicating about people's names, along with their title or position. You really would rule out all such statements from your writing?

A. I will try to learn to. Yes.

Q. We find uses of the verb "is" in a great many situations where people engage in labeling: "That is the Bar-X cattle brand."; "If this is 'Choice,' let's disregard beef grading."; "He is a terminal case."; "This car is a lemon."; "It is a non-performing loan. (No one has made a payment on it for years)." These uses of "is" show one of the strongest, most emphatic, most direct ways of expressing the labeling relationship. You wish to eliminate "is" from all of your written contexts involving labeling?

A. Yes.

Q. Surely you don't want to stop using "is" in dealing with the classes of animals and plants of the natural sciences, Zoology and Botany, and other widely used classes and hierarchies of classes. For example, you wouldn't restrict your freedom to write "A monkey is an animal."?

A. Yes I would — in the very little amount of writing I do on these matters. Whether using common or scientific names or referring to relationships between more or less rigorously defined individuals or classes, I want to learn to write without "is."

Q. If you forbid yourself the use of "is," does this mean that you can't even say that something *is a fact*?

A. Yes, indeed, it definitely means that I must *not* write the verb "is" to try to express or establish a truth.

Q. As one of the most frequently used verbs in the language, and certainly the most verbally economical, "is" must furnish some measure of help in conceptualizing and expressing similarities and differences. Otherwise its use probably would have disappeared long ago. Surely you accept that it plays some linguistically beneficial role in establishing and fixing relationships and in recalling, recognizing, organizing, and ordering relationships between the things we encounter in our daily life? Don't you agree?

A. Yes.

Q. Then why work so hard to try to get rid of it? Why fight a lifelong habit, a habit almost universally supported by other speakers of English, trying to learn to write without "is" (and other forms of "to be")?

A. I agree that in a great many contexts "is" produces unrivaled verbal economies. Where could we find a briefer, stronger, more concentrated, more emphatic way to express so many different relationships than "A is B," where A can refer to *anything* and so can B? But these seductive benefits come with unacceptable semantic and logical costs.

Q. Semantic costs? Would you give a definition of "semantic cost"?

A. I use "semantic cost" here to designate the kind of misunderstanding occurring when the mind (the evaluational system) suffers unclarity and confusion regarding what its words refer to. "Semantic cost" means the referential misunderstanding the mind pays (undergoes) for a given use of a word or words.

Q. I take it that the unacceptably high semantic cost of using "is" accounts for one of the reasons you have decided to try to write in E-Prime. You have given a vague, highly general notion of "semantic cost." How about tying this free-floating definition to some concrete examples?

A. In the question on naming, you gave the example "Fred Smith is a Vice President." The "is" in this statement tells both writer and reader that Fred Smith *now* has the title of Vice President. But, apart from instantaneous communication, how can the writer know, when making the statement, whether Fred Smith has accepted a higher title, or a lower title, or a golden handshake, or whether he has resigned, or received a notice of dismissal? The "is" in "Fred Smith is a Vice President." gives to me, and surely a great many other writers and readers of English, the certainty of a *factual statement*. But given a dynamic, highly mobile society like ours, titles can get conferred, change, or disappear with startling rapidity. In the midst of such changing conditions and uncertainty, do we want to use "is" to cast relationships of people and their titles into what many will interpret as *factual statements*?

In the Summer 1989 issue of *ETC.*, Ruth Gonchar Brennan tells of attending a class on general semantics (in the early 1960s) where students had spent the period trying to learn to distinguish between statements of fact and inference:

> Toward the end of the class, Dr. [Harry] Weinberg offered us some statements and we were asked to determine whether they were statements of fact or inference. Harry Weinberg offered us the following example: "Fact or inference," he said, "John F. Kennedy is President of the United States." "Fact," we shouted in unison. "Fact?" he responded. "We've all been in class for almost an hour. Who's to say as a matter of fact that John Kennedy is President of the United States? It is an *inference*, although it's a highly probable one. He might have resigned, his back pain may have incapacitated him, he might even have been killed. Such a statement is *not* one of fact."

Class was over and I started to walk across campus. It was just slightly after noon on November 22, 1963. A young woman sat on the ground with tears streaming down her face. "Someone shot the President," she said. "Which President?" I asked. "Our President," she cried.

A. (continued) Your question on labeling included the statement "He is a terminal case." If these words came from a physician, they may amount to an inference based on the patient's vital signs. But this brief message gives no prognosis in terms of probability, of what could possibly happen: It tells nothing of the prospect of recovery as one might anticipate from the usual course of disease or peculiarities of the case. Here, again, the "is" lends an air of the certainty of a factual statement, this time about how long a patient will live. Surely "terminal" would appropriately label death within 10 days, perhaps death in 10 months, but death in 10 years or more? On rare occasions doctors have had to wait a decade or longer for a "terminal" patient to die.

Now let me touch on the matter of classification and "is." To write about classifying — the sorting of persons, places, things, processes, etc. — requires expressing relationships between individuals, between individuals and groups, and often relationships between groups and still other groups. Previously classified individuals and groups will surely carry names or labels familiar to one writing about them. Using the names and labels, the writer goes on to discuss relationships in some classificatory system or other. Thus, the discussion may well involve relationships between each of the following: the name of the individual *and* the individual; the name of the group *and* the group; the name of the individual and the individual *and* the name of the group and the group; and perhaps on into the greater complexities of one or more hierarchical organizations of groups. Consider the following statements:

A monkey is a primate and a gorilla is a primate, but Ping Pong is not a gorilla. Ping Pong is the name of my monkey.

Let those who find no confusion using "is" to express different classificatory relationships, translate, quickly and easily, the above statements to clearly reveal the following different relationships: between the name of the individual and the individual; between the names of groups and groups; between the individual and groups; and between groups and groups.

The writer attempts clarification with the following classificatory statements which he arrived at neither instantaneously nor all that easily:

> The group called primate includes subgroups that carry the names of gorilla and monkey. Of these two subgroups, only the one named monkey includes the individual named Ping Pong who belongs to me.

Before going on, I should offer a closely related example illustrating how "is" and another form of the verb "to be" can sow seeds of confusion in a syllogism:

> Primates are a Zoological group.
> Ping Pong is a primate.
> Therefore Ping Pong is a Zoological group.

We have here another exercise in reformulation: to both clarify referential meaning and to correct the logic. Little wonder that, in dealing with individual members and groups, students of set theory must learn *different* symbols to distinguish the quite different relationships that use of "is" so often confounds.

To repeat an answer to one of your earlier questions, I want to learn to eliminate "is" when writing about facts; I want to learn to stop using "is" to express or to establish a truth. Points illustrated in the following dialogue bear on this decision to discard "is" and to look for less misleading, clearer, more reliable formulations in E-Prime:

> C. It is a fact that the United States is a North American country.

D. No, it is not a fact — the State of Hawaii lies many hundreds of miles outside of the North American continent.

C. Well, in the first half of the 20th century people accepted it as a fact. I guess it must have stopped being a fact the day Hawaii became a state.

D. Rubbish! Surely you can't mean that one day it was a fact and the very next day it was false!

C. You're probably right. If something is a fact, how can it become false? What is the point in something being a fact if you can't depend on it for the next 24 hours?

The different meanings these participants give to "It is a fact" — meanings they find so frustrating and confusing — would receive scant attention from cartographers. Map makers must remain aware that people not only give names to land masses, but laws get passed requiring the use of names in many situations; and more or less frequently laws get enacted that change such names. As cartographers, their responsibilities include noting and publishing such name changes: After Hawaii acquired statehood, map makers stopped producing maps and charts marked with "Territory of Hawaii" and started calling the islands "State of Hawaii." Cartographers also know that land masses undergo constant changes and that their duties involve observing and charting such changes when of sufficient magnitude. A single eruption of one of Hawaii's volcanoes can dramatically change the height and shape of the mountain as well as closely surrounding land.

From the various widespread uses of "It is a fact ..." I infer that for many it has a semantic role of building an unchanging world welded to a fixed language and the security that such stability provides. *Webster's Ninth New Collegiate Dictionary* gives at least two quite different referential meanings gleaned from past uses of the word "fact": reference to an actual occurrence, an event or something that has actual existence; and reference to a piece of information presented as having objective reality. Such pieces of information commonly come to us in the form of written statements. Evidently we learn to use the word "fact" to refer to *both* actual occurrences and events *and* statements about occurrences and events *simultaneously*. No wonder that, in using "fact," we so often weld words to things, confuse verbal statements with occurrences, events, or processes. Or, as general semanticists say, confuse maps with territories.

Such semantic welding assists those who would influence the direction of our thoughts: those who covertly dictate (instead of overtly suggest) which words for us to use.

For example, in labeling people and behavior they might say: "It is a fact that she is virtuous." Or "It is a fact that she is puritanical." "It is a fact that he is a chauvinist." Or maybe "It is a fact that he is a patriot." Thus, such words may offer certainty regarding the *true* label to use.

In more than a few contexts "It is a fact ..." assures continuity; it introduces a truthful history of the past and an unfailing prediction of the future — a world we can anticipate with total confidence. No such world, of course, exists.

Q. You have made clear your desire to learn to write in E-Prime. If possible, would you forbid all other writers from using "is" and other forms of "to be"?

A. No. Although writing only in E-Prime would probably help some of the poets I have read, it would restrict the poetic license needed by others. How about e. e. cummings' line, "Bang is the meaning of a gun." Or Gertrude Stein's "A rose is a rose is a rose...."?

Who would rule out future analogies as insightful as Barnett Newman's "Aesthetics is for the artist as ornithology is for the birds."?

Playwrights certainly must have freedom to put *any* words into the mouths of their characters and so must novelists. Unable to predict the future, I would never dictate the use of E-Prime by others. Nevertheless, I feel convinced that *all* writers of English could benefit enormously by learning to write skillfully in E-Prime — not to write with the time-consuming effort of translating into a "foreign" language (as I have spent doing this interview), but to write E-Prime with the ease and familiarity of a second language.

Q. Would you briefly summarize what your answers in this interview have to do with general semantics and E-Prime?

A. In originating general semantics Alfred Korzybski dealt with many different kinds of human misevaluations, including the confused thinking and unsane behavior resulting from certain uses of "is" and other forms of the verb "to be." He developed the structural differential, a training device for describing and differentiating relationships: relationships between reduced and expanded ranges of attention; between processes over time; between individuals; between groups; between names, labels, and other verbal maps and the non-verbal world of objects, events, and processes; and between many other relationships as well.

It remained for one of Korzybski's most inventive students, D. David Bourland, Jr., to conceive of E-Prime and develop it as a study and practice. By showing how "is" and other forms of "to be" promoted misevaluations spelled out in Korzybski's general semantics, Bourland demonstrated important benefits of E-Prime; both as a means of alerting language users to the pitfalls of using "to be" and as a medium for producing more reliable verbal formulations.

In this interview I have dealt with only a *few* examples stemming from *one* form of "to be." Other students of general semantics and E-Prime have investigated different uses of "to be" and offered other evaluations of E-Prime. But we can rest assured that *much* about E-Prime and closely related matters remain for exploration. Shall I go on?

Q. Would you like to?

A. Another time, perhaps — we must consider the reader.

THE PRIME PROBLEM

JAMES D. FRENCH* ## WITH GENERAL SEMANTICS

THE SUMMER 1992 issue of *ETC.*, contains my article, "The Top Ten Arguments Against E-Prime." (1) David Bourland criticized the article (and other essays leery of the E-Prime movement) in that same issue. (2) This essay constitutes my response.

Just as some individuals use Zen meditation to achieve one of the goals of general semantics (silence on the objective levels of abstraction), other individuals use E-Prime to become more mindful of language structure. I do not object to the use of virtuous methods such as Zen, E-Prime, the Alexander Technique, or any other discipline for the purpose of attaining the goals of general semantics; but I would object (and in the case of E-Prime, I do object) to any attempt to weave those disciplines directly into the fabric of our non-Aristotelian system. Why? Because, as I see it, E-Prime, Zen,

* James D. French, a Director of ISGS, works as a computer programmer at the University of California, Berkeley (1993). His articles on logic, general semantics, and other subjects have appeared in various publications, including *The Journal of Symbolic Logic*.

and some other practices, have aspects about them that are discordant with our science-oriented methodology.

So, in this essay, I will state my case against E-Prime, starting with my reactions to Mr. Bourland's paper. (3)

I was particularly struck by the title of Mr. Bourland's paper: "E-Prime and Un-Sanity." From his writings, I gain the impression that Mr. Bourland considers "un-sanity," and the use of the verb "to be," as inexorably linked. And so, using the verb "to be" leads to un-sanity, in his view, even for persons trained in general semantics. But there is simply no evidence[1993] that trained general semanticists who include "to be" in their language are any more "un-sane" than those who adopt E-Prime. Until there is such evidence, we can and should reject flatly any writing that might smear others with a label like that.

In his paper, Mr. Bourland resorted to ridiculing the E-Prime critics by listing his negative responses to their efforts in an "Agony Matrix." And incredibly, he criticized six people for not writing their criticisms of E-Prime in E-Prime. William Dilworth, in a letter to me, responded with the following comments: "I find it amusing that in the explicitly forensic *ETC.* article, Bourland includes 'failure to write in E-Prime' among pejoratives he attributes to the other side. Evidently his mastery of E-Prime does not prevent his begging a question."

If we should eliminate the verb "to be" from the English language, other, more subtle (and difficult to detect) ways of expressing identity may increase. As even the advocates of E-Prime admit, the is-of-identity belongs as an element to a larger set of problems called, "the confusion of the orders of abstraction," and so eliminating the verb "to be" from the language does not necessarily eliminate identity from the nervous system. For example, in response to something that I had written, Mr. Bourland said, "And where did you get that nonsense about 'expedient'?" (4) I see little difference between identifying something strongly as "that nonsense," and saying, "It is nonsense," except that the "is" expression seems easier to detect.

Mr. Bourland said that my Argument 8 discusses "trivial examples of how to live with use III." (5) What is the difference between denigrating someone's arguments as "trivial," and saying, "They are trivial"? One dissimilarity might be that, in the E-Prime case, we have no trip-word (is) to alert us to a possible identification.

So far, I have not discovered anything in the attitude of the E-Prime advocates toward their own assumptions (and toward criticisms of E-Prime) that would lead me to conclude that their approach to general semantics works better than any other.

In their enthusiasm for E-Prime, it seems quite possible that even experienced general semanticists may come to slight the training methods that have served us so well in the past. If so, one wonders whether or not novices introduced to general semantics through E-Prime will also neglect them. Actually, I regard that as highly likely, considering that some of the core training phrases — for example, "The word *is not* the thing," and "Smith$_1$ *is not* Smith$_2$ *is not* Smith$_3$," and so on — are not even permitted in E-Prime.

General semantics was built on the pillars of *negative* premises. The "is not" statement has served for sixty years as the linchpin for a whole system. Remember "The map *is not* the territory"? Unlike E-Prime, which targets only identities expressed with the "to be" verb, "is not" works against identity in general, no matter *how* it is expressed. The strength of the "is not" statement derives from its ability to provoke an "emotional" response, and thus affect the nervous system. Because of its strong, affective qualities, the "is not" statement has been assigned a major role in retraining our semantic reactions with the structural differential (Korzybski's physical model of the abstracting process). It is also featured prominently in dating, e.g., Smith$_1^{1992}$ *is not* Smith$_1^{1993}$. Losing that particular ability to draw a *simple* and *sharp* distinction between different individuals, different times, different orders of abstractions, etc., may give us pause. At the very least, it should alert us to the *possibility* that, far from enhancing Korzybski's system, E-Prime undermines it.

I could see many E-Prime novices largely ignoring the fundamental writings of general semantics; and even if they did read them, it would be quite difficult for them to take those works seriously, it seems to me. Readers of Irving Lee, for example, might find his use of "is" *distracting.*

I infer that some new members of the Society lose some of their interest in *ETC.,* when they discover that it includes few articles written in E-Prime. Would such persons be willing to read *Science and Sanity* with the respect and diligence that real learning requires?

Dismissive attitudes toward Korzybski are encouraged by the E-Prime proponents when they say that he spoke against certain of the "is" language forms but at the same time used them in his writings.

Korzybski based his system explicitly on the *denial* of identity, not on the removal of "is" from the language. He claimed to have developed techniques that, if applied, would effectively eliminate identity through *consciousness of abstracting.* To him, identity was not just a language problem, but an "over-emotional" generalization of the human nervous system. In the introductions to the second and third editions of *Science and Sanity* (written years after the book proper) he clarified his position, saying, "I must stress again that this difficulty [orientation by intensional definition rather than extensional facts] is not inherent in our language as such, but depends exclusively on our *attitude* toward the *use* of language." (6) (The emphasized words are his.) Korzybski's solutions were based on "changing not the language, but the *structure* of the language, achieved by the habitual use of the extensional devices in our evaluational reactions." (7) Note that he said, "in our evaluational reactions," not "in our speech."

Take indexing — as in lawyer$_1$ *is not* lawyer$_2$ *is not* lawyer$_3$, for example. As indexing becomes an habitual and integral part of our reactions, a marked change takes place in our response to "is." Identification involves what Korzybski called "affective pressure," as when you have a generalized dislike of lawyers, and you say that someone is "that lawyer." Absent that pressure — and general semantics methods such as indexing consistently train against it — where do we find the identification?

When someone well-trained in general semantics says, "John is a lawyer," she is not likely to *over-associate* the person with the word (that is, with *what the word "lawyer" means to her*), because "all" of her general semantics reading and training have warned her and drilled her against such a reaction.

Yes, the is-of-identity and predication have their dangers; but, to date, no one has shown that general semantics does not perform well as an antidote against those dangers.

Without E-Prime, a host of tools are available to the general semanticist to drill the nervous system against identification. We even have the option of rewording is-of-identity and predication statements, an option that has long been a general-semantics tradition. Contrary to what many novices may believe, the practice of wording certain sentences to avoid those types of statements did not originate with the E-Prime movement. One can approve of that practice, but oppose E-Prime, just as one can approve of the idea of attaching a date to certain statements, but oppose the idea of dating *every* statement.

If the idea of dating all of our statements were defined as "The English language dated"; and if it were called "E, sub-D" (E_D); and if people began to describe the general-semantics practice of dating as "writing in E_D," we could hardly be blamed for objecting to it.

Wording certain of our sentences to more closely reflect the relational, structural realities of situations has always been part of general semantics; but eliminating even structurally correct instances of the verb "to be" — as E-Prime surely does — has not. We have every justification for opposing the adoption of E-Prime as the name for rewording structurally limited or faulty statements. Where is the structural error in saying, "I am going to the store"?

If we could identify one element that distinguishes the sciences from the other, less successful forms of human endeavor, we might point to the insistence in science on the strict, rigorous formulation of basic procedures. Yet, E-Prime fails to live up to that standard. It targets the verb "to be" as the problem, when the known facts[1993] indicate that the problem occurs with only *certain forms* of the verb "to be." Are we going to allow a map into our system that we *know* does not fit the territory? E-Prime *should* have been defined as "the English language without the 'is' of identity and the 'is' of predication." Then its advocates could have said, "To achieve E-Prime, you may find it necessary to eliminate even seemingly benign forms of the verb 'to be' from your language." That would have been consistent with the known facts, and no one would have objected to the definition of E-Prime on formulational grounds, at least.

Perhaps the general-semantics community should consider finding a more fitting term for the practice of wording sentences to eliminate the is-of-identity or predication; otherwise "E-Prime" will become the de-facto name.

William Dallmann has proposed the term "E-Prime$_{mod}$." (8) I regard that suggestion as appealing, but I think a more appropriate name could be found because the notion of avoiding certain is-of-identity and predication statements arose prior *to* and independent *of* E-Prime. E-Prime$_{mod}$ has the drawback that one must first define E-Prime before explaining E-Prime$_{mod}$.

I nominate a term suggested by Charlotte Read — the term "rewording" — defined as, "the practice of wording or rewording one or more sentences to avoid the is-of-identity and the is-of-predication in the English language." Rewording should fit nicely with the other extensional devices, e.g., "indexing, dating, rewording"; and since, like "indexing" and "dating," "rewording" says what it does, students of general semantics should find the name easy to understand. As with the other extensional devices, rewording could be used as much or as little as one desired. But of course, students would be encouraged to *reword* their more pernicious is-of-identity and predication statements, just as they are encouraged to *date* or *index* other statements. The prohibition against "all" uses of "to be" could be retained as a rewording *exercise*, to be used in the classroom, and for individual practice on one's own, if desired. (The vast majority of E-Prime devotees seem to use it only as an exercise anyway. As of the date of this writing, I know of only five persons who claim to both speak and write in it consistently. As I see it, the so-called lesser forms of E-Prime are not "E-Prime" by its own definition.)

Of course, outside of general semantics, nothing would prevent individuals from adopting the practice of E-Prime, just as nothing prevents them from using Zen meditation or any other technique.

By adopting rewording as an extensional device, we could accomplish most of the laudable goals of E-Prime, and allow a more flexible approach to the problems of "is," while maintaining the integrity of our discipline.

Finally, let me say that, although I have quite a few objections to E-Prime as a *formulation*, I have even more objections to it as a *movement*. Three things in particular come to mind. One has to do with the tendency of E-Prime promoters to add items willy-nilly to the agenda of general semantics, such as opposing the use of the passive voice, without the long period of review and debate which should precede the adoption of new items. Novices are left with the impression that these things are basic tenets of general semantics, which is not the case. The second objection has to do with the inclination to display a strongly disparaging attitude toward any use of the verb "to be" by others, a penchant that seems reminiscent of witch-hunting. The third objection is the tendency to make sweeping, unverified claims about the benefits of eliminating the verb "to be" entirely from English, e.g., that it improves one's writing. (For arguments against that claim, see note 9.) None of these propensities is consistent with a discipline grounded in science, in my view.

For these and other reasons, I hope that the Society will cease to promote E-Prime; otherwise, these problems, and the divisiveness they have engendered, will continue (I predict) to plague our discipline indefinitely. Unlike any other "extensional device," E-Prime tends to seize the minds of certain people so strongly that general semantics itself gets relegated to the sidelines. Apparently, some writers now think that the major purpose of general semantics is to eliminate the verb "to be" from the English language. Should we retain E-Prime, we can expect such distorted interpretations to isolate general semantics further from the educational mainstream.

NOTES AND REFERENCES

1. James D. French, "The Top Ten Arguments Against E-Prime," *ETC., 49* No. 2 (1992), 175-179.
2. D. David Bourland, Jr., "E-Prime and Un-Sanity," *ETC., 49* No. 2 (1992), 213-223.
3. I thought that the following argument was too technical for the body of my paper, and so I have put it here in the reference section:

   In my original essay I pointed out that the language called "mathematics" facilitates time-binding. Mathematics relies heavily on the notions of equivalence and equality, notions that, to me, seem inherent in some uses of the verb "to be." Mr. Bourland reminded me that the equals sign translates into "equals" in English, not "is"; but I was not asserting that the equals sign means "is" — rather my point was that the equals sign in mathematics, and the "to be" verb in English, perform a similar *logical function.* When we say that $9 = 3 \times 3$, we are logically asserting that the symbol "9" and the symbols "3 X 3" denote the same number; similarly, when we say, "John Jones is that professor," we are logically asserting that the words "John Jones" and "that professor" denote the same person (in that particular context). Symmetrical mathematical relations are characterized by the fact that the *order* in which the symbols are presented does not matter; we can say, "$9 = 3 \times 3$," or we can say, "$3 \times 3 = 9$." Similarly, in English, if we say, "John Jones is that professor," we can say, "That professor is John Jones." As Mr. Bourland pointed out, some teachers of mathematics occasionally substitute "is" for "equals," as in "4 plus 2 is 6." The fact that they can do that and the mathematics still works confirms my point that the two symbols perform equivalent logical functions.

   Mr. Bourland says that even the slowest student can see that "1/2" *is not* "2/4," but surely even the slowest student can be made to understand that the intention of the phrase "1/2 is 2/4" is not to say that the symbol "1/2" *is* the symbol "2/4," but rather that the symbols "1/2" and "2/4" denote the same number. When we say, "John Jones is that professor," we do not intend, and few would take it to mean, that the words "John Jones" are the *words* "that professor."

None of these arguments should be understood to mean that I think it is the "same thing" to substitute "is" for "equals" in the teaching of mathematics, or that I advocate doing it. I do not, of course. Given that the verb "to be" in English performs a similar logical function to the equals sign in mathematics, and given that the equals sign appears fundamental to mathematics — a language that clearly facilitates rapid time-binding — there *may* exist considerable benefits for humankind in the continued use of the verb "to be." None of that is to deny the considerable *dangers* associated with the naive use of "to be" as an identification term, of course, as pointed out by Korzybski and others.

4. D. David Bourland, Jr., "E-Prime and Un-Sanity," *ETC.*, *49* No. 2 (1992), p. 219.

5. Ibid, p. 217.

6. Alfred Korzybski, *Science and Sanity*, 4th Ed. 1958, p. liii. International Non-Aristotelian Library Publishing Company, Lakeville, CT.

7. Ibid. p. xxii. His emphasis. The structure of the language is changed *at the system level* by adopting a new methodology and a new terminology as permanent habits. The language of orders of abstractions, for example, has ordinal and relational (structural) implications different from the terminology of the Aristotelian system. But when we adopt the new terms, and when we use the extensional devices we do so *within* the English language, which remains essentially untouched.

8. William Dallmann, "Is Is Not Is Is Not Is," *ETC.*, *49* No. 2 (1992), p. 134.

9. E-Prime advocates attempt to show, by citing selected examples, that substituting another verb for the verb "to be" improves one's writing. However, no attempts are made to improve the examples while occasionally retaining forms of the verb "to be," and then contrasting those sentences with the E-Prime versions. Furthermore, the E-Prime versions go far beyond simple substitutions. For example, a phrase having nothing to do with the verb "to be" — "I believe that your involving other people made the situation much worse" — is improved to say, "I believe that involving other people with your problems made the situation much worse." [This illustration is taken from Elaine C. Johnson's paper, "Discovering E-Prime," published in *ETC.*, *45*, No. 2 (1988)] Because individual words, short phrases, and entire sentences are altered in many of the samples, often in ways not

directly related to eliminating the verb "to be," the evidence appears questionable, to say the least.

Even if more rigor were applied in such cases, the attempt to prove a general proposition by inductive methods (selected examples) has an uneven record at best. Many science-oriented persons would consider that form of proof unacceptable.

Besides, we have no reliable, scientific means to prefer one person's subjective evaluation over that of another educated person. Suppose someone says, "It does not seem better to me"? Then what?

I do not think that the sentence, "I see rain falling," is necessarily superior to "I am looking at the rainfall," for example. (Nor do I think that the latter sentence is more "static" because it contains a form of that "static" verb "to be.")

Even when we prefer a revised sentence without "to be" to the "to be" version, the E-Prime rule cannot claim an *essential* role in that result, because the exact same revised sentence could have come about as a result of a completely different rule, a rule such as, "*Cut back* on your use of 'to be.' "

A writing paradigm that says, "*Never* use the verb 'to be,' " seems inconsistent with the flexibility sometimes required of effective writing. Consider these two writing examples that critics have ranked with the finest in the language: "It was the best of times, it was the worst of times..."; "To be or not to be: that is the question." Both prominently feature forms of the verb "to be." Had Dickens and Shakespeare written those sentences in E-Prime, I seriously doubt that the E-Prime versions would have become as widely quoted or esteemed as the "to be" passages are today.

Obviously, for any given sentence, there are scores if not hundreds of ways to word it differently; so we should not be surprised that we can often find alternatives that we like better (in our personal judgment). *Any* rule that forced us to alter our writing, such as "never use the word 'and,'" could lead us to alternatives that we might prefer. But most of the improvement, if any, would come from working harder at seeking and discarding alternatives until a more pleasing one was found, not from eliminating a word like "and" from our language.

This much should be clear: I am not arguing that E-Prime fails to improve one's writing. I am saying that the testimony, examples, and arguments used by advocates to show that E-Prime improves one's writing do not meet established standards of scientific verification, and so they carry no weight in a *science-based* discipline. General semantics is not an English class, and lowering our standards to fit what *may* pass for evidence in an English class violates one of the goals of our system, the goal of bringing scientific standards of evaluation into our lives.

The author is thankful to Professor Charles Chihara, Emory Menefee, and Greg Sawin for their helpful remarks.

COMMENTS ON AND
A PUBLIC SPEAKING TEXT
CHARLES R. GRUNER* *IN E-PRIME*

A FTER SOME ENCOURAGEMENT from a publisher, I wrote a public speaking textbook titled *Plain Public Speaking*. I tried to
write the book as a concise text containing simple directions
on how to make speeches — a manual that any college fresh-
man could easily read and then put into practice with a little
hard work. In fact, to produce the manuscript I basically
wrote up and "fleshed out" my lecture material for the basic
public speaking course that I taught.

In other words, I wrote the book to and for *students.* Perhaps I should have written it for my professional colleagues
in other schools who make the adoption decisions — decisions usually made using criteria other than whether the
book would prove "user-friendly." But I did not "scholarize"
the book by including many quotations, citations, and gar-
lands of *ibids* in hopes of footnoting the work of all possible
text adopters. As a result the book sold only moderately well;
but it paid for my childrens' orthodontia and sent me to several professional conventions, and otherwise satisfied me for
the effort I had put into it.

Now, what makes for good public speaking, unlike what
makes for good chemistry, has not changed much since Aris-

---

* A professor in the Department of Speech Communication at the University of
Georgia, Athens, Charles R. Gruner teaches a graduate seminar on "Humor in
Communication."

totle's *Rhetoric*. (And, I apologize to all us *non*-Aristotelians.) No one has done it, but I imagine that an experiment with two groups of students, one using *The Rhetoric* and the other using some modern speech textbook, would produce two groups of speakers of equal quality.

When you revise a public speaking text, what do you change?

Well, you can shuffle and/or rename chapters. You can (and should) update any material whose place in history would prove puzzling or irrelevant to today's students. You can add material, perhaps a new chapter or new research findings. And you can alter the *style*.

I did update, of course. I renamed chapters, on the advice of my editor. And I added a chapter. But, most relevant to this article, I decided to alter the style — to E-Prime.

I teach general semantics as a graduate seminar and occasionally as an undergraduate "special-number" course; I also teach it on an "individual projects" basis for undergraduates. And, since I touch upon E-Prime in this teaching (I require one assignment, the rewriting of a newspaper editorial), I decided that I would practice what I teach.

I finished the manuscript before the recent flurry of publications on E-Prime, primarily *To Be Or Not*, a collection of papers, and the Summer, 1992 issue of *ETC*. But before getting into the revising of the text into E-Prime, I feel impelled to comment on the "controversy" over E-Prime, especially that found in *ETC*. E-Prime Symposium.

After reading the articles by Dallman, Gozzi, Lakoff, French, Kenyon, Parkinson, Wanderer, and Menefee, plus the responses to them by Kellogg and Bourland in that issue of *ETC*., I will try to summarize the arguments "against" E-Prime and what its devotees (and/or I) would say in response. I simplify here perhaps, but not too much, I hope. I put each criticism in italics:

1. *One cannot call oneself a "real" general semanticist unless one practices E-Prime completely and all the time.* I do not think anyone really has said this. I call this a straw man.

2. *One can lie, distort, project, show prejudice, etc. even when using E-Prime; and E-Prime does not convert all illogical statements to completely logical statements.* True, but no one really denies this criticism.

3. *Some ("foreign") languages do not use "is" much at all.* So what? Those that do can still make trouble for people.

4. *Adopting E-Prime would be too large an adjustment for the entire English-speaking world.* Granted, but no one proposes such a grandiose change-over.

5. *There are other ways to avoid any "harm" that "is" can cause, such as context, other extensionalization features (plurals, "to me," etc.) etc.* Agreed. Let us use all these tools, too, like good general semanticists. Who objects?

6. *"Is" identifies identification, so that we can deal with it, whereas "no is" can hide the identification.* I refer here to the "subterranean is," as in "Tyrant George Bush today proclaimed that..." makes it harder for an intelligent human to realize that the speaker asserts that "George Bush, whom we all agree is a tyrant, today proclaimed..." I cannot imagine that eliminating "ises" could result in such a gain for propagandists.

7. *Using "exists as" for "is" does nothing to remove "identification."* True, but who recommends this substitution for every instance of "is"? Creativity can even overcome use of "exists as."

8. *Denying us writers the word "is" when its use serves purposes other than identification and predication, takes from us tools and thus subtracts from our abilities as writers.* After doing an entire book in E-Prime, I would tend to agree with this point of view. Changing "My name is Chuck" to "I call myself Chuck," or "It is raining" to something like "I perceive rain falling here and at this time" can look and sound a little silly. About the only argument against this part-time use of E-Prime is that using "is" part of the time for purposes other than for identification and predication purposes makes the habit just too durned hard to break.

I really cannot buy this rebuttal favoring "total" E-Prime. The only defense of it I can find offered comes from the analogy to quitting smoking and drinking — that the smoker and the alcoholic cannot really just "cut down"; they must

completely abstain. The analogy does not hold up. I quit
both drinking and heavy smoking cold turkey, but I find that
I can still ration my "ises" to any rate I choose, and do it with
alacrity.

9. *Lastly, an ad hominem argument attacks the advocates of E-
Prime for using the "deity mode" metaphor applied to using "is."*
Like many figures of speech, this comparison contains logical
flaws, of course, and even potentially emotional content that
renders it vulnerable to attack. These qualities make it easy
for detractors to pick it apart with aplomb. But Kellogg and
Bourland convince me that they choose "deity mode" as a
metaphor, for emphasis and vividness, not as an analogy to
adopt as *strictly literal* in all respects. Come on folks, let's
lighten up!

In summary here, I most appreciated the stance of Mr. Earl
Hautala in his short, sweet *ETC.* piece. You might remember
that he concluded:

> Let's stay within the bounds of choice and self-respon-
> sibility. Eventually those who study general semantics will
> choose for themselves, how and when E-Prime will serve
> them best.

But then I believe in freedom of choice and moderation in
most things.

Now, back to that textbook rewrite.

One thing I learned on this project: Kellogg and Bourland
correctly state that you don't achieve E-Prime by writing material and then going back and converting all the forms of "to
be" into other wordings such as "exist(s/ed as"). When you
rewrite, you truly *translate*. For example:

> You will have to know the satisfactions to be derived from
> believing or doing as you ask. This should be ridiculously
> simple. You already believe in your idea or already do what
> you are going to urge others to do. So you ought to be able
> to figure out why *you* believe or do it.

became:

In order to persuade others, you must know your *own* reasons (or motivations) for believing or doing as you want others to. So it should follow as the day the night, you should have no trouble in discovering those reasons or motivations for your audience.

(Note: an indefinite "*this*" in the original disappeared in the translation, also.)

The overall task of translating the entire book into E-Prime (except for in direct quotations, of course) proved less difficult than I first imagined. The reason: originally I wrote the book in a personal "I-to-you" format ("When you speak to persuade, you provide your listeners with information, but not just for the sake of teaching them that information..."). Thus I had much less passive voice to transcribe into the active sentences of E-Prime than usual.

But another aspect of the original style challenged my skill as a detective. As a *speech* teacher I tried to write in more of an *oral style* than a written style such as an English teacher would probably prefer. For instance, this *oral* style included the use of contractions, which would give my old English schoolmarms the heebie-jeebies. These contractions, then, hid away some "ises," as in "Be sure to thank the man who introduces you. He's usually a..." These "is contractions" sneakily hide from you, and even your word processor's word search feature cannot find them.

Although much of the original book spoke directly to the reader, prescribing specific behavior, some of it merely provided information for one substantive reason or another. Translating this "straight information" required a bit more linguistic rethinking, as in the following:

When Franklin D. Roosevelt was struck down by polio, his political ambitions were only delayed, not killed. In order to keep his name before the public, he asked his wife, Eleanor, to fill in for him on his extensive public-speaking schedule.

Eleanor, a private and shy person, was terrified of taking on these speaking engagements. But out of fierce loyalty to her husband, she hitched up what courage she could manage....and was not entirely successful at first, but she kept doggedly working at it.

I translated that passage to:

Franklin Delano Roosevelt's political career appeared ended when he contracted the deadly disease, polio (infantile paralysis). In order to keep his name before the public, he asked his wife, Eleanor, to fill in for him on his extensive public-speaking schedule.

Eleanor, a private and shy person, cringed with terror at the thought of all those public speeches. But, out of fierce loyalty to her husband, she hitched up what courage she could manage....[and] did not succeed completely at first, but...

After rewriting (and, of course, updating, etc.) the old, original text, I next took up the task of writing from scratch a new chapter, one on "The Speech To Entertain."

This chapter did not represent my very first original writing of new material in E-Prime; but it did embody my *lengthiest* effort at the medium. Perhaps the difference lay in my own motivation, but I seemed to have less difficulty *creating* in E-Prime than I had had in *rewriting* the other. I wound up, in fact, creating a chapter which my editor considered overly-long! But in the ensuing correspondence over my chapter's length I managed to convince her to cut not a word.

Any book should profit from rewriting. I feel that mine did, and improved even more by conversion to E-Prime. I also feel that the discipline of eschewing all forms of the verb "to be" added insight and character to my writing ability in general. And I also feel that writing in that style forces one to more carefully consider how words need to fit reality just as maps ought to reflect territory; and don't all general semanticists wish for that outcome?

REFERENCES

Bourland, D. D. Jr. (1992). E-Prime and Un-Sanity. *ETC.*, *49*, No. 2 (Summer), 213-223.

Bourland, D. D. Jr. & Johnston, P. D. (Eds) (1991). *To Be or Not: An E-Prime Anthology.* San Francisco: International Society for General Semantics.

Dallman, W. (1992). Is Is Not Is Is Not Is. *ETC.*, *49*, No. 2 (Summer), 134-137.

French, J. D. (1992). The Top Ten Arguments Against E-Prime. *ETC.*, *49*, No. 2 (Summer), 175-179.

Gozzi, R. Jr. (1992). Metaphor and E-Prime: Of the Subterranean "Is," Paradoxical Commands, and Tilted Abstraction Ladders. *ETC.*, *49*, No. 2 (Summer), 138-141.

Gruner, C. R. (1982). *Plain Public Speaking.* New York: Macmillan.

Gruner, C. R. (1993). *Essentials of Public Speaking.* San Diego, Collegiate Press. [Second edition of Gruner (1982)]

Hautala, E. (1992). General Semanticists and E-Prime. *ETC.*, *49*, No. 2 (Summer), 165-167.

Kellogg, E. W. III. (1992). The Good, the Bad, and the Ugly: Comments on the E-Prime Symposium. *ETC.*, *49*, No. 2 (Summer), 205-212.

Kenyon, R. (1992). E-Prime: The Spirit and the Letter. *ETC.*, *49*, No. 2 (Summer), 185-188.

Lakoff, R. T. (1992). Not Ready For Prime Time. *ETC.*, *49*, No. 2 (Summer), 142-145.

Menefee, E. (1992). 'S Word Play at the Grammar Reform School. *ETC.*, *49*, No. 2 (Summer), 196-203.

Parkinson, T. (1992). Beyond E-Prime. *ETC.*, *49*, No. 2 (Summer) 192-195.

Wanderer, R. (1992). The Word "E-Prime" Is Not the Thing. *ETC.*, *49*, No. 2 (Summer), 189-191.

EMORY MENEFEE* **ONE GRUNT OR TWO?**

M Y NAME IS ALFRED. This sentence, besides giving my name,
demonstrates what we used to call an "is of identity"
construction, which early believers in E' thought was the
most deadly use of the verb "to be." You who someday read
these words will most likely not know that E' (E-Prime) was
the name given to a variety of English without *any* of the
forms of "to be." It became popular for a while, because its
champions claimed that it would reduce or eliminate statements of identity (equating one abstraction with another as
in the first sentence above), the passive voice, notions of permanence, and other problems that caused people to misuse
and misinterpret the language with often unfortunate results.
The E-Primers were a group of otherwise nice folks who
started us on a fatal spiral of language "correctness," leading
finally to our present deplorable situation, though I suppose
one could say that we have succeeded in achieving "communication" with no ambiguity whatsoever.

---

* Dr. Menefee, a resident of Richmond, California, divides much of his time
between general semantics and research in physical chemistry (mostly polymer
physics and hair growth).

But I'm ahead of myself. The E-Primers zealously spread their message, and after a few years it became mandatory to teach only E' in our schools. Amazingly, speakers of the rest of the world's languages fell into line. Unfortunately, life and strife went on much as before (people managed to misunderstand each other just as well without "to be" as with it). Eventually, though, a shattering discovery was made: identification could occur using verbs besides just "to be." Saying, for example, "Charlie has the brains of an ass" left little doubt about identifying Charlie with an ass, and seemed even more insulting than, "Charlie is an ass," because it was clear to most people that Charlie couldn't bray. Obviously the next step was to legislate against the "to have" verbs. Soon, many more equally troublesome verbs were identified and added to the list: appear, become, come, consist, continue, feel, get, go, grow, involve, keep, lie, look, prove, remain, resemble, run, seem, sit, sound, stay, turn, wax, and others too numerous to mention. People promoting this change called themselves Double Primers, and though there was some grumbling, before long the schools were teaching this new version, now called E". Luckily, many graduates found work rewriting already published literature.

The Double Primers waxed eloquent about the new English, but the reform proved futile: people were still able to make trouble for each other through language. Inevitably, one day the Triple-Primers came along, a group that had realized adjectives are forms of identification, too. For example, if somebody said, "That beautiful flower," it surely meant pretty much the same thing as saying "that flower is beautiful." Obviously, all adjectives had to be eliminated, and so E''' was born. Heavy penalties were exacted for anybody caught with an adjective. Unfortunately, the goal of creating harmonious communication still wasn't within reach: people developed such stress and worry about incorrectness and punishments that they fought over almost nothing.

At long last, theoreticians among the Triple-Primers recognized the core of the problem: *language.* People talk and write and incite with language, they tell each other off in language, they plan, scheme, cheat with language. The ultimate solution thus became crystal clear: complete elimination of all language, with capital punishment (or even worse) for anyone caught using any form of recognized speech. What a stroke! Disagreement virtually stopped, except for occasional local tribal battles over who got the most food around the fire. Industry and commerce vanished, and, except for all the bodies that resulted from rampant starvation and fighting, pollution became nearly nonexistent.

I remember an old story about someone named Gulliver who visited the School of Languages in Laputa. The scholars there had decided that using words shortened life, so they should communicate by showing the "things" that words stand for. Serious talkers had to carry a huge bag of these "things," though one could stuff enough under one's arms for a short conversation. Maybe this is where Korzybski, another old timer, got the idea that the most basic communication is pointing at something. Anyway, that's what we do these days: point at things — though most people find it helps to grunt now and then, by way of emphasis.

I'm scratching this message into a rock; I may be the last person either crazy enough or able to write in the old way. It's dangerous, but perhaps someone will understand it one day.

Andrew Lohrey* *E-PRIME, E-CHOICE, E-CHOSEN*

E-Prime or E-Choice "is" a choice. I could have written "appears as a choice" but that would have detracted from my point. A point isomorphic with Emory Menefee's argument ("E-Prime or E-Choice," *ETC.*, Summer 1991) that not all identificational verbs "to be" should be eliminated from our discourse. I agree with Menefee's concern that we should become conscious of when to use and when not to use identificational verbs. Such consciousness of expressive devices and rhetorical uses (of abstracting) contrasts with the straightforward involuntary rejection of all identificational verbs under the regime of E-Prime.

But how much choice do we really have in eliminating identification and identity from our expressions, and should we try and erase them anyhow? I know these questions are heresy to E-Primers, but I suggest they should be asked as a matter of course in examining this "thing" called "language." Should we try for instance, to do away with identities produced by nouns? This has been the argument by C. A. Hil-

* A former member of the Tasmanian (Australian) Parliament, Andrew Lohrey is currently in a doctoral program at the University of Technology, Sydney, Australia.

gartner *(General Semantics Bulletin* No. 44/45) in "Some
Traditional Assumings Underlying Western Indo-European
Languages." In this paper Hilgartner concludes that noun
phrases as well as verb phrases produce identity through ob-
jectification. His remedy: where possible make nouns into
verbs by adding the suffix "ing," thus "noun" is replaced by
"nouning" and "verb" by "verbing" and so on.

   Hilgartner's ascetic approach incorporates the elimination
of identificational verbs as well as an attempt to dispose of
objectifying nouns. But what was the result? Did Hilgartner
manage to eliminate identity from his own writing? The answer is clearly no. For pages he carefully avoided identities
produced by the verb "to be" and most nouns, but Hilgartner
nevertheless wrote, as all E-Primers have to write, by using
the first person singular pronoun. Reflection for a moment
on the semantics of pronouns will be enough to make most
readers aware that every pronoun produces an identity of
nonverbal referent and symbol. "I," "me," "you," "she," "it,"
"him," "her," "we," "us," "they," "them," "this" are pronounal
identities. One can write in E-Prime or express oneself by
adding "ing" to the end of nouns, but one cannot write in
these styles and not use pronouns. It is quite impossible and
I challenge anyone to try it.

   We could go further than pronouns and look at identities
produced by other aspects of grammar. For instance, what
about the identities produced by adjectives of quality?
Should we not try for a semantic hygiene that eliminates
such adjectival identities as "hot," "cold," "clever," "absurd,"
"beauty," "absent," "eternal," et cetera? Such a style which
attempts to eliminate these may be possible (although I
doubt it) but even if we did succeed in erasing these terms
from our expressions it would be rather dull prose.

   The point I wish to make here is that the semantic construction of identity is a basic part of every discourse. If identity does not come in the form of the verb "to be" then it is
produced by nouns, pronouns, and adjectives as well as other grammatical forms. In other words, I discovered, as Hilgartner did, the impossibility of expressing myself without
using identities. Therefore to believe that we should attempt
to simply eliminate identity from our expressions, as

E-Primers endeavor so to do, appears a futile exercise. I would go further and suggest that in particular, the use of the verb "to be" is in many circumstances an important generic classificational and differential device. For instance, where is the semantic difficulty in saying, "that is a starling and not a blackbird," or "flour is an ingredient of bread"?

Rather than attempting the impossible perhaps our semantic concerns should be focused on the manner in which identities can combine together to produce the pernicious identification of mythologised and reified discourses. I refer here to such powerful meanings as found in the serious and harmful use of stereotyping in the formulaic narrative, film, or television story or in the political report that appears as an "objective" piece of journalism or in the partisan voice of censorship disguised as a patriotic call against un-American or un-Australian activity, or in the many other mythologised discourses in contemporary society. The power of these discourses comes, not from any single identity produced by the verb "to be." Rather persuasion comes from the combinations of identities (produced by a variety of grammatical constructions) which are fused into an overall pattern of identification: a "reality" made as a seamless web of meaning producing a sense of "the way things are."

Detecting patterns of identification by looking at sentence construction is not easy but some of the semantic hallmarks of discourses of power can be found in such telltale phrases as the following:

(1) *The agent-less phrase.* This is a common device favored particularly in television and news reports, in academic writing as well as biblical texts. Here the authors delete themselves from their expressions by the expedient of never using first person singular pronouns. In this manner, omnipotence, authority, and a sense of truth is created. The missing identity in these cases is transformed by the semantic identification of expression with author into an "isness" of authority and power. Taken together with the use of identificational verbs the "agent-less phrase" is a powerful semantic building block for myth and propaganda.

(2) *Deletion of the actor.* In this device the cause of the process referred to is deleted. For example, "Jerry Brown was

accused by Clinton of buying votes" is changed to "Jerry Brown was accused of buying votes" or even "Jerry Brown bought votes." The effect of this deletion is to increase the authority and power of the expression by reducing the qualification inherent in an explicit reference to an actor. Once again the deletion produces an identification, this time of actor and process. When this deletion combines with identificational verbs the effect is powerful and persuasive meaning.

(3) *Collapsing participants into a single model.* This is a form often used in news reports, for example "workers picketing the hospital" is collapsed into "picketing," or "Mr. Freeman delivers food" is collapsed into "food deliveries." The semantic effect of such collapsing is to reify the process by identifying participants and causes of actions with the process. In this sense at least three identities are identified together as one.

(4) *Decontextualisation.* This represents a major mythological device and it functions under several conditions. For example, it comes about when an author omits the social and generic context of their expressions. This omission is common to fiction, particularly to traditional realist narratives, but this erasure is also common to the traditions of science and religion. For example, the so called "Laws of Nature" are often decontextualised to the extent that these "Laws" are described as if they were written in cement by non-human scientific or religious hands. The context omitted from these "Laws" is the social and linguistic community which had agreed to these principles and which constructed them in the first place. Decontextualisation can also function when a proposition is expressed so that it omits its own classificational context. Examples of decontextualised propositions are the so called universal logic found in truth tables and universal classifications such as "she is mad." The semantic affects of decontextualisation are universalism, (the expression applies universally throughout time and space), and a sense of the a-political, a-social, and a-historical, (the expression appears innocent of all vested interests and socio-historical contexts). With decontextualisation a series of identities are combined together by way of identifying the author, the generic frame-

work, the historical and social setting with the rhetorical devices of the expression itself so that together these different identities make for a single unified totality of meaning.

In each of these four semantic building blocks (and there are many others) several identities have been combined together into what appears often as a singleness of meaning. The process of combining various identities is itself one of identification. Identification in this sense is the process of unities building on unities to form larger totalities. From this perspective, myth and propaganda represent the semantic processes of combination in which a series of identities (embedded in phrases) combine into larger and more persuasive patterns of identification (embedded in sentences). These large patterns of identifications are pernicious for they block enlightened and critical communication and detached responses to communication.

In following Emory Menefee's argument for E-Choice, I would submit that the attempt to rid our expressions of the identity produced by the verb "to be" has marginal semantic significance. As it appears impossible to eliminate identity in its varying forms from language and still have language, we could choose instead how and in what manner identities are used. The problem, as I see it, is one of hierarchy rather than of type: as a basic unit of language, identity is fine when it produces relatively discrete classifications. Identity becomes a problem however, when through the use of rhetorical devices a variety of them are welded together forming complexes of meaning that appear indivisible. I have therefore argued that rather than E-Prime our E-Choice should be to eliminate the large patterns of identification which occur in reified and mythological discourses.

Paul Dennithorne Johnston* **TALKING TO THE WALL**

I T WOULD SEEM that certain upholders of the faith have deemed it necessary to protect us from the insidious influence of a new trend which threatens to undermine the very core of civilized life. I refer, of course, to that heinous, noxious, baneful, deleterious, mischievous, malicious, and offensive habit that so threatens to destroy our mental acuity — the practice of E-Prime.

Like the proverbial fool, I naively waltzed into those dangerous quagmires where angels so wisely fear to tread. I wrote many compositions in E-Prime, ranging from articles and essays to short stories, a novella, and a novel-in-progress (if you can call it progress), not to mention a hundred percent E-Prime personal telephone directory. Little did I know of the dangers with which I flirted. I shudder now to think of my close scrape with moral and intellectual ruin. Thankfully, I have seen the light.

* Paul Dennithorne Johnston serves as Executive Director of ISGS.

At first, when I observed that many who criticized E-Prime most vociferously had not actually indulged in this pernicious and reprehensible activity, I thought of that old saw which goes something like "Don't knock it if you haven't tried it."

After much agonized soul-searching, I realized the error of my ways. Does the pious person sample sin in order to warn us against its dangers? Must one experiment with radioactive waste or suicide in order to claim the authority to warn us against such evils? Must a doctor contract a deadly disease in order to cure it?

And so began my tortuous wrestling with the E-Prime question — to do or not to do, whether to suffer the slings and arrows of outraged critics, or in confronting them, add more fuel to the fire.

Unlike Menefee who has Mr. Itchy the cat, or Bourland who consults Schnapps the dog, I had no one to advise me. Our feline Nip refused to get involved in this contentious and controversial matter.

"I will discuss tuna fish. I categorically refuse to talk nonsense," said Nip dogmatically. "Meow."

Like Shirley Valentine, I had to talk to the wall.

"Tell me, Wall," I said. "Have I gone beyond the pale?"

"You could use a little sun," said Wall noncommittally.

"I don't know," I wavered. "I find E-Prime useful in helping me think more clearly."

"You need help," muttered Wall.

"For example, E-Prime won't let me think in the deity mode, so I have to take responsibility for my own conclusions."

"Without the deity mode, we'll have atheists running riot all over the place," warned Wall ominously.

"I must admit, the deity mode helps me impose my prejudices on others. Bigotry needs a strong higher authority."

"Exactly," said Wall. "If you start to quail, think about family values."

"But Wall," I said nervously. "What about this paradigm thing? I heard that we sit on the edge of a new linguistic paradigm which might solve some problems of identification."

"Never sit on the edge. Sit safely in the middle. Especially if you have a picket fence."

"When you approach a new paradigm, you get a backlash. The clerics refused to look through Galileo's newfangled telescope. They made Galileo recant, but as he did so he stamped his foot and muttered, 'The earth moves.'"

"Hemingway said that," said Wall contemptuously.

"Pareto said you decide your position first, then find rational explanations."

"That cuts both ways," said Wall grimly.

"The Swiss dragged their feet over making digital watches and lost much of the market."

"Watchmakers drag their hands," said Wall dourly.

"It seems as if people have forgotten their common goal. They just want to win the debate, whichever side they happen to take," I mumbled sadly.

"The first amendment," said Wall. "Everybody has the constitutional right to badmouth everybody else. Now let me give you some advice. Don't get in a corner. Keep your back to the wall. Look for a window of opportunity opening doors to thresholds of the future while you put a ceiling on innovation and keep a firm foundation of tradition."

"I'll keep my ear to the ground," I replied cautiously.

"Don't use clichés," said Wall with disgust.

"But E-Prime takes me off 'automatic.' The seeking of alternative structures provides a beneficial exercise in logical awareness because it makes me think hard about what I write."

"You find it hard to think, generally," snorted Wall derisively.

"I must admit that E-Prime doesn't automatically prevent identification or other misevaluations," I said pedantically. "Look at such phrases as *the pompous professor* or *the noble nutcracker*."

"...or *the literate lunatic*..." muttered Wall.

"You can *imply* identity. Some call this more dangerous because of its insidiousness."

"Do I perceive a glimmer of intelligence in your ramblings?" asked Wall caustically.

"One must remember that *intent* plays a vital role," I continued philosophically. "If you don't *want* to deal with problems
of identity, E-Prime won't mitigate them. But if you do, E-
Prime provides a tool.

I continued hurriedly while I had the chance. "E-Prime
helps my writing because it eliminates the passive voice. It
makes writing more descriptive because I must use active
verbs. It tightens sentences for that same reason. It brings
you closer to the level of experiences as you avoid higher abstractions, thus making your writing more extensional..."

"Personally, I could use more long-winded highfalutin abstractions like yours," interrupted Wall. "When people write
on me, they usually keep it graphically short. Speaking of
writing, I suggest you give up that cheap literary device of
talking to animals to make your point."

"Censorship! Animals have a right to free speech," I cried
self-righteously. "Only if they do it in E-Prime, of course," I
added hastily.

"Ha!" retorted Wall victoriously. "Do *you* speak in E-
Prime?"

"When I avoid 'to be' verbs I do. I can tell you that I'm the
only person in the known world who *eats* in E-Prime."

"How do you do that?"

"I eschew all calorie-loaded *to be* verbs, not to mention *B*
vitamins, honey and beeswax. However, once a year I use a
be-word just to prove I have an open mind."

> *"Nothing in speech,*
> *Became him like the talking of it,"*

recited Wall Shakespearefully.

"Perhaps Menefee's Alfred has the right idea — eliminate
language altogether," I said sarcastically.

"Humor has no place in epistemological discussions,"
growled Wall angrily.

"Eliminate humor, too. It encourages avoidance of serious
issues."

"You're a nincompoop," said Wall. "That's it."

"Ah," I replied condescendingly. "The insult-of-identity."

"I've had enough, I'm out of here," said Wall in disgust.

"Does that mean you currently undergo the process of departure, or that you intend to leave at some future moment, or that you have actually left?" I asked E-Primefully.

"You figure it out," said Wall.

"Seriously," I said. "A sense of humor would..."

"Traitor!" screamed Wall.

As I crept from the room, the doorknob caught my sleeve and hissed conspiratorially: "It all hinges on..."

Dodging some malevolent passive verbs clogging up the hall, I ran for my epistemological life.

IS-Y WHITE HATS

Stewart W. Holmes* # AND IS-Y BLACK HATS

I N RECENT ISSUES OF *ETC.*, we've been treated to arguments for
E-Prime and to arguments for E-Choice. In presenting my
two-cents worth, I shall abandon the faintly carnivorous
metaphor and switch into the Hollywood Western mode:
good guys wear white hats and bad guys wear black hats.

The principal E-Prime advocate, Dave Bourland, places
black hats on all uses of the verb *be*. Korzybski explicitly goes
along with putting a black hat on the "is of identity." As I
read his statement in *Science and Sanity*, he means by "is of
identity" only the copulative use of forms of *be* followed by a
noun or noun construction. This use definitely gets a black
hat from him.

This doesn't mean that he avoided such use of *be* consistently. He admits that he has not sufficiently retrained himself in this aspect of being invariably conscious of abstracting.
But he used this verb frequently in other ways. I think he
would put white hats on the following uses.

* Stewart Holmes, who lives in Hendersonville, North Carolina, has written two
books, *Meaning in Language* and *Zen Art for Meditation*. His essays have
appeared in *ETC.* since its first year of publication, 1943.

The "is of existence." "I am here." This has no connotation of identicalness.

The "auxiliary is." "I am writing this letter." This *is* has no more connotation of identicalness (of *is* and *writing*) than its root verb, "writing," has.

The "passive is." "This letter is being written to *ETC*." This use may lack semantic clarity, but it has at least two useful functions. One, to conceal the doer of the deed: "This letter was written." Two, to describe simply a clearly observable operation. "A computer was used to type this letter."

The "is of identity" and the "is of predication" used with a consciousness of abstracting qualifier. "It seems to me that he is a crook." "I believe him to be venal." Such a usage may profitably be followed by an operational description of a reason for the classification, such as "His votes usually support the position of wealthy contributors to his reelection."

The uses of "is of identity" and "is of predication" in conditional mode forms such as "may be," "might be," "could be," "should be." "He may be a crook." Such uses open up possibilities of other perceptions and interpretations and judgments. "But then again, he may be honest."

And now for the "is of predication." "The sky is blue." This tempts me to reach for a gray hat, if such exists. This label, used in a context not evidencing consciousness of abstracting, does imply identicalness. Shall we give it a black hat? But what if the adjective is used attributively rather than as a predicate adjective following a copulative verb? "The jagged snow peak seemed to pierce the blue sky." I can't imagine anyone placing a black hat on an attributive adjective — of which each of us utters a few thousand every day. Yet it seems to me that there is an equal possibility of identicalness in each kind of usage. Maybe we shall have to give the "is of predication" a white hat with a black feather in it, warning us to call to mind a picture of the structural differential — plus a subvocal chanting of the mantra: "Whatever you say it is, it isn't."

A REVIEW OF

TO BE OR NOT:

RETTA WEST
WHINNERY* **An E-Prime Anthology** †

To Be Or Not: An E-Prime Anthology. D. David Bourland, Jr., and Paul Dennithorne Johnston, editors. San Francisco: International Society for General Semantics, 1991. 185 pages. $14.00 (softcover).

A S TECHNICAL WRITERS, we continually strive for clarity. An accurate explanation of how a software program functions enables the user to employ it more effectively. We try to show the user what it does by using descriptive verbs; in this context, most of us have discovered that verbs of "being" muddle the explanation, especially in the passive voice. E-Prime, a system of writing without the verb "to be," requires active voice and thus shows the true relationships between subjects and objects.

---

* Retta West Whinnery works as a technical writer for an environmental consulting firm in Kansas City, Missouri. She has done graduate work in linguistics.
† Reprinted with permission from *Technical Communication*, 4th Quarter, 1992, published by the Society for Technical Communication, Arlington, VA.

For example, a typical instruction in a software manual might read —

> If a directory containing K9 database files *is* specified, the following message will *be* displayed: "If you wish the files to *be* converted, press any key to continue. Press Ctrl/Break to exit and the files will not *be* converted."

Rewritten into E-Prime, this instruction would read:

> If you specify a directory containing database files, the K9 screen displays this message: "To convert the files, press any key. To prevent file conversion, press Ctrl/Break."

Not only does the E-Prime instruction more clearly explain the relationship between the user's actions and the program's function, it also results in a 30 percent reduction in verbiage.

This anthology describes the E-Prime system of writing, which consists of a more descriptive derivative of English that brings the user back to the level of first-person experience. One of the book's twelve essays defines E-Prime as —

$$E' = E - e$$

where *E* represents the whole of the English language, *e* represents the linguistic element "to be" with all its inflectional forms, and *E'* represents a subset of English minus verbs of being. Bourland coined the term E-Prime in the 1960s, though he had used the concept in his own writing since 1949.

Linguists estimate that one English sentence in two employs some form of the verb "to be" and most paragraphs have at least a dozen. The subtraction of "to be" influences the sentence structures we choose — no passive voice, less use of the subjunctive mood, and fewer participial usages. Actors re-enter the picture. To illustrate, "If I were king of the forest..." would become "As king of the forest, I...." "Being queen for a day, she..." would require recasting as "Crowned queen for a day, she...."

On the downside, however, eliminating all forms of "to be" results in loss of the present progressive. In E-Prime you cannot say "it is raining" and the alternatives "it rains" or "it continues to rain" sound awkward.

To Be or Not consists of three parts. Part 1, "E-Prime in Action," includes introductory essays written by two English teachers after they discovered E-Prime and got rid of the "to be" crutch. An essay by Paul Dennithorne Johnston presents us with his personal awakening to semantics.

Part 2, "Epistemological Foundations of E-Prime," includes essays on writing in E-Prime, *Is*-less grammars, and using E-Prime as a tool for critical thinking.

Part 3, "Further Applications of E-Prime," contains a short story, demonstrating the use of E-Prime in creative writing, and a linguistics thesis, showing its application to scholarly works.

In "Getting Rid of the *To Be* Crutch," Ruth S. Ralph describes the concepts of general semantics:

> [Alfred] Korzybski believed that the verb *to be* causes serious communication disturbances and other psychological problems for modern man [sic]. In his book *Science and Sanity*, Korzybski referred to these problems as the "*is* of predication" and the "*is* of identity." In both, he blamed the verb *to be* for misleading people into making untrue and unwarranted statements....

> A pair of common enough sentence structures employ *to be* to tempt man [sic] into mistaken value judgments. Korzybski called the Subject - Linking Verb - Adjective sentence pattern the "*is* of predication" and the Subject - Linking Verb - Noun sentence pattern the "*is* of identity."
> A sentence like "Robert is stupid" exemplifies the first, while "Marcia is a genius" demonstrates the second....

> "For example," he [Bourland] continues, "in a case where most people might judge themselves harshly by saying, 'I'm no good at math,' I would advise them to say in-

stead, 'I got poor grades in sixth grade arithmetic,' or 'I did better in other subjects than I did in math.' "

According to David Bourland, "Using E-Prime can improve a person's outlook on life. Once you realize that every time you say *is* you tell a lie, you begin to think less about a thing or person's 'identity' and more about its function."

By "telling a lie" Ms. Ralph means that although certain "to be" statements tell facts (i.e., Mr. Thompson is my boss), they still prevaricate in that the sentence directs our attention away from all the other aspects of Mr. Thompson's personality. It makes us believe that Mr. Thompson's "bossness" takes precedence over anything else about him.

Most "to be" statements have the *appearance* of fact because the linking verb functions as a fulcrum or "equal" sign (i.e., Mr. Thompson = boss; Robert = stupid). But such "to be" statements do not distinguish verifiable fact (Mr. Thompson is my boss) from the speaker's opinion (Robert is stupid).

Is-less grammars discourage labeling (Joan is smart; Cleve is smart) and encourage fact-reporting (Joan makes $500,000 a year; Cleve scored 160 on an I.Q. test).

One of the best works in this anthology, "Coping with Semantic Problems in Systems Development" by Karen L. Ruskin, describes some of the benefits that ensued from persistently using E-Prime in the development of a large, complex, real-time computer system. This essay will grab the attention of software documenters.

Because one essayist contributed five articles to the anthology, some examples appear more than once and seem somewhat redundant. Most of the contributors to this anthology had previously published their essays in professional journals, and many included footnotes and references to supplement their research. Lack of an index did not detract from the book's usability.

Overall, this anthology introduces a dynamic concept that technical writers may adopt to improve clarity and precision.

ROBERTA WEDGE* **LETTER OF COMMENT**

D EAR SEMANTICIANS:

I claim no particular expertise in your field, and have not even read *To Be Or Not,* but I recognize a fish when I smell one, and smell one I did upon reading the correspondence concerning E-Prime in your fall 1991 issue. My sympathies ought to lie with the proponents of this particular technique of language modification, for in adolescence I came up with a line of thought quite similar, in which I tried to replace, as far as feasible, all descriptive nouns by their corresponding adjectives, and, if possible, to compress their meaning into one clear verb. Thus from saying, "I am a Canadian," a state, if you'll excuse the pun, that tries to push all of me into this one word, an unbearable limitation, I moved to, "I am Canadian," a phrase which only encompasses part of me. It would change my meaning, however, to dump the "am" with absolutist finality, for no alternative suffices. "I hold Canadian citizenship" reaffirms the paper power of Ottawa (and while monarchs may claim that "l'état, c'est moi," this *moi* feels no

* Roberta Wedge lives in Montreal.

affinity to any *état*), "I think of myself as Canadian" obscures how others see me, and "I live in Canada" simplifies matters into falsehood. Saki wrote that, "A little falsehood sometimes saves tons of explanation," but this journal exists, like most academic publications, precisely for tons of explanation.

Vegetarians have no bones to pick. (Too definitive. Rewrite: "Those who eat no meat....") Nor can I adopt the persona of canine companion or feline familiar. Instead I shall have to speak as myself, as one who has taken a long time to find herself, and indeed has not come to the end of the path of self-discovery. My main discomfort with what I understand of E-Prime I can state briefly: it denies me the right to assert myself in the simplest way possible, to stand up and say, "I am, I exist, I am here." There are so many pressures in this society that try to persuade me not to exist, not to *be* myself. A chillingly flip example of this appeared on p. 316 beneath the article on dieting: a cartoon depicting the forces of commerce and industry literally pressing, squeezing, torturing a fat person into an acceptable shape. Explicit or what?

It strikes me that with all this denial of being and emphasis on having and doing, the main changes evident in prose constructed or reconstructed in E-Prime rings of the typically male Western pursuits: rush rush, scurry scurry, define oneself by work and achievements and possessions. Thus it comes as no great surprise to find your editorial board and society, as listed on the inside front cover of *ETC.*, overwhelmingly male. In E-Prime I see acceptance neither of what I could call, with gross oversimplification, "Zen knowledge," the insight of sitting quietly and, yes, just *being*, nor of female experience, the intimate bonds of relationships — not "having" (possessing) a child, a lover, a friend, but *being joined* to them. In this sense "being" describes not a fixed state but a dynamic, an action, the vibrating tension of the web of life. E-Prime misses this.

You've got some good ideas, boys, but you've got a lot to learn.

SEMANTICS

Semantics
Helps us understand people's antics
It lays some secrets bare
It makes us more aware
For sure!
Inferring
Can often result in a blurring
So, cautious we must be
Distilling carefully
What's pure!
Ah, Ruth dear,
We've had fun with the abstraction ladder
And so we've emerged wiser, not sadder.
Please note, dear
That I've used "to be" verbs only twice here!

CORRIE ERNST

[*Note from Ruth Ralph*: I taught a class in general semantics at the Institute for Learning in Retirement at American University, Washington, D.C., this last spring. At the end of the course one of the students, Corrie Ernst, presented this poem.

The students and the teacher of this class are all 65+ but that didn't make it any less lively.]

LETTER TO

Charles Stade* *D. DAVID BOURLAND, JR.*

THE Special Issue of *ETC.* on E-Prime [*ETC.*, Summer 1992] has generated much correspondence that I have seen, and I hate to think of how much that I have not seen. After carefully studying the published articles and these letters I would conclude that the Special Issue has taken a confusion level that was already too high and raised it even more. I would assume that most of the contributors to this issue were well acquainted with your book *To Be or Not.* Even in the extreme case that E-Prime turns out to be a total farce, I should think that a serious investigation of it would be very educational and contribute to time binding. This the Special Issue and the reactions have not done. There are many areas here in need of clarification. I have a list of specific matters relating to E-Prime on which I would like to get your comments. Such comments should at least provide a basis for the investigation I would like to see.

I E-Prime supposedly provides its users with certain psycho-social benefits. Many people in the world speak languages that do not have forms of the verb "to be" to be eliminated. Do you think individual speakers of these non-identifying languages enjoy the benefits of E-Prime, and if not, why not?

* Charles Stade, producer of a video tape lecture series on general semantics and coordinator of research studies in advanced semantic technology, does computer data system redesign work in Chicago.

II You have said that we cannot expect E-Prime to solve all of our semantic problems, but it has now been on the academic scene for over 25 years. I would like from you three short lists; I will settle for, say, three entries in each category. (1) Problems that *have been* solved by the use of E-Prime. (2) Problems that *could be* solved by the use of E-Prime. (3) Problems that *cannot* be solved by means of E-Prime. Let us grant that people who learn to write in E-Prime derive great pleasure from such a difficult achievement. However, I would not accept that as an example of an E-Prime solved problem.

III Over the years I have encountered many arguments about the meaning of the term "identity." If you think this term has only one, or a few, possible meaning(s) I would like your interpretations. If you think some of the employed meanings are invalid I would like your explanation. If you think more than one of the possible meanings are valid I would like to know how you tell which one the user intended in some particular case. By valid I do not mean semantically correct, but commonly understood, say in a dictionary sense. Here you may draw your examples from this letter.

IV As stated above many people/societies employ languages that do not contain forms of the verb "to be." However, the greatest philosophic, scientific, cultural, economic, and artistic achievements of the human race have been made by people speaking languages heavily dependent on is's. (I will not make any claims for the spiritual accomplishments of the Western world.) If the use of is's is so detrimental, could you please explain these cultural/scientific imbalances?

V For purposes of discussion, let us assume that E-Prime confers significant advantages on its users. In this case I am concerned with the possibility that people making this assumption will *identify* general semantics with E-Prime. I do not think that you personally hold this position, but I would like you to describe some of the advantages you think could be derived from general semantics *as distinguished* from E-Prime.

D. David Bourland, Jr.* **_TOO FAR?_**

1. Introduction

I N THE LIST of my peak intellectual life experiences I would
surely have to include the following three: (i) During Korzybski's last summer seminar (August, 1949), at Great Bar-
rington, Mass., and at his last winter seminar (Christmas,
1949), at Sharon, Conn., I had the honor of sitting on the
same platform with him as his "recording student," taking
notes for him to go over to see what he had said, to keep him,
as he put it, "from getting lost in the footnotes." How would
you like for Korzybski to study carefully *your* notes of a seminar on general semantics? (ii) At that same summer seminar
during the workshop week, I had the honor of sharing the
platform with Dr. George K. Zipf, lecturing on socio-logics
and his Principle of Least Effort. (iii) At the San Francisco
Conference on General Semantics in the summer of 1965, I
received the honor of Dr. Sam Bois' inviting me to join him
from the audience and discuss E-Prime.

* D. David Bourland, Jr., a retired Associate Professor of Linguistics, has written
on general semantics topics for many years. In 1965 he "invented" E-Prime.
Copyright © 1993 by D. David Bourland, Jr.

From time to time people would write Korzybski and ask him why he continued to use the verb *to be* in the Identity and Predication modes. They cited pages in *Science and Sanity* (1) for examples. I heard him deny that he did employ such uses on the given pages. You may turn to your copy of *Science and Sanity* and make your own analysis. Just remember:

Identity: Noun Phrase + a form of *to be* + Noun Phrase;

Predication: Noun Phrase + a form of *to be* + Adjective Phrase.

Korzybski occasionally went out of his way during a seminar to say that one could not communicate in English without the verb *to be*, since he believed that one would need the Auxiliary and perhaps other uses. Of course, we must take into account the fact that English did not constitute one of his maternal languages: he claimed that he "grew up" in four — Polish, Russian, German, and French.

Bois included a brief mention of E-Prime in the first (1966) edition of his *The Art of Awareness* (2, p. 292f). By the time the third edition appeared in 1978, two changes had become incorporated in the E-Prime comments. In the first place, a typo made hash of the "semantic equation" that provided the origin of the name. E-Prime, symbolized as E', has had the following as its definition:

$$E' = E - e,$$

where E represents the one to two million words of the English language, and e represents the various conjugated forms of the verb *to be*. The typo in question replaced the " = " with " ≠ ". The resulting non-equation must have puzzled some readers, who probably blamed this writer, who hopes the publisher will correct the error in future editions of this classic. But Bois had also had second thoughts about E-Prime (certainly his prerogative): "Personally, I find Bourland's suggestion [to avoid all forms of *to be*] too sweeping. I retain two uses of the verb 'to be,' the 'to be' of existence (the lamp is on the table) and the 'to be' as an auxiliary (he is speaking)." (3, p. 360) Unfortunately, Bois also retained the Identity and Predication uses, as one may readily determine by checking his book.

In 1992 the Institute of General Semantics issued a book list that, among many others, included mention of the anthology on E-Prime prepared by Paul Dennithorne Johnston and myself. (4) With an air of pompous judiciality, they asked: "Does E-Prime go too far?"

In May, 1993, Dr. David F. Maas kindly invited me to speak on E-Prime to his class in general semantics at Ambassador College in Big Sandy, Texas. After the presentation a student asked me whether I felt (meaning that he *did* feel) that I had gone...right: "Too far?"

I have to admit that it has gradually become extremely boring to have to go over this same material every year. It seems similar not just to teaching the same class, year after year, but to teaching the same class *to the same people* year after year! And some of them keep earning terrible grades! I have even taken to asking certain colleagues for their views on why some supposedly intelligent people, with a background in general semantics, still seem to have a semantic blockage concerning the need for E-Prime.

Suggestions have included: (a) Poor babies! They just don't understand. (b) Frightened bunnies! They feel insecure with something so new. (c) Jerks! Ignore them. (d) Low IQ overachievers! Some have become professional *pars pro toto* folks, claiming to avoid two uses only (which they do not). Come *on* out there: try to pay attention!

2. E-Prime as an Extensional Device

Starting with the first paper written concerning E-Prime, the writer has offered this subset of English as an extensional device. Korzybski stated the noble goal of the extensional devices as that of "Changing the [semantic] structure of the language, without changing the language itself." Some might suggest that the preceding statement consists of a logical impossibility, but that belongs to some other argument.

He gave the following as his extensional devices: indexes, dates, use of the etc., quotes, and hyphens. He subsequently added chain-indexes for their excellent assistance in dealing with problems involving hierarchical structures. To the writer, E-Prime clearly belongs with this group, although E-Prime does in fact affect the syntactic structure of the language more severely than do the other devices. Since this linguist agrees with the late Uriel Weinreich in recognizing "the deep interpenetration of syntax and semantics," (5) ...so what?

Now no one, so far as the writer knows, has ever attacked the extensional device status of the *hyphen*, say, because it does not solve/resolve all the problems of language. (Shall we review the second "Non-Aristotelian Law"?) Indeed, no one has snarled at the even more useful *quotes* or the enshrined *etc.*, in view of their undoubted inability to fix *every* difficulty that afflicts us time-binders when we interact/transact with the world, including other time-binders. Similarly, E-Prime does not make it impossible to talk like a ninny, or a bigot, or a confused human, etc. However, it can help significantly in preventing the development of many serious problems.

After discussing the formulation of *time-binding*, in terms appropriate to the age/intelligence level of the group, the writer cannot imagine a more felicitous way to present the exciting major facets of general semantics than to begin with the extensional devices, *including* E-Prime. This emerged as the writer's opinion after having taught general semantics to second-year graduate students for ten years, using *Selections from Science and Sanity* with its excellent index as the text. (6) Please keep in mind that almost any beginning student can start *applying* the seven extensional devices immediately upon learning of them, with reflections upon their deep significance to follow at leisure.

3. A Certain Verb vs. the Human Nervous System

If anyone would like to review the usages of the verb *to be*, please check the treatments in references (7) and (8). Those two papers contain reasonably comprehensive discussions of the drawbacks involved in the routine application of that static verb, with special attention to Identity and Predication uses (as defined above), plus the inherent elementalism of the passive voice, which may become awkward without *to be* in the Auxiliary use.

As if the major steps toward resolving those three language problems did not suffice to encourage one to use the extensional device known as E-Prime, we have recently received some material that shows the evil one can do to oneself with *to be* in the Existence use. Roberta Wedge had the following comment on the Existence use of that verb: "My main discomfort with what I understand of E-Prime I can state briefly: it denies me the right to assert myself in the simplest way possible, to stand up and say, 'I am, I exist, I am here.' There are so many pressures in this society that try to persuade me not to exist, not to be myself." (9) The writer regrets that Ms. Wedge evidently perceives herself as so ill-used by "this society." Do we see here the high order abstraction "this society" receiving the blame for her callous treatment by specific individuals? Korzybski suggested the application of dates and indexes to help in efforts to clarify and allocate such a seemingly wide-ranging hostility. E-Prime, of course, denies Ms. Wedge *nothing.* If she used E-Prime in ways discussed in reference (10), Ms. Wedge *might* find her focus changing to "I can allow myself to feel, etc.; the here-and-now includes unique and wonderful me!" Please treat yourself to a strong dose of linguistic sensitivity, Ms. Wedge. Only you can do that, but E-Prime can probably help.

The frequency studies cited in reference (8) indicate that professional writers tend to employ some form of *to be* in half or more of their sentences. If a writer used any other verb that often, he or she would most likely have trouble getting the material published. (Word freaks may enjoy noting that the preceding sentence has a passive clause that does not involve *to be*.) We should remain conscious of the well-known fact that each time we use and re-use a given semantic structure, such as those involving *to be*, we wear a deeper groove — so to speak — in our brain, making the continued use of that structure more likely, and almost surely rendering us less likely to change such a pattern.

Too far? I don't think so.

REFERENCES

1. Alfred Korzybski. *Science and Sanity: An Introduction to Non-Aristotelian Systems and General Semantics.* Lakeville, Conn.: International Non-Aristotelian Library Publishing Co., 1933. Fourth edition, 1958.
2. J. Samuel Bois. *The Art of Awareness.* Dubuque, IA.: Wm. C. Brown Co., First edition, 1966.
3. J. Samuel Bois. *The Art of Awareness.* Dubuque, IA., Wm. C. Brown Co., Third edition, 1978.
4. D. David Bourland, Jr., and Paul Dennithorne Johnston, eds. *To Be or Not: An E-Prime Anthology.* San Francisco: International Society for General Semantics, 1991.
5. Uriel Weinreich. Explorations in Semantic Theory in *Current Trends in Linguistics III:* p. 395-477, 1966.
6. Alfred Korzybski. *Selections from Science and Sanity.* Lakeville, Conn.: International Non-Aristotelian Library Publishing Co., 1948. Seventh printing, 1972.
7. D. David Bourland, Jr. E-Prime and Un-Sanity, *ETC. 49*, No. 2, 1992.
8. D. David Bourland, Jr. E-Prime and the Crispness Index, [published in the present volume].
9. Roberta Wedge. Letter of Comment, (in this second Symposium).
10. E. W. Kellogg, III, and D. David Bourland, Jr. Working with E-Prime: Some Practical Notes, *ETC. 47*, No. 4, 1991.

TOO FAR?

Part Three:
APPLICATIONS

GENERAL SEMANTICS
AND RATIONAL EMOTIVE

Albert Ellis # BEHAVIOR THERAPY *

I NEVER WOULD HAVE ORIGINATED rational emotive behavior therapy (REBT) had I not been strongly influenced by phi-losophers rather than psychotherapists. For when I founded REBT (which I formerly called RET) in 1955, the field of therapy was almost completely run by clinicians, ranging from psychoanalysts to behaviorists, who firmly, and rather dogmatically, believed that people's early experiences, espe-cially with their parents, made them or conditioned them to become emotionally disturbed.

This theory, of course, has some degree of validity because all humans live in an environment. As Korzybski (1951) put it, a person is "an organism-as-a-whole-in-an-environment." People seem to be born teachable and self-teachable and therefore partly acquire their feelings from their experiences with others and with the objects and things they encounter in their early and later life. Also, because they are more gull-ible or influenceable when they are young, they may well — though not necessarily always — be more disturbable in their childhood and adolescence than when they are older.

* Dr. Ellis adapted this text from his 1991 Alfred Korzybski Memorial Lecture, sponsored by the Institute of General Semantics.

Fortunately, however, as philosophers have shown for many centuries, a crucial aspect of people's disturbance stems from the part they play in their interactions with the environment — from what they think about and tell themselves about the unfortunate events that occur in their lives. As Epictetus (1890), a Greek-Roman stoic, said 2000 years ago, "People are disturbed not by things, but by the *views* which they take of them." Asian philosophers, such as Confucius and Gautama Buddha, said something similar; Marcus Aurelius echoed Epictetus' view; and many Western philosophers — especially Spinoza, Kant, Dewey, Russell, Heidegger, Sartre, and Popper — all seem to agree that what people feel and do largely, though not completely, stems from the way they actively and creatively construct and reconstruct reality rather than from their passively reacting to it.

Some early psychotherapists, such as Janet (1898), Dubois (1907), Munsterberg (1919), and Adler (1927, 1931), were also cognitive and believed that their clients' ideas about their experiences, rather than only the experiences themselves, made them neurotic. Even Sigmund Freud temporarily espoused this view and in his first book said that neurosis is ideogenic (Breuer & Freud, 1897). Unfortunately, he largely later retracted this view and insisted that it almost completely stemmed from childhood experiences, especially sex experiences. Although modern psychoanalysts of the object-relations school have repudiated Freud's sex theories, they have replaced them with the view that the early love or interpersonal relationships of children make them neurotic and borderline if they do not receive sufficient nurturing from their parents and other early love objects (Guntrip, 1971; Kernberg, 1975; Klein & Riviere, 1964; Kohut, 1977).

Largely believing in psychoanalysis in the 1940s, especially in the neo-analytic views of Horney (1945), Fromm (1950), and Sullivan (1953), I got analyzed, was supervised by a training analyst of the Horney Institute, and practiced psychoanalysis for six years. Although my clients liked analysis and usually felt better as a result of it, I was not impressed and became quite disillusioned with all forms of psychoanalysis, except that of Alfred Adler (1927, 1931) who really opposed its main tenets and called his system individual psychology. I also was influenced by Alexander & French (1946) and by Sullivan (1953) who considerably modified psychoanalytic technique. I saw that most of my clients *felt* better as a result of my psychoanalytic sessions with them, but virtually none of them *got* better. Why? Because they still strongly believed the same basic, largely self-created *philosophies* that originally made them and now kept them neurotic.

Looking for a better model of human disturbance and for a distinctly more efficient method of helping people become less neurotic, I abandoned psychoanalysis in 1953, did eclectic psychotherapy for a while, and founded rational-emotive therapy (RET), now known as rational emotive behavior therapy (REBT), at the beginning of 1955. Going back to philosophy, I combined the best elements of Stoicism, Epicurianism, and several other phenomenological-humanistic-existential philosophies and formulated the ABC theory of emotional disturbance, which then became the core of most of the other cognitive-behavior therapies that began to follow REBT in the 1960s and 1970s. (Beck, 1976; Burns, 1980; Glasser, 1965; Goldfried & Davison, 1976; Mahoney, 1974; Maultsby, 1975; Meichenbaum, 1977).

The ABC theory of REBT, which I have revised over the years but is still similar to what I said at the American Psychological Association Convention in Chicago in 1956 (Ellis, 1957a, 1957b, 1958, 1962), states that people have goals and values (G's), especially to stay alive and be happy. When their Goals (G's) are blocked by Activating Events or Adversities (A's), such as failure, rejection, and discomfort, they have a choice of making themselves feel and act with appropriate Consequences (C's), such as sorrow, regret, and frustration, that tend to encourage them to change or improve their A's. Or they have a choice of making themselves panicked, depressed, enraged, and self-hating and thus creating inappropriate Consequences (C's) that tend to make their A's worse and block their achieving their Goals. Some of the main behavioral C's they choose to construct are withdrawal, procrastination, inertia, compulsions, and addictions (Bernard, 1986, 1991; Dryden, 1990; Ellis, 1957a, 1962, 1971, 1973,

1977, 1985, 1988; Ellis & Dryden, 1987, 1990, 1991; Yankura & Dryden, 1990).

REBT, in other words, hypothesizes that people do not mainly *get* disturbed by unfortunate Activating Events or Adversities, which *contribute to* but rarely directly *cause* their self-defeating feelings and actions. Instead, they largely (not completely) *create and construct* their neuroses by their philosophies or Beliefs (B's). When, says REBT, their Beliefs stay within reality, and only consist of *preferences, wishes,* or *desires,* they make themselves feel appropriately frustrated and displeased when these preferences are thwarted. Thus, if they stick to, "I strongly *want* success and approval, *but* I don't absolutely *need* these desirable results," they feel appropriately sorry and disappointed but rarely upset themselves about not achieving their goals and values.

However, when people change their wants and preferences to absolutist, dogmatic musts and demands, they often bring on emotional trouble. For these absolutist musts are not in accord with reality and lead to awfulizing, I-can't-stand-itis, damning of oneself and others, allness and neverness, and other kinds of unrealistic overgeneralization. Thus, if you take your preferences for success and approval and you transform it into an unconditional must, you come up with Beliefs like, "Because I very much *desire* to do well in my work and *want* Mary Jones to love me, I *must* at all times and under all conditions succeed and *have to* always win her affection. If I don't, it's *awful,* I can't *stand* it. I'm a *worthless person,* and I'll *never* achieve any success in life and will *always* fail to win any decent partner!"

When you create absolutist, unconditional demands like this, you clearly put yourself in emotional jeopardy. For you often make yourself panicked before you try to fulfill your goals because you know that you may not succeed, as you *must,* at these goals. You severely depress yourself if you actually do fail. And even if you are doing very well at work and if Mary Jones happily returns your love, you keep worrying and worrying whether this fine state of affairs will continue tomorrow and into the future. As, of course, it *must!*

As you can see — and as I think Alfred Korzybski was a pioneer in seeing — thinking realistically about yourself, about others, and about the world in which you live leads to both *Science and Sanity*, the title of his seminal book (Korzybski, 1933). On the other hand, perceiving and thinking in unrealistic, absolutist, all-or-nothing, either-or, overgeneralized terms very likely leads you to what we call emotional disturbance and to your doing poorly in both your intrapersonal and interpersonal relationships.

Korzybski (1951, p. 172) seems to have had a picture of human functioning similar to that of the ABC theory of REBT. Thus, he said that when we "perceive" a happening or event we "silently" or "nonverbally" react with *evaluations* about it and our "emotions" and "evaluations" are organismically combined together and interact with our verbalizations, which quickly follow our silent thinking-feeling level. He quotes George Santayana as showing that humans are much better at believing than seeing.

In my first paper on REBT, at the American Psychological Association Convention in Chicago (Ellis, 1958, 1962), I specifically said that people's cognitions, emotions, and behaviors are not pure, but are part of an organismic or holistic interaction. Again, Korzybski seems to have predated me by seeing each human as "an organism-as-a-whole-in-an-environment" (Korzybski, 1951, p. 7). As he states (1951, p. 187), "There is no perception without interpolation and interpretation." Obviously, before REBT was formulated he endorsed some of its basic ABC theories.

As I noticed after practicing rational emotive behavior therapy for a short while — and as I think Korzybski would have again agreed — once you demand and command that you absolutely *must* do well and that you always *have to* be approved by others, and once you thereby make yourself panicked, depressed, enraged, or self-hating, you frequently show what a natural self-misled musturbator you are by dogmatically telling yourself, "I *must* not be panicked! I *must* not be depressed!" You then become — or much more accurately stated, *make* yourself — panicked about your panic, depressed about your depression, and self-hating about your self-hatred. You thereby create a secondary neurosis that is often more intense and pervasive than your primary disturbance and that, in fact, tends to stop you from clearly seeing how you first made yourself upset and what you can do to change your thinking and to unupset yourself (Ellis, 1962, 1973, 1985, 1988).

I think that Korzybski would have endorsed REBT's continual crusading against people's absolutistic, dogmatic, overgeneralized *shoulds* and *musts*. Thus, he noted "the fact that we do abstract on higher orders becomes a danger if we are not conscious that we are doing so and retain the primitive confusions or identifications of orders of abstractions" (1951, p. 218). He also advocated our increasingly using the term "etc." because it "facilitates flexibility, and gives a greater degree of conditionability in our semantic reactions. This device trains us away from dogmatism, absolutism, etc." (1951, p. 192). Korzybski also first formulated the REBT concept of secondary symptoms (such as anxiety about anxiety) by talking about "second-order reactions ('thinking' about 'thinking,' 'doubt of doubt,' 'fear of fear,' etc.)" (1933, p. 440; 1951, p. 190).

Once again, Korzybski, from 1920 to 1951, presented some unusual ideas that I seem to have taken from him and other philosophers and have solidly incorporated into REBT along the lines I have stated in the previous several paragraphs. Thus, he endorsed physico-mathematical methods of thinking and said that they link science, "and particularly the exact sciences, with problems of sanity in the sense of adjustment to 'facts' and 'reality' " (1951, p. 189). He warned that "elementalistic or metaphysical terms are not to be trusted and that speculations based on them are misleading or dangerous" (1951, p. 192). In my various criticisms of mystical and transpersonal ideas and practices in psychotherapy (Ellis, 1972b, 1986; Ellis & Yeager, 1989) I have expanded upon Korzybski's crusading against dangerous kinds of mysticism.

Science and Sanity

The more I think about Korzybski's masterpiece, *Science and Sanity*, the more I am enthralled by its revolutionary title. For after practicing REBT for several years and trying to assess its effectiveness by using the scientific method to check its results, and after helping hundreds of disturbed people by scientifically, realistically, and logically Disputing — at point

D in REBT — their neurosis-producing irrational Beliefs, I saw that REBT and the other cognitive-behavior therapies that Dispute people's dysfunctional Beliefs tend to show that neurosis and antiscience are very similar and that mental health and science distinctly overlap.

Why is this so? Because science includes four main attributes: First, it is realistic and tries to make its theories consistent with the facts of "reality." It postulates no absolute "reality" — because all "things" and "facts" are viewed phenomenologically, through human perceptions and interpretations. But science thinks that there is some kind of "reality" out there, apart from human perception, and it tries to check and falsify or partially verify its theories in relation to external "facts."

Second, science uses logic, both Aristotelian and non-Aristotelian, to check its hypotheses, and usually ends up with theories that are not self-contradictory and are not falsified by other views of people and the world. It rules out magic, cavalierly jumping to conclusions, and many illogical nonsequiturs.

Third, and perhaps most important, science is invariably open-minded and nondogmatic. It holds even its best theories tentatively and sees them as always subject to change, and does not claim that they describe the nature of things for all possible conditions and for all times. It is exceptionally flexible and never devout.

Fourth, science is alternative-seeking and keeps looking for new, better theories, and interpretations. It is never absolutist and has no final or invariant technique or answer.

REBT holds that neurosis, unlike science, tends to be replete with the kind of thinking, feeling, and behavior that is unrealistic, illogical, dogmatic, devout, and rigid. In this sense, as I think Korzybski strongly implied, and as REBT agrees, science and unneurotic sanity tend to be similar (Korzybski, 1921, 1922, 1933, 1951).

Why is this so? Why do so many people much of the time think crookedly, misperceive reality, reason illogically, become dogmatic and devout, and stick rigidly to misleading perceptions, overgeneralizations, and conclusions? REBT's answer is that they largely are innately predisposed to do

this. They are strongly inclined by both their biological tendencies *and* their human experiences *and* their social learning
to often make themselves self-defeating and socially sabotag-
ing. As Piaget (1963) noted, children actively *construct* their
view of the world and their adjustments to it; and REBT and
other constructivist therapies say that they keep *re*constructing their thoughts, feelings, and actions all their lives (Ellis,
1991b; Ellis & Dryden, 1991; Guidano, 1988; Mahoney, 1991).
That is their "nature" to do so, even though this "nature" is
changeable.

Moreover, once people adopt and create unrealistic, rigid,
non-alternative-seeking ideas, they have a strong biosocial
tendency to carry them into dysfunctional action, to repeat
these actions many times, and to habituate themselves to destructive behaviors. They don't *have to* do this — for they always have *some* degree of choice. But they very frequently
are innately *propended* to habituate themselves to dysfunctional thoughts, emotions, actions, and find it difficult,
though not impossible, to change them.

Fortunately, however, the very nature of human construc-
tivism includes a strong proactive changing and self-
actualizing element. People are not merely born and reared
to defeat themselves — for if that were so the human race
would soon die out. They are also born and raised with a
powerful tendency to choose, to remember, to think, to think
about their thinking, to change, to grow, and to develop.
What is more, if they choose to do so, they can use their abilities to think and to change to largely, though probably not
completely, overcome their propensities to perceive, think,
and interpret crookedly (FitzMaurice, 1989, 1991; Johnson,
1946; Korzybski, 1923, 1933, 1951).

This, of course, is the goal of general semantics — to show
people how they can become aware of their misperceptions,
overgeneralizing, and poor judgements and how they can
reconsider and reconstitute them so that they help themselves to more accurately perceive, accept, and live more
comfortably with "reality."

This goal of general semantics is remarkably similar to that
of rational emotive behavior therapy. REBT has faith in disturbed people's ability to reconstruct their adopted and self-

constructed distorted views of themselves, of others, and of the world with which they needlessly disturb themselves. It teaches them how to strongly Dispute their absolutist musts, shoulds, and demands; to reduce their overgeneralizing, aw-fulizing, and I-can't-stand-itis; to evaluate and rate only what they and others think, feel, and do while rigorously refraining from judging others' *self, being, essence,* or *personhood* (Ellis, 1962, 1971, 1972a, 1973, 1976b, 1985, 1988, 1991a, 1991b; Ellis & Dryden, 1987, 1990, 1991).

REBT has two main goals: First, to help people see and correct their dogmatic, absolutistic attitudes and dysfunctional feelings and behaviors and to make themselves, as Korzybski called it, subject to greater sanity. Second, as people are making themselves less disturbed and more functional, REBT tries to help them fulfill more of their human potential, to actualize themselves, and to enjoy themselves more fully (as Epicurus more than Epictetus advocated) (Ellis, 1985, 1988, 1991a; Ellis & Dryden, 1991). Korzybski also strongly urged people to try to achieve more of their human potential. Thus, he said, "With a time-binding consciousness, our criteria of values, and so behavior, are based on the study of human potentialities, not on statistical averages on the level of *homo homini lupos* drawn from primitive and/or un-sane evaluational reactions which are on record" (1951, p. 189).

In other words, both general semantics and REBT hold that if people think about their thinking, and minimize their "natural" tendency to overcategorize, they can significantly — though perhaps never completely — free themselves from some of their thought-language limitations and achieve a more self-fulfilling life.

We can speculate that humans in primitive times had to jump to quick conclusions, to make their wishes into musturbatory demands, and to act over-emotionally because they were thin-skinned animals living in a very dangerous world. Perhaps their imprecise perception, their seeing part of the picture as a whole, their rigid ways of approaching life, and their other cognitive weaknesses which Korzybski (1933) pointed out and that REBT often details (Ellis, 1962, 1987a, 1987c; Ellis & Dryden, 1987, 1990, 1991), helped them survive in a grim and hostile world. Thus, by insisting that they *must* perform well and that others *had to* do their bidding, they may have made themselves needlessly anxious and angry thousands of years ago but may have survived better than if they were more reasonable. Perhaps. In any event, they did survive with their innate tendencies to reason better than other organisms *and* to often think sloppily. Now, using general semantics and REBT, they can use more reason and less dogma to survive more freely and more happily.

The Is of Predication

Let me continue with the agreements between general semantics and REBT. Korzybski showed that using the *is* of predication leads us to think imprecisely. Thus, statements like, "I *am* good" and "I *am* bad" are inaccurate overgeneralizations, because in reality I am a *person who* sometimes acts in a good and sometimes in a bad manner. In REBT, we teach our clients not to rate *themselves* or their *being* but only what they *do*. All *self*-ratings seem to be mistaken, because humans are too complex and many-sided ever to be given a *global* evaluation. Moreover, REBT holds, if you aim to be a *good person* you are too fallible to achieve that all-good status. And if you say, "I *must* be *good*," you will fail and then see yourself, quite falsely, as being *bad*. When you think in terms of dichotomous, good and bad terms, you will tend to demand that you *always* act well, for otherwise you will "become" bad. So even when you are doing well, you will be at great risk and will be quite anxious.

Moreover, when you strive to be a *good person* (rather than a person who tries to do *good things*), you make yourself grandiose, try to be better than other *humans*, tend to deify yourself; and then when you fall back and do stupid things, you see yourself as a *bad person*, and consequently devil-ify yourself. This is the essence of much neurosis! So REBT is perhaps the only therapy that specifically teaches, "*You* are not good and *you* are not bad. You are only *you*, a *person who* acts well and badly."

We can avoid the *is* of predication, as Korzybski points out by saying, "I see myself as good" or "I see myself as bad," for then we do not claim that our "goodness" or "badness" really exists in the universe, but only that we *choose* to interpret our-selves in a "good" or "bad" manner. Because we are entitled to our personal definitions, we can *decide* to see ourselves as "good" because that will help us function better, rather than *decide* to see ourselves as "bad," for that will help us bring about worse pragmatic results.

So REBT teaches people that they can arbitrarily *define* themselves as "good" and that that will work much better than if they define themselves as "bad." They can attach their "goodness," for example, to their existence and tell them-selves, "I am *good* because I am human and alive." This is a pretty "safe" definition of themselves because they then will always be "good" as long as they are human and alive — and will only have to worry about being "bad" after they are dead. Quite safe, you can see!

The trouble with this definition of human worth is that it *is* definitional and cannot be validated nor falsified. Thus, you could say, "I am good because I am human and alive" and I can object, "But I think you are bad because you are human and alive." Which of us, then, is correct? Neither of us is, be-cause we are both definitional; and definitions are useful but cannot be checked against "facts" or "reality."

Moreover, both statements — "I *am* good" and "I *am* bad" are overgeneralizations because, as noted above, all people do *both* "good" and "bad" deeds, and cannot really be catego-rized under a single, global heading — as *being* "good" or as *being* "bad." So the pragmatic solution to the problem of hu-man "worth" is not a very good one, and had better be re-placed by the REBT *more elegant* solution: "I *am* neither good or bad; I am just *a person who* sometimes acts 'well' and some-times acts 'badly.' So I'd better rate or evaluate what I *do* and not what I *am*." I am pretty sure Korzybski would endorse this *more elegant* REBT solution to the very important prob-lem of *self*-rating.

Korzybski's writings on the *is* of predication encouraged me to help REBT clients to stop using several kinds of over-generalizations. For if they say, "I am good," they strongly imply that they have an essence or "soul" of goodness, that they *only* do "good" things, and *therefore* deserve to live and enjoy themselves. This is misleading, because they cannot prove that they have any *essence* (which is a very bad, vague, and mystical word); and if they do have one, they cannot show that it always at all times *is* "good."

To be much more precise, as Korzybski would put it, I help my clients say, "I am a person who *does* good things (e.g., helps others in *trouble*) but who *also* does many 'neutral' and 'bad' things (e.g., harms others). I am never really *entirely* 'good,' 'bad,' nor 'neutral.' Because I am, as a human, much too complex and many-sided to perform *only* 'good' or 'bad' or 'neutral' behaviors."

REBT particularly follows Korzybski in this respect, largely because before I even formulated it I read Hayakawa (1962, 1965) and other general semantics writers and saw that the *is* of predication is not only a misleading overgeneralization but that it also leads people to rate and evaluate their *self*, their *being*, their *totality*, rather than to only evaluate what they *do* and what they *don't* do.

Since its very beginnings in 1955, REBT has taught people *not* to rate their *self* or their *personhood* but only to evaluate their *acts*, *deeds*, and *performances* in relation to their goals and purposes. Thus, if you choose to stay alive and happy, you are acting *well* or *sensibly* when you keep your eyes open and avoid cars as you cross the street. But if you choose to commit suicide, you may be acting *badly* or *foolishly* when you carefully cross the street.

Let me repeat this important point: Following Korzybski, REBT is one of the very few psychotherapies that tries to help people only rate, measure, and evaluate what they *do* and *don't do* and not to rate their *self, totality*, or *personhood* (Bernard, 1986, 1991; Dryden, 1990; Ellis, 1962, 1972a, 1973, 1976b, 1985, 1988, 1991c, 1991d; Ellis & Dryden, 1987, 1990; FitzMaurice, 1989, 1991; Hauck, 1992; Yankura & Dryden, 1990).

Let me say that teaching clients and other people *merely* to rate their acts, feelings, and thoughts and *not* to give themselves a misleading *self*-rating is quite difficult. For, as Korzybski implied, humans *naturally and easily* conclude that "Because I act in a 'good' manner, I am a 'good person' and that because I act 'badly' I am a 'bad person.'" Obviously, both these views are mistaken and will often produce poor results. Because if you view yourself as a "good person" when you behave well, you will almost immediately see yourself as a "rotten person" and thereby produce anxiety, depression, and self-hatred, when you fall back, as you inevitably will, to behaving "badly" again.

To make matters worse, when you say, "I am a *good person* when I do *good acts*, you are not really proving, factually, that your entire *self* is good because of your good *deeds*, for there is no exact way of validating or falsifying this proposition. You are merely *defining yourself*, tautologically, in terms of one set of acts, which are good according to your goals and purposes, and you could theoretically *define yourself* in terms of *any kinds* of acts, "good," "bad," or "neutral." Thus, Hitler could say, "My goal is to kill Jews and Gypsies, and therefore I am a *good person* when I kill more of them." Would you agree with him? Or someone could say, "The human race is no good and deserves to die out. Therefore, If you do 'good' deeds by helping other humans to survive, you are really a *bad* person!" Would this individual who rates *you* as "bad" for your supposedly "good" deeds be right or wrong? Who can really say?

REBT uses another kind of Disputing (D) of people's irrational Beliefs (iB's) when they think and say, "Because I do many bad *things*, I am a *bad person*." I tell such disturbed people, "When you say you are a *bad person* for doing bad things, you are engaging in what Bertrand Russell called a category error. For the *bad things* you are doing are in one category and you, the doer of these things, are in a quite different category. You do *all* kinds of things, good, bad, and indifferent. So if you categorize these things as "good" or "bad," you jump to a different category when you call *yourself*, the doer, "good" or "bad." You *are* not what you *do*. So you'd better rate only the *things* you do and not identify them with your *youness*, which is quite a different category."

I got the idea for this kind of Disputing from Bertrand Russell; and in recently re-reading Korzybski in order to write the present paper I was pleased to note that he gives Russell due credit for his "epoch-making work in his analysis of subject-predicate relations" (1951, p. 181). Even before I read Korzybski I was significantly influenced by Russell; so I am happy to acknowledge that REBT owes a real debt to both these modern philosophers. Russell, Korzybski, and REBT all join in examining and revealing the limitations of the *is* of predication.

The Is of Identity

Korzybski (1933, 1951) objected to the *is* of identity, to people saying, "I am a man," "I am a woman," "I am a good (or bad) person." I think he was correct about this, because once again these statements are all crass overgeneralizations. Moreover, as REBT points out, to identify with *any* group or concept implies *loss* of oneself and leads to what Helmuth Kaiser (1965) called neurotic fusion. Thus, to identify with your peer group gives you a sense of belonging and security. But ironically it also takes away your *own* identity, makes you over-conforming, and therefore less of an individual in your own right. You are really a *person who* chooses to be in the group but had better *not* be a devout follower of the group. When the latter occurs, you are believing something like, "I absolutely *must* be a group adherent, else I am *nothing*." That is hardly a good state of mental health!

Identity is a poor word because it has conflicting meanings. I am I, myself, and am not really any other person. So that is fairly clear. But I also call myself a New Yorker, an American, or a man; and as I do so I partly lose my identity as myself, a unique human. Of course, as a person I am normally a member of a social group; and, as Sampson (1989) and others have pointed out, I take *some* of the main parts of my personality from the group — such as the way I dress, the kind of foods I eat, and the language I speak. So I am never *just* myself; nor had I better even be *just* a group member. For me to say that I am *only* I or *only* a member of a certain class is wrong on both counts.

Korzybski seems to solve this problem by noting that I am *neither* only myself *nor* only identified with a group. He would presumably say I am *both/and* rather than *either/or*. That is what REBT says, too. I am partly an individual in my own right but once I choose to be in or to remain in a group that I was put in at birth (e.g., choose to remain an "American"), I no longer am *only* responsible for and to myself but *also* to the group I choose to remain a member of.

REBT, like Korzybski I think, gives me *some* degree of human choice (for I can even choose to be a hermit) but it also says that I have *limited* choice, because my biology and my upbringing help make me a *social* creature; and therefore I am never completely a person in my own right. If I accept this "reality" I shall probably get along fairly well *both* as an individual *and* a social person. If I reject or deny it, I shall probably get into both personal and social difficulty.

To make things still more confusing, you will practically insure that you will end up by making yourself anxious and depressed, if you believe, "I am a good person when I do good things" for you will tend to "logically" conclude, "And I am a bad person when I do bad things" — as, I would say, most people in the world now often conclude. If so, you will be very anxious even when you are acting in a "good" manner, for as a fallible human you will know that you can easily act "badly" tomorrow and your acts will then "make" you a *bad person.* When you do *behave* "badly," you will then tend to view *yourself* as a *rotten* individual and will thereby make yourself depressed. So unless you are perfect and *always* perform well, defining your *self* or your *personhood* in terms of your "good" and "bad" behaviors is, as Korzybski held, an anti-factual overgeneralization. From an REBT standpoint, it just won't work!

If you insist on rating your *self* or your *person*, therefore, REBT advises that you pick a safe or self-helping definition, such as, "I am 'good' or 'okay' just because I exist, just because I am human, just because I choose to view myself this way." This is still a definitional or tautological self-rating that cannot really be validated or falsified. But, pragmatically, it is safe and will get you into little trouble!

Better yet, as noted above, REBT helps people to refuse to rate their *self*, their *totality*, at all but merely to evaluate what they do. Then, when they act "badly," they can tell themselves, "*That* was 'bad' or 'foolish' but I am a *person who* acted that way. I am *not* a *bad person* and therefore I am capable of changing my behavior and of probably acting better next

228 More E-Prime: To Be or Not II

time. If *I* am 'bad' I am hopelessly stuck. But if what I *do* is 'bad' I can usually change."

Absolutist Shoulds and Musts

Korzybski did not clearly differentiate between people's preferences and their demands, as REBT does, nor did he show how when they take their *preferably shoulds* and change them into *absolute, unconditional shoulds*, they make themselves neurotic. But he implied that virtually all absolutist, unconditional thinking encourages us to make ourselves "unsane."

Thus, when speaking against identity, he said, " 'Identity' as a 'principle' is defined as 'absolute sameness in "all" ("every") respects.' It can never empirically be found in this world of ever-changing processes, nor on silent levels of our nervous systems" (1951, p. 184).

REBT shows that when you believe, "I *preferably should* succeed and win the approval of significant others," you explicitly or tacitly include *buts* and *alternative solutions* to your desires, such as: "*But* if I don't succeed, I can try harder next time." "*But* if I'm not approved, too bad, but it's not the end of the world." When your *preferably shoulds* are not fulfilled, REBT holds, you normally feel *appropriately* sorry, disappointed, and frustrated (rather than *in*appropriately panicked, depressed, and self-hating).

On the other hand, when you strongly believe, "Because I want to succeed and to be approved by significant others, I *absolutely, under all conditions and at all times must do so,*" you create severe anxiety when you *may not* do well and severe depression when you *do not* act well or win others' approval. For with your *absolute, under all conditions* shoulds and musts you allow yourself no alternative solutions to your desires, box yourself in, and needlessly make yourself miserable (Ellis, 1957, 1973, 1985, 1988, 1991b, 1991c, 1991d).

Korzybski wasn't as clear as REBT is about this, but he fought vigorously against absolutist, dogmatic, allness and neverness thinking. Therefore, general semantics obviously opposes self-statements like, "Because I want to succeed at my profession and want to win the approval of significant others, I *absolutely, under all conditions, at all times must* do so." In REBT, we frequently encourage people to change their inaccurate self-defeating language to more precise languages, and we therefore show our clients how to change this all or nothing sentence to something like, "Because I want to succeed at my profession and to win the approval of significant others, I very much *prefer* to do so. But if I don't, I can find other things to succeed at. If I never succeed at any important project, I can still enjoy doing what I can do and can still have a reasonably happy life. As for winning the approval of significant others, I *want* very much to do so, but I never *have* to. If I keep trying, I can practically always find *some* people who will like me as I like them. But if I never somehow do, there are many other aspects of life that I can enjoy, so I'll keep looking until I find them."

Precise Thinking and Language

Alfred Korzybski was a pioneer in linguistics and pointed out that when we think imprecisely our crooked thinking works its way into our language and then our dysfunctional language leads us into engaging in more imprecise thinking. Ever since I started doing REBT, I found that people habituate themselves to poor language habits that then interfere with their accepting reality, that they largely are responsible for their own dysfunctional language, feelings, and actions, and that therefore they can change them.

Thus, when my clients say, "Joe lied to me and that made me furious," I interrupt, "How could *that*, or *Joe*, get into your gut and *make* you furious?" "Oh, I see," they often reply. "Yes, Joe lied to me, and *I* chose to infuriate myself *about* his lying." "Yes," I say. "Isn't that a much more accurate description of what happened and how *you* chose to create your fury?"

Again, a client says, "I'm not getting the love I want Martha to give me, and she makes me feel like a worm." I ask, "Do you only *want* Martha's love, or aren't you telling yourself you *need* it?" "Mmm. Yes, I guess I am believing that I absolutely *need* it." "And does Martha's lack of loving you make you feel like a worm?" "Uh, no. I guess I'm putting the two together and *making myself* feel like a worm." "And how could you not win Martha's love and still not label yourself as a worm?" "I guess I could tell myself that because I want Martha's love and don't have it, my relationship with her is somewhat wormy. But that doesn't give me, a total person, the label of a worm." "Right! So hereafter try to watch your language that includes your *demanding* instead of *wanting* and that keeps you giving inaccurate labels of *you*, rather than descriptions of what you and others *do*."

So REBT often shows people how to correct their language and their thinking, and to stop sneaking in overgeneralizing, labeling, demandingness, and other unscientific verbalizations into their thinking and behaving. It employs a specific technique called *semantic precision* or *accurate language* to do this and in this respect is one of the very few therapies that puts Korzybski's theory of language and meaning into therapeutic practice (Ellis, 1988; Ellis & Velten, 1992).

Biological Underpinnings of Behavior

Although I was mainly an environmentalist as a young psychologist, when I practiced REBT for a few years, I saw that people are born as well as reared to think irrationally and dysfunctionally and to sink their crooked thinking into inappropriate feelings and self-sabotaging behaviors (Ellis, 1962, 1976a, 1985, 1988; Ellis & Dryden, 1990, 1991). I believe that Korzybski held similar views. For he consistently shows how practically all people at all times in all parts of the world make profound semantic errors and thereby help upset themselves and others. If our parents and our culture mainly taught us to overgeneralize, label, and commit the cognitive misperceptions and jumping to conclusions that Korzybski talks about, some of us would do so and some of us would not. But all of us, to one degree or another, often seem to be embroiled in these kinds of errors. So although there appears to be some environmentally-inculcated factors in our doing so, we also seem to be innately prone to distorted semantic processes.

Thus, Korzybski notes: "Practically all humans, the most primitive not excluded, have some types of either-or orientation" (1951, p. 186). And: "Our old habits of evaluation, ingrained for centuries if not millenniums, must be re-evaluated" (1951, p. 194).

And again: "A 'name' involves for a given individual a whole constellation of configuration of labeling, defining, evaluating, etc., unique for each individual, according to his socio-cultural, linguistic environment and his heredity" (1951, p. 177).

REBT and general semantics, then, seem to fully acknowledge the important biological as well as environmental roles in human dysfunctional thinking.

Self-Change and Self-Actualization

While general semantics and REBT seem to agree that people are innately predisposed to create and construct semantic errors, they also agree that people can learn to minimally do so. REBT says that just because humans are active constructivists, rather than are passively conditioned to be disturbed by their parents, teachers, and culture, they also have the innate tendency to change themselves and to choose to behave less defeatingly. Thus, they are able to think about their thinking, to realistically assess their unrealistic attitudes, to dispute their irrational beliefs, and to work hard at reconstructing their disordered thoughts, feelings, and behaviors (Ellis, 1962, 1973, 1985, 1988). Moreover, once they keep working at reformulating their disturbed ideas and feelings, they can also creatively work at growing, developing, and bringing about greater degrees of happiness and involvement (Ellis, 1988, 1991a; Ellis & Becker, 1982; Ellis & Harper, 1975).

Korzybski and his followers obviously have similar ideas. The Institute of General Semantics and many members of the Institute solidly believe that people can be taught the principles of general semantics and can be shown how to think and communicate more clearly with themselves and each other and thereby help themselves to change. REBT and general semantics are both psychoeducational approaches to helping humans improve their intrapersonal and interpersonal relationships (Crawford, 1980; Crawford & Ellis, 1982, 1989; Ellis, 1975; Johnson, 1946; Mosher, 1966).

The Use of E-Prime

In order to encourage people to give up the *is* of predication and the *is* of identity, Bourland (1965-6, 1986; Bourland
& Johnston, 1991) advocated and used E-Prime, the English
language without any inclusion of various forms of the word
to be or its various tenses. Although writing in E-Prime is difficult and does not completely make a writer and the reader
avoid all linguistic and semantic errors, it does offer some
help. REBT, through the advocacy of Dr. Robert Moore of
Clearwater, Florida, of Dr. William Knaus of Springfield,
Massachusetts, and myself, has favored E-Prime more than
has any other form of psychotherapy; and I think it is still the
only form of therapy that has some of its main works written
in E-Prime (Ellis, 1957a, 1977; Ellis & Harper, 1975; Ellis &
Knaus, 1977).

Use of Forceful Persuasion

Korzybski noted that we humans have "to change our habitual methods of thinking, and this is not so easy as it seems"
(1951, p. 196). He implied that our overgeneralized, misleading thinking gets into our body-mind system and into our
action habit patterns. REBT has always said that thinking,
feeling, and behaving are not disparate, but importantly influence and affect each other. As I noted in my very first paper on REBT, delivered in 1956: "Thinking...is and to some
extent has to be sensory, motor, and emotional behavior...Emotion, like thinking and the sensory-motor processes, we may define as an exceptionally complex state of
human reaction which is integrally related to all the other
perception and response processes. It is not one thing, but a
combination and holistic integration of several seemingly
diverse, yet actually closely related, phenomena (Ellis, 1958,
p. 35).

Because of its holistic emphasis, REBT has always favored
strong and direct cognitive, emotive, and behavioral methods of showing people exactly what they are doing to needlessly disturb themselves and what they can do to active-
directively minimize their self-disturbance. In consonance

with Korzybski's disavowal of either/or solutions to human problems, REBT does not favor *either* thinking *or* emotive *or* behavioral methods of therapy. It consciously and actively employs all three kinds of therapy; and, following and/also and et cetera facilitations, it has no hesitation in combining psychotherapy with pharmacological treatment, with environmental changes, and with any other kinds of psycho-physical methods that are likely to help various clients (Ellis, 1985, 1988, 1989; Ellis & Abrahms, 1978; Ellis & Dryden, 1987, 1991; Ellis & Velten, 1992).

Realism and Profound Philosophic Change

Korzybski was in many ways a profound realist and empiricist, and noted that the revised structure of language that he advocated "necessitates 'thinking' in terms of 'facts,' or visualizing processes, before making generalizations" (1951, p. 193). He also noted that while Aristotelian either-or language fosters our evaluating "by definition" or "intension" his own "non-Aristotelian or physico-mathematical orientation involves evaluating 'by extension,' taking into consideration the actual 'facts' in the particular situation confronting us" (1951, p. 194).

REBT's original method of helping people to Dispute (at point D) their self-defeating ideas, inferences, attributions, and overgeneralizations, showed them how to scientifically challenge these ideas in the light of "reality" or "facts." Thus, if Joan asks Harry to marry her and he refuses to do so, she may foolishly conclude, (1) "I made a mistake in asking him," (2) "He hates me!" and (3) "That proves I'm no good, that I am a bad person!" REBT, and the main other cognitive-behavior therapies often confront Joan with the "facts," which tend to show that her inferences about Harry's refusal are invalid overgeneralizations. Because: (1) Joan was probably right, not wrong, in asking Harry to marry her — for by doing so she has gained some valuable information about his feelings for her. (2) There is no evidence that Harry hates her, but only evidence that he doesn't want to marry and live with her. Actually, he may deeply love her and still, for various reasons, not want to marry her. (3) His refusal to marry her never proves, of course, that she *is* no good nor *is* a bad person, though it may possibly show that "factually" or in Harry's eyes, she has some undesirable traits.

REBT and cognitive-behavior therapy (CBT) therefore use "facts" or "reality" to show Joan her dysfunctional Beliefs and they therefore accord with Korzybski's views. But REBT goes further than the other therapies and asks, in Joan's case, "What is the underlying musturbatory overgeneralization that leads an intelligent woman like Joan to make such silly inferences that are obviously unsupported by the 'facts' or 'reality'?"

Seek and ye shall find. Looking for Joan's tacit, implicit, or unconscious *musts* that she probably believes and from which she largely *derives* her antifactual inferences, we find that she very likely *brings to* her proposal to Harry the basic, core philosophy: "Whenever I ask *any* person I really like, such as Harry, to grant me *any* important favor, such as marrying me, he *absolutely must under all conditions* accede to my request — or else (1) I made a mistake in asking, (2) he or she hates me, and (3) that proves I am no good and that I am a bad person."

I am contending, in other words, that if Korzybski were a psychotherapist — which, actually, he partially was — he would surely have Disputed Joan's irrational inferences and refuted them "factually" and "empirically." But he would also, I suggest, look as REBT does (and as most other cognitive-behavior therapies do not) for the higher-order abstractions that seem to lie behind and to help instigate many of Joan's disturbance-creating inferences.

Korzybski noted that "making us *conscious* of our *unconscious assumptions* is essential" (1951, p. 195). He also said that "abstracting by necessity involves evaluating, whether conscious or not, and so the process of abstracting may be considered as a *process of evaluating stimuli*" (1951, p. 172). Again: "The fact that we do abstract on higher orders becomes a danger if we are not conscious that we are doing so and retain the primitive confusions or identifications of orders of abstractions" (1951, p. 178).

If I interpret Korzybski correctly, he is saying here that to understand ourselves *in depth* we had better not just look for our conscious inferences about unfortunate events in our lives (such as Joan's conscious inferences about her self when Harry rejects her) but we had better *also* look for our unconscious, tacit assumptions that underlie many of our self-disturbing inferences. This is what REBT does when it looks for core musturbatory philosophies behind Joan's (and other people's) anti-factual inferences. In this respect, REBT is not only more depth-centered than most other cognitive-behavior therapies, and is not only one of the most construc-tivist therapies in today's world, but it also — ironically enough! — seems to be considerably more depth-centered than psychoanalysis. Why? Because psychoanalysis is not particularly philosophic, does not explore and look behind people's disturbing assumptions, creates vague, almost unde-finable higher-order abstractions of its own (such as ego, id, and superego) and almost entirely ignores the depth-centered semantic problems that Korzybski raised and went a long way toward solving.

A purely Korzybskian analysis of people's cognitive-emotional-behavioral problems, such as Wendell Johnson (1946) attempted, will, I wager, do people more good and much less harm than will psychoanalysis. When REBT is employed, incorporating as it does much of Korzybski's work with other important elements of cognitive-behavior thera-py, even more depth-centered, philosophically profound therapy will, I predict, often occur. Compared to this kind of "deep" analysis, psychoanalysis seems to be quite superficial!

Conclusion

As I think can be seen by many of the parallels between rational emotive behavior therapy and Korzybski's general semantics, the two disciplines overlap in many important respects. This is hardly coincidental, as I was distinctly in-fluenced, when formulating and developing REBT, by sever-al of Korzybski's ideas. This does not mean that were Alfred Korzybski alive today he would enthusiastically endorse REBT and place it above all the other psychotherapies. Per-haps he would — and, quite likely, for one reason or another, he wouldn't. In keeping with his own extensional thinking, I would guess that he would agree with *some* of REBT's theory and practice *some* of the time under *some* conditions. As my own life and my practice of REBT continues, I try to take a similar attitude. Rational emotive behavior practice works quite well some of the time under some conditions with some people. It is not, and will never be, a panacea for all of all people's cognitive-emotive-behavioral problems. There is no reason for it to take an either-or position nor to claim that all people with all disturbances have to be treated with REBT or else they will not improve. Rubbish! As Korzybski would probably have recommended and as I have previously noted (Ellis, 1987b, 1989), REBT had better be integrated with the most useful of other therapies so that it becomes and remains effective with many (not all) people much (not all) of the time.

REFERENCES

Adler, A. (1927). *Understanding Human Nature*. New York: Greenberg.
Adler, A. (1931). *What Life Should Mean to You*. New York: Blue Ribbon Books.
Alexander, F., & French, T.M. (1946). *Psychoanalytic Therapy*. New York: Ronald.
Beck, A.T. (1976). *Cognitive Therapy and the Emotional Disorders*. New York: International Universities Press.
Bernard, M.E. (1986). *Staying Alive in an Irrational World: Albert Ellis and Rational-Emotive Therapy*. South Melbourne, Australia: Carlson/Macmillan; New York: Carol Publications.
Bernard, M.E. (Ed.) (1991). *Using Rational-Emotive Therapy Effectively: A Practitioner's Guide*. New York: Plenum.
Bourland, D.D., Jr. (1965-6). A Linguistic Note: Writing in E-Prime. *General Semantics Bulletin, 32-33*, 111-114.
Bourland, D.D., Jr. (1968). The Semantics of a Non-Aristotelian Language. *General Semantics Bulletin, 35*, 60-63.
Bourland, D.D., Jr. & Johnston, P.D. (eds.) (1991). *To Be or Not: An E-prime Anthology*. San Francisco: International Society for General Semantics.

Breuer, J., & Freud, S. (1897). Reprinted in *Studies in Hysteria.* Vol. 2 of *The Standard Edition of the Complete Psychological Works of Sigmund Freud.* New York: Basic Books, 1965.

Burns, D. (1980). *Feeling Good: The New Mood Therapy.* New York: Morrow.

Crawford, T. (1990, May 7, May 11, May 26). Letters to Albert Ellis.

Crawford, T., & Ellis, A. (1982, October). Communication and Rational-Emotive Therapy. Workshop presented in Los Angeles.

Crawford, T., & Ellis, A. (1989). A Dictionary of Rational-Emotive Feelings and Behaviors. *Journal of Rational-Emotive and Cognitive-Behavioral Therapy,* 7(1), 3-27.

Dryden, W. (1990). *Rational-Emotive Counseling in Action.* London: Sage.

Dubois, P. (1907). *The Psychic Treatment of Nervous Disorders.* New York: Funk & Wagnalls.

Ellis, A. (1957a). *How to Live with a Neurotic: At Home and at Work.* New York: Crown. Rev. ed., Hollywood, CA: Wilshire Books, 1975.

Ellis, A. (1957b). Outcome of Employing Three Techniques of Psychotherapy. *Journal of Clinical Psychology, 13,* 344-350.

Ellis, A. (1958). Rational Psychotherapy. *Journal of General Psychology, 59,* 35-49. Reprinted: New York: Institute for Rational-Emotive Therapy.

Ellis, A. (1962). *Reason and Emotion in Psychotherapy.* Secaucus, NJ: Citadel.

Ellis, A. (1971). *Growth Through Reason.* North Hollywood, CA: Wilshire Books.

Ellis, A. (1972a). *Psychotherapy and the Value of a Human Being.* New York: Institute for Rational-Emotive Therapy. Reprinted in A. Ellis & W. Dryden, *The Essential Albert Ellis.* New York: Springer, 1990.

Ellis, A. (1972b). What Does Transpersonal Psychology Have to Offer the Art and Science of Psychotherapy? *Voices, 8*(1), 20-28.

Ellis, A. (1973). *Humanistic Psychotherapy: The Rational-Emotive Approach.* New York: McGraw-Hill.

Ellis, A. (1976a). The Biological Basis of Human Irrationality. *Journal of Individual Psychology, 32,* 145-168. Reprinted: New York: Institute for Rational Emotive Therapy.

Ellis, A. (1976b). RET Abolishes Most of the Human Ego. *Psychotherapy, 13,* 343-348. Reprinted: New York: Institute for Rational-Emotive Therapy.

Ellis, A. (1977). *Anger — How to Live With and Without It.* Secaucus, NJ: Citadel Press.

Ellis, A. (1985). *Overcoming Resistance: Rational-Emotive Therapy with Difficult Clients.* New York: Springer.

Ellis, A. (1986). Fanaticism That May Lead to a Nuclear Holocaust: The Contributions of Scientific Counseling and Psychotherapy. *Journal of Counseling and Development, 65,* 146-151.

Ellis, A. (1987a). The Impossibility of Achieving Consistently Good Mental Health. *American Psychologist, 42,* 364-375.

Ellis, A. (1987b). Integrative Developments in Rational-Emotive Therapy (RET). *Journal of Integrative and Eclectic Psychotherapy, 6,* 470-479.

Ellis, A. (1987c). A Sadly Neglected Cognitive Element in Depression. *Cognitive Therapy and Research, 11,* 121-146.

Ellis, A. (1988). *How to Stubbornly Refuse to Make Yourself Miserable About Anything — Yes, Anything!* Secaucus, NJ: Lyle Stuart.

Ellis, A. (1989). *The Treatment of Psychotic and Borderline Individuals With RET.* Rev. ed. (Orig. publication, 1965). New York: Institute for Rational-Emotive Therapy.

Ellis, A. (1990). Is Rational-Emotive Therapy (RET) "Rationalist" or "Constructivist"? In Ellis, A., & Dryden, W., *The Essential Albert Ellis* (pp. 114-141). New York: Springer.

Ellis, A. (1991a). Achieving Self-Actualization. In A. Jones & R. Crandall (Eds.), *Handbook of Self-Actualization.* Corte Madera, CA: Select Press.

Ellis, A. (1991b). Using RET Effectively. In M.E. Bernard (Ed.) (1991). *Using Rational-Emotive Therapy Effectively* (pp. 1-33). New York: Plenum.

Ellis, A. (1991c). The Philosophical Basis of Rational-Emotive Therapy (RET). *Psychotherapy in Private Practice, 8*(4), 97-106.

Ellis, A. (1991d). The Revised ABC's of Rational-Emotive Therapy. In J. Zeig (Ed.), *Evolution of Psychotherapy: II.* New York: Brunner/Mazel. Expanded version: *Journal of Rational-Emotive and Cognitive-Behavior Therapy, 9,* 139-172.

Ellis, A., & Abrahms, E. (1978). *Brief Psychotherapy in Medical and Health Practice.* New York: Springer.

Ellis, A., & Becker, I. (1982). *A Guide to Personal Happiness.* North Hollywood, CA: Wilshire Books.

Ellis, A., & Dryden, W. (1987). *The Practice of Rational-Emotive Therapy.* New York: Springer.

Ellis, A., & Dryden, W. (1990). *The Essential Albert Ellis.* New York: Springer.

Ellis, A., & Dryden, W. (1991). *A Dialogue with Albert Ellis: Against Dogma.* Milton Keynes, England: Open University Press.

Ellis, A., & Harper, R.A. (1975). *A New Guide to Rational Living*. North Hollywood, CA: Wilshire Books.

Ellis, A., & Knaus, W. (1977). *Overcoming Procrastination*. 2nd ed. New York: Signet Books.

Ellis, A., & Velten, E. (1992). *How to Quit Addictive Drinking and Stinking Thinking*. New York: Barricade Books.

Ellis, A., & Yeager, R. (1989). *Why Some Therapies Don't Work: The Dangers of Transpersonal Psychology*. Buffalo, NY: Prometheus.

Epictetus (1890). *Collected Works*. Boston: Little, Brown.

FitzMaurice, K. (1989). *Self-Concept: The Enemy Within*. Omaha, NE: Fitz-Maurice Publishing.

FitzMaurice, K. (1991). *We're All Insane*. Omaha, NE: Palm Tree Publishers.

Freud, S. (1965). *Standard Edition of the Complete Works of Sigmund Freud*. New York: Basic Books.

Fromm, E. (1950). *The Sane Society*. New York: Holt, Rinehart & Winston.

Glasser, W. (1965). *Reality Therapy*. New York: Harper & Row.

Goldfried, M.R., & Davison, G.C. (1976). *Clinical Behavior Therapy*. New York: Holt, Rinehart & Winston.

Guidano, V.F. (1988). A Systems, Process-Oriented Approach to Cognitive Therapy. In K.S. Dobson (Ed.), *Handbook of Cognitive Behavioral Therapies* (pp. 307-356). New York: Guilford.

Guntrip, H. (1971). *Psychoanalytic Theory, Therapy and the Self*. New York: Basic Books.

Hauck, P. (1992). *Overcoming the Rating Game*. Louisville, KY: Westminster.

Hayakawa, S.I. (1962). *The Use and Misuse of Language*. Greenwich, Connecticut: Fawcett.

Hayakawa, S.I. (1965). *Language in Thought and Action*. New York: Harcourt, Brace and World.

Horney, K. (1945). *Our Inner Conflicts*. New York: Norton.

Janet, P. (1898). *Neuroses et Idée Fixes*. 2 vols. Paris: Alcan.

Johnson, W. (1946). *People in Quandaries*. New York: Harper & Row.

Kaiser, H. (1965). *Effective Psychotherapy*. New York: Free Press.

Kernberg, O. (1975). *Borderline Conditions and Pathological Narcissism*. New York: Aronson.

Klein, M., & Riviere, J. (1964). *Love, Hate and Reparation*. London: Hogarth.

Kohut, H. (1977). *The Restoration of the Self*. New York: International Universities Press.

Korzybski, A. (1921). *Manhood of Humanity*. Lakeville, Conn.: International Non-Aristotelian Library Publishing Co.

Korzybski, A. (1923). Fate and Freedom. In I.J. Lee (Ed.), *The Language of Wisdom and Folly* (pp. 341-357). San Francisco: International Society for General Semantics.

Korzybski, A. (1933). *Science and Sanity*. Lakeville, Conn.: International Non-Aristotelian Library Publishing Co.

Korzybski, A. (1951). The Role of Language in the Perceptual Processes. In R.R. Blake & G.V. Ramsey (Eds.), *Perception: An Approach to Personality* (pp. 170-205). New York: Ronald Press.

Mahoney, M.J. (1974). *Cognition and Behavior Modification*. Cambridge, MA: Ballinger.

Mahoney, M.J. (1991). *Human Change Processes*. New York: Basic Books.

Maultsby, M.C., Jr. (1975). *Help Yourself to Happiness: Through Rational Self-Counseling*. New York: Institute for Rational-Emotive Therapy.

Meichenbaum, D. (1977). *Cognitive-Behavior Modification*. New York: Plenum.

Mosher, D. (1966). Are Neurotics Victims of Their Emotions? *Et cetera, 23*, 225-234.

Munsterberg, H. (1919). *Technique of Psychotherapy*. Boston: Houghton Mifflin.

Piaget, J. (1963). *The Origin of Intelligence in Children*. New York: Norton.

Sampson, E.E. (1989). The Challenge of Social Change in Psychology. Globalization and Psychology's Theory of the Person. *American Psychologist, 44*, 914-921.

Sullivan, H.S. (1953). *The Interpersonal Theory of Psychiatry*. New York: Norton.

Yankura, J., & Dryden, W. (1990). *Doing RET: Albert Ellis in Action*. New York: Springer.

E-PRIME AND THE

D. DAVID BOURLAND, JR. *CRISPNESS INDEX* *

1. *Introduction*

A FTER REVIEWING BRIEFLY the potential contributions E-Prime can make to our written or spoken behavior, I will present a quantitative measure for one aspect of excellence in writing, an aspect so far ignored.

For some time now I have had a growing concern that perhaps Kellogg, Johnston, Joyner, and I have not adequately captured/explored/discussed some aspects of the key benefits offered by E-Prime (you know, English without any form of the verb "to be"). (1, 2, 3, 4, etc.) I feel that we need to do this before proceeding to further efforts to train others in the challenging process of learning to write, speak, "think," dream (etc.?) in E-Prime. I invite you to join us in this endeavor.

Some of our colleagues have written polemics *against* E-Prime, in one case writing *in E-Prime*, evidently without *understanding* E-Prime. (5, 6) I believe these misadventures with E-Prime illustrate dramatically the need for further discus-

---

* See Note 1. Copyright © 1992 by D. D. Bourland, Jr.

241

sion of what E-Prime can do for us, and why, and how. (See Note 2.)

2. What E-Prime Provides

With E-Prime, writers (speakers, etc.) can help free themselves from an important set of handicaps from which the English-using people have suffered for at least the last thousand years. (8) See Table I for some of the details. All this time people have extensively used what we now call the verb "to be" in their writing (i) to suppress role players in the passive voice, an inherently elementalistic act;** (ii) to identify a structure belonging to one order of abstraction with another structure on the "same" or on a different order of abstraction; (iii) to identify a structure at one date with "itself" at another date; (iv) to project transactional aspects of personal perceptions upon the "outside world"; and (v) to write and to speak statically about dynamic happenings. (See Note 3.) Unfortunately, we have behaved in those ways almost completely unconsciously, and hence it has become extremely difficult to correct such abuses through conscious processes. Korzybski pointed out the debilitating consequences of (i) through (v) as just noted; E-Prime provides a readily teachable technique to avoid many aspects of those problems.

In addition to removing most of those confusions and miseries, E-Prime also offers the *increased possibility* of vivid descriptions, limited generalizations, and the more adequate characterization of what one person (the writer or speaker) has perceived. All of those improvements can contribute to our becoming more aware of the abstractions we make: fostering a heightened *consciousness of abstracting*, regarded as the central goal of general semantics. Anyone who believes that the improvements just described do not have much value evidently subscribes to a very poor model of general semantics, and perhaps also of the "real world." (See Note 4.) Anyone who believes that E-Prime does not tend to increase the likelihood of the beneficial possibilities as just described,

---

** For a discussion of "elementalism," see Note 1 to reference (3). For a more extensive and definitive presentation, see reference (15, e.g., p. 105f).

in my opinion, needs to review the literature on E-Prime, for he or she may have missed something.

The epistemological justifications for E-Prime given by several great men over the centuries has confined itself almost entirely to the level of the sentence. These intellectual titans include Thomas Hobbes (10), Augustus de Morgan (11), Bertrand Russell (12), George Santayana (13), Alfred North Whitehead (14), and Alfred Korzybski (15). An early paper of mine on E-Prime (16) addressed the matter of larger bodies of text, with an emphasis on the uses of "to be" in the Identity and Predication modes (Use III in Table I in this paper) in political documents. I now believe that while the approach taken in reference (16) provided (as advertised) quantitative support for one of Korzybski's positions — always worth the effort — it did not give an adequate basis for wider applications.

E-Prime in fact emerged from basic epistemological conclusions brought to our attention by the previously mentioned greats. However, from my vantage point, I wonder why more literary people did not follow the lead of Ernest Fenollosa and Ezra Pound on the matter of eschewing the verb "to be" (17) strictly for stylistic reasons. I say this because, while essentially every fledgling writer knows to avoid repeating any given verb in sentence after sentence, few seem to find it odd when half or more of one's sentences include the verb "to be." Of course, the conjugated forms of "to be" remove some of the repetitive sting, but the basic point remains. I will return to related literary issues shortly, but first let us consider the complicated matter of dealing with a process world by means of various kinds of language.

3. Static, Dynamic, and Non-Static Forms of Representation

Even within the serious limitations of what I have chosen to refer to as "Lieutenant Semantics" (see Note 5), people genuflect toward the "Map-Territory Analogy." Nevertheless, some otherwise astute folks seem willing to ignore one of the most unfortunate facets of the verb "to be." This verb, almost uniquely, signifies a *static* condition. As Kellogg put it recently, the verb "to be" "encourages 'false to facts' habits of thought through which we see a world made up of unchanging independent objects." (18) This undercuts, *devastatingly* in my opinion, the pussyfootery of such fence-sitting approaches as "E-Prime mod" by Dallmann (19) and the even fuzzier attempts at waffling by Menefee. (20) Maps containing "to be" just do not fit territories very well.

On the other hand, we must not underestimate the difficulty of trying to develop a more "dynamic" language to deal with events in the process world. The only really effective effort along these lines so far consists of the differential equations of mathematical analysis, as applied to physical, economic, biological, etc., problems. See Note 6 for an illustration of the *complexities* and, for most of us, the *difficulties* involved in even a comparatively simple problem explained by, and solved by, a differential equation. I believe the material given there illustrates once again the assertion by Korzybski that the language of mathematics gives a precise way to describe and deal with problems, with severe limitations on what you can "discuss." One can properly use the term "dynamic" to refer to differential equations (and other mathematical formulations) because *they explicitly include quantities which vary with time, and not just simply one or more time variables.*

Korzybski's extensional device of "dating" probably comes closer than any other linguistic procedure for dealing with processes. However, I believe that we must recognize that dating suffers from several handicaps: (i) one must explain carefully and early in a paper the *what* and the *so what?* of dating, in the event that a non-indoctrinated person happens upon the writing in question; (ii) the awkwardness of the dates, from a printing point of view, tends to limit the application of dating, despite its value. The biological sciences use descriptions of stages of development of various life forms, a somewhat cumbersome technique for handling changes. Other procedures of this general type exist, as appropriate for various sciences. Now let us consider where E-Prime fits in with such considerations.

E-Prime falls somewhere between standard English and mathematical analysis, obviously much closer to the former than to the latter. The discipline of E-Prime provides a teachable way to give the basis for what I believe we could call "non-static representations." I say "basis," because of course a variety of additional static verbs in English can assist those who might wish to speak in an avowedly static manner, including "to stay," "to remain," "to continue," and so on, when used without time-dependent modifiers. Of course, you can say, "Sit! Stay!" to a dog, and it may come to pass. If you say, "Stay as sweet as you *are*," to a human, you may court emotional disaster. E-Prime tends to move us in the non-static direction. This tendency does not come cheaply, but most of those who have tried it regard it as worthwhile. Furthermore, readers or listeners can easily understand written or spoken E-Prime *without any explanation*.

4. The Matter of "Crispness"

Quite apart from its epistemological justifications, as just discussed in the preceding two sections of this paper, it turns out that E-Prime overlaps with what English and Journalism teachers have advocated for some time. People often have told me that their teachers have tried to get them to use "action verbs" rather than "to be" in their writing. I must admit that I have heard this, in effect, only from Alfred Korzybski, but Hey! That does it for me! Let us now investigate the degree to which certain writers (or their editors) who, primarily, have never heard anything about E-Prime have dealt with the matter of "to be," without any theoretical framework to guide them. To do this I must request your forebearance to define yet another quantitative measure of writing excellence. At least I will do you the favor of not reviewing in detail the several previous efforts along such lines. Suffice it to say that over the past 50 years or so we have seen a number of attempts to develop quantitative techniques for the analysis of a variety of characteristics of writing. Some of these measures even appear as a part of the computer programs provided to characterize work done on word processors. Most often the quantitative measures have had to do with the length of sentences or the length of words used. The silent assumption behind such efforts went something like this: "If you can say it with short words in short sentences, *good!*" (See Note 7.) I propose an improved form for that pre-scription. Let us investigate the *crispness* of various offerings, defining the *Crispness Index (C.I.)* for any body of writing (see Note 8) as follows:

$$C.I. = \text{Nr. of E-Prime Sentences/Total Nr. of Sentences,}$$

or, in other words, the number of sentences without any form of "to be" divided by the total number of sentences in the sample. In the following sub-sections I will show you the results of doing such counts on a rather extensive number of writings. From time to time, when appropriate, the tables introduced below will include an "Overall" Index for several novels, stories, or articles. These do not consist of *averages* of the components, but rather the results of dividing the sum of the number of E-Prime sentences in the individual samples by the total number of sentences in the piece of writing stud-ied. An average, in such instances, usually gives a biased statistic.

   a. *General Semanticists, etc.* Table II contains the results of several studies of books known to the general semantics com-munity, some outstanding political documents, and a few recent articles by writers who understood Korzybski's meth-odology in various degrees. The indices given for books rep-resent the results of sampling; the indices for articles include the whole piece. Appropriately enough, from our non-Aristotelian viewpoint, the indices range from the .180 of Aristotle to the meritorious .724 of our colleague, Robert Pula, a former Director of the Institute of General Semantics. This amounts to a truly vast range, and demonstrates that we may indeed find a considerable difference in the Crispness In-dices for various pieces of writing. It seems worth pointing out that Aristotle probably did not enjoy the benefits of a stern editor who could rap him on the intellectual knuckles and say, "For Zeus' sake, man, write more crisply, won't you?"

   b. *Novels by Hemingway.* Table III summarizes my study of five of Hemingway's novels from the viewpoint of the Crisp-ness Index: *The Sun Also Rises, A Farewell to Arms, For Whom* the *Bell Tolls, Across the River and Into the Trees,* and *The Old Man and the Sea.* Whatever other (frequently inappropriate, in my opinion) comments effete literary critics have flung at Hemingway over the years, most of them have, however grudgingly, commented on the clarity of his writing. I submit that from the very beginning he wrote very *crisply,* perhaps in part as a consequence of the editorial advice he enjoyed from Ezra Pound. Note that in Table III *Across the River and Into the Trees* has the lowest Crispness Index. Critics in the early 1950s generally excoriated this novel. Perhaps in part the somewhat lower Crispness Index contributed to this. (See Note 9.) Notice what comparatively high Crispness Indices describe all five novels. Only the paper by Robert Pula, no doubt reflecting the recommendations of Korzybski, had a higher one (as shown in Table II). Of course, those who consciously write in E-Prime should have a Crispness Index approaching unity, but sometimes even this does not work out absolutely: apart from quoted material, Parkinson's infamous paper had one sentence with an "are," (6) and the very first paper written in E-Prime contained a "was." (21) The Hemingway material has an Overall C. I. of .651.

c. *Stories by Welty.* Table IV shows the results of doing a Crispness Index study of three stories by Eudora Welty, the well-known and distinguished Southern writer. Although not my cup of tea, by a long shot, many current critics seem to regard her writing very highly. I felt that, perhaps as a conterpoint to the macho Hemingway, we might learn something from a study of these well-received short (well, medium length) stories. And here we see "good writing" giving an Overall Crispness Index of .568.

d. *Movie Reviews by Travers.* Let us now seek data from a vastly different region of printed material. Table V contains the results for Peter Travers' reviews of movies that appeared in a recent issue of *Rolling Stone* magazine. The several reviews have only a comparatively few sentences individually, so it does not seem worthwhile to make much of them on that level, but the Overall C.I. equals .544.

e. *National Enquirer.* The well-known supermarket tabloid, *National Enquirer,* has (according to them) "the largest circulation of any paper in America." Although held in somewhat low esteem by the intelligencia, due to the studiedly lurid subject matter that evidently preoccupies the writers of articles in this paper, it evidently receives the benefit of professional editing. I did a Crispness Index study of the first 20 pages of their issue for November 17, 1992, which produced an Overall C. I. of .501.

f. *Four Short Essays.* Table VI contains the results of Crispness Index studies of end-paper essays that appeared recently in *Time* and *The New Yorker* magazines. Since professional writers wrote them all, with help from probably extraordinary editors, I personally find it quite surprising that their Crispness Indices show such variation: from .269 (Updike) to .600 (Arlen), both appearing in the "Shouts and Murmurs" department of *The New Yorker,* with the two *Time* essays (by Kinsley and Brookhiser) falling between those extremes.

g. *Scarlett & Rhett.* Over the past 56 years *Gone With the Wind* has remained one of the most popular novels in English. If media hype can manage it, the sequel *Scarlett* will stay around a like amount of time. It gives one the fantods to reflect on the amount of treasure Hollywood moguls will invest sometime soon in a movie based on the sequel. I will conclude this investigation into various Crispness Indices with the presentation of studies on those two novels. See Table VII for details. The Margaret Mitchell original has a Crispness Index of .547, while Alexandra Ripley's sequel weighed in at .562!

5. Concluding Remarks

This paper must, by its very nature, leave a number of interesting problems dangling. Why did Updike write that specific essay so uncrisply? Hurried? Would it improve *his* writing if he'd stop using "to be" so much? Would he like to punch this writer in the mouth? What kind of Crispness Indices do "really bad" writings have? (See Note 10.) "Really bad" according to whom?

I feel that I should add a caution: even now I seem to hear some of my critics switching on their word processors to castigate me for suggesting that a high Crispness Index somehow assures "high quality" in a piece of writing. Let us calm down while I remind whoever needs it that *the Crispness Index addresses only one aspect, but evidently a very important aspect, of an extremely complex whole.* I understand this: readers should not feel a need to tell me about it. Indeed, I presented data pertaining to material in *Rolling Stone* and the *National Enquirer* that has no literary pretentions and, for that matter, data on the popular (but rather lowly regarded) novels *Gone With the Wind* and *Scarlett*, to demonstrate that the Crispness Index refers most particularly to professional editing, which may or may not have much to do with the literary quality of the material edited. On the other hand, I do suggest that, if one insists on writing or publishing drivel, it will probably seem like more readable drivel if one can increase its Crispness Index.

Many people have had the vague, unquantified feeling that "good writing" has at least *something* to do with avoiding or minimizing the use of the verb "to be." The Crispness Index gives a quantitative measure for the degree to which one does so. (See Note 11.) I invite the reader to investigate his or her own writing, plus writing that particularly pleases him or her. How does it compare in crispness with Hemingway? With Aristotle? May I invite you to make your personal Crispness Index equal 1.00? Or, as a waiter at breakfast recently asked me, "Just how crisp would you like your English?"

TABLE I

EARLIEST ATTESTED USES OF THE VERB "TO BE"*

I. 1. Existence: c 1000 "Ic eom se 4e eom cw24 he ... se 3e ys me sende to eow." [Roughly, "Ik eom se the eom cwaeth he ... se the ys me sende to eow."]
2. To come into existence: c 950 "Cue3, hoenne 3as bi3on." [Roughly, "Cueth, hoenne thas bithon."]

II. Location: Before 1000 "On swa hwilcum husee swa he bi4." [Roughly, "On swa {as} hwilcum husee swa he bith."]

III. With Noun Phrase or Adjective Phrase: c 1000 "Min 5eoc is wynsum and min byr3yn ys leoht." [Roughly, "Min gheoc is wynsum and min byrthyn is leoht."]

IV. Auxiliary Tenses (Passives): c 825 "Du on-stri5des mec mid ysopan ... 3u 3wes mec, & ofer snaw, ic beom ge-whitad." [Roughly, "Thu on-strighdes mec mid ysopan ... thu thwes mec, & ofer snaw, ik beom ge-whitad."]

V. Phraseological Combinations: c 1300 "4e were betere habbe [it were better for thee to have] bileued stom, 4an icome me to fonde." [Roughly, "The were betere habbe bileued stom, than icome me to fonde."]

TABLE I (Continued)

Note: The earliest use given by the OED for a form of the verb "to be" consists of a present subjunctive of c 732 from the *Death-Song* of B2da [Baeda]: "Naeni5 uuiurthit snotturra than him tharf sie." [Roughly, "Naenigh uuiurthit snotturra than him tharf sie."] What we now call "Old English" amounted to a blend of "several West Germanic dialects taken to Britain from the north-western European mainland in the middle centuries of the first millenium AD. Germanic settlement was very limited during the late Roman period, but expanded greatly after the departure of the Romans in the early fifth century." (9, p. 722)

* Source: *The Oxford English Dictionary.* Old English "had speech patterns similar to those of its fellow North Sea Germanic languages, Old Frisian and Old Dutch. It was written first in runic letters, then in an adaptation of the Roman alphabet to represent distinctive" Old English sounds. (9, p. 722) The following forms no longer appear in our alphabet, which I have chosen to represent in numbers: (i) ash = 2, (ii) eth = 3, (iii) thorn = 4, (iv) yogh = 5.

Today we call *ash* the "digraph," approximately the vowel sound in "lamb." *Eth* (also called *edh*) and *thorn* could represent both voiced and unvoiced apico-dental fricatives. *Yogh* consisted of a loosely written form of the letter *g*, which subsequently came to represent *y* and *gh*. Unfortunately, the OED does not give a gloss in Modern English of their examples. If you *really* want to know their "meanings," check with your local scholar of Old English.

TABLE II A VARIETY OF CRISPNESS INDICES*	
a. Various Books**	C.I.
A. Korzybski (*Science and Sanity*)	0.413
J. S. Bois (*Art of Awareness*)	0.332
K. Popper (*Conjectures and Refutations*)	0.303
A. Rand (*Introduction to Objectivist Epistemology*)	0.275
b. Various Political Documents**	
U. S. Constitution (w/o Amend.)	0.428
U. S. Constitution (w/ Amend.)	0.400
Communist Manifesto	0.546
Welch's *Blue Book*	0.260
Machiavelli's *The Prince*	0.222
Aristotle's *Politics*	0.180
c. Various Articles***	
Pula	0.724
Menefee	0.524
Lakoff	0.430
Perlman	0.331

* C.I. = Nr. of E-Prime Sentences/Total Nr. of sentences.

** From reference (16), with C.I. = 1 - Measure #1.

*** From *Et cetera: A Review of General Semantics*, Vol. 49, No. 2 (1992).

TABLE III
C.I. STUDY OF FIVE HEMINGWAY NOVELS*

	C.I.
1. *The Sun Also Rises* (1926)	0.681
2. *A Farewell to Arms* (1929)	0.647
3. *For Whom the Bell Tolls* (1940)	0.712
4. *Across the River and Into the Trees* (1950)	0.545
5. *The Old Man and the Sea* (1952)	0.636

* Based upon 16 pages of the Easton Press Edition of these novels (1992): 8 pages beginning with p. 20 plus 8 pages beginning with p. 80.

TABLE IV
C. I. STUDY OF WELTY STORIES*

	C.I.
1. "Showers of Gold"	0.511
2. "Losing Battles"	0.620
3. "The Ponder Heart"	0.577
OVERALL	0.568

* Source: Eudora Welty: *Three Stories*. New York: Quality Paper Back Book Club Edition. 1992.

TABLE V
C. I. STUDY OF MOVIE REVIEWS*

		C.I.
1. "Husbands and Wives"		0.527
2. "Sneakers"		0.364
3. "School Ties"		0.714
4. "Swoon"		0.700
5. "Glengary Glen Ross"		0.700
6. "Simple Man"		0.417
7. "The Lover"		0.400
OVERALL		0.544

* Source: Peter Travers. "Trouble in Paradise."
Rolling Stone magazine, Issue 640, October, 1992.

TABLE VI
FOUR ESSAYS

	C.I.
Michael Arlen, "Perot: The Sequel," *The New Yorker* magazine, Nov. 16, 1992.	0.600
John Updike, "Hostile Haircuts," *The New Yorker* magazine, Nov. 2, 1992.	0.269
Richard Bookhiser, "Two Centuries of New World Orders," *Time* magazine, May 6, 1991.	0.528
Michael Kinsley, "Election Day Fraud on Television," *Time* magazine, Nov. 23, 1992.	0.404

TABLE VII
SCARLETT & RHETT*

	C.I.
Gone With the Wind, by Margaret Mitchell. New York: Macmillan, 1936 (Avon edition, 1973).	0.547
Scarlett, by Alexandra Ripley. New York: Warner Books, 1991.	0.562

* Both indices calculated from four 8-page samples, beginning with pp. 40, 80, 380, and 580.

NOTES

1. In the middle 1960s Charlotte Schuchardt Read kindly referred to something I had written (in E-Prime) as "crisp." In recognition of and appreciation for this encouraging comment, and despite the fact that by now she (and most particularly her husband, Dr. Allen Walker Read) seems somewhat negative about E-Prime, I have selected this particular term (i.e., "Crispness Index") for a measure of relative independence from the verb "to be."

2. In contrast with what some might consider a more temperate and accomodating position of the past, I now believe quite strongly that the verb "to be" has no place in the semantic reactions, and hence the lexicon, of those of us who try consciously to struggle toward "sanity" (see reference 15, p. 371), and *certainly* that verb has no place in the writings of those who consider themselves serious students of general semantics, or perhaps I should say, more correctly, those who seriously wish to apply to their own lives the great contributions of Alfred Korzybski. The epistemological reasons for the position just given have appeared repeatedly in *Et cetera*, the *General Semantics Bulletin*,

and elsewhere (for example see the references cited above). Earl Hautala, currently President of the International Society for General Semantics, has recently pointed out the folly of using E-Prime as a litmus test: "We might end up with an organization with five members, more or less." (7) I certainly agree, up to a point, with Mr. Hautala, an unusually astute and gentle man. However, I personally believe that considerations of this kind may blur the extremely important distinctions between valid political *decisions* ("Hey! Let's vote on E-Prime ... quickly now: pro or con?") and a *simple language modification* which can contribute importantly to problems involved in matching language processes with processes in the "real world." Perhaps "simple" slightly overstates the case, but remember: I personally understood the value of this matter *and began to apply it* at a very tender age. Surely others, in their more mature wisdom... In any event, I submit that it would amount to the sheerest folly to try to convert the application of E-Prime to something like a political issue, rather than recognizing it as a powerful tool of epistemological engineering.

3. The *Oxford English Dictionary* calls this "an irregular and defective verb [from the writer's point of view this amounts to a *vast* understatement], the full conjugation of which in modern English is effected by a union of the surviving inflexions of three originally distinct and independent verbs, viz. (1) the original Aryan substantive verb with stem *es-* ...; (2) the verbstem *wes-* ... Gothic *wis-an* to remain, stay, continue to be ...; (3) the stem *beu-* ... Old English *beo-n* to become, come to be. ... By the beginning of the 13th c., the Infinitive and Participle, Imperative, and pres. Subjunctive of *am-was*, became successively obsolete, the corresponding parts of *be* taking their place, so that the whole verb *am-was-be* is now commonly called from its infinitive, 'the verb *to be*,' although *be* is no part of the substantive verb originally, but only a later accretion replacing original parts now lost." (8, Vol. II, p.1) On the basis of the foregoing material it would seem more appropriate to speak of this unique verb as *is-am-was-be*. This issue lies outside the scope of this paper.

4. For examples of such misguided (or, in some cases, simply ignorant) positions, you may wish to see papers by Dallmann, Gozzi, Lakoff, French, Kenyon, Wanderer, Parkinson, and Menefee in the first *Et cetera* E-Prime Symposium, reprinted in this volume.

5. For me, as presented piecemeal in several communications to *Et cetera*, "Lieutenant Semantics" consists of a debased form of Korzybski's

methodology that I deduce some readers of (and, *worse*, some writers for) *Et cetera* unaccountably seem to espouse or prefer to Korzybski's methodology. Lieutenant Semantics has the following characteristics: (a) Apotheosis of the Map-Territory Analogy, without proceeding to the Non-Aristotelian Laws and their significance; (b) Ignoring such messy matters as the problems with Identification and Allness [and *forget* Self-reflexiveness]; (c) Lack of discussion of the extensional devices, with the possible exception of indexing; (d) Refusal to address what amount to perhaps the greatest of Korzybski's contributions: multiordinality, non-elementalism, and consciousness of abstracting; (e) Occasional allusion to the "Abstraction Ladder" without going on to the Structural Differential with its inter-relatedness to the other largely ignored issues mentioned in (a) - (d). Yes, Virginia, Lieutenant Semantics seems better than No Semantics; however, from the very 1933 beginning one did not need to stop so far short of "The Real Thing."

6. To illustrate the power and also the limitations of the mathematical technique of differential equations, I want to show explicitly how one particular application leads to the value of the escape velocity from the Earth. Experiments have produced the formulation that, if we represent the acceleration caused by gravity at the Earth's surface by g, then at time t, we can express the distance r from the center of the Earth of a particle moving vertically upward by this differential equation:

$$(N\text{-}1) \quad d^2r/dt^2 = -g\,(R/r)^2$$

where the operator d^2/dt^2 represents the second derivative with respect to time (t), and R represents the radius of the Earth (about 4000 miles at the equator). If we set the initial velocity of projection at V, then we have for the initial conditions of position and velocity at $t = 0$ the following:

$$(N\text{-}2) \quad r = R, \ dr/dt = V.$$

In order for the particle to escape the Earth's gravitational field, $(dr/dt)^2$ must exceed zero for all r. It turns out that to satisfy this condition V^2 must equal or exceed $2gR$. Hence the value for the escape velocity, V_e, consists of:

$$(N\text{-}3) \quad V_e = (2gR)^{1/2}.$$

Source: Reference (22).

7. This silent assumption, which relies heavily on brevity, has several major flaws. In the first place, absolute balderdash could receive high scores, because the brevity measures do not deal with content. Secondly, those measures tend to foster the use of "to be," since obviously *is, am, was, were,* etc., rank among the shortest and most frequently used verbs in the language. These forms of "to be" produce, as Russell Joyner has pointed out, writing about as uncrisp as a wilted lettuce leaf. Specifically, to give an example of the measures alluded to above, the "Readability Statistics" package produced by Ami Pro includes Gunning's Fog Index, the Flesch-Kincaid Score, the Flesch Reading Ease Score, and the Flesch Reading Ease Grade Level.

8. We have to deal separately with the more basic (and of course older) matter of oral speech in contrast with written material. So far as I know, those who have shifted over to E-Prime in speech have had a hell of a time, but eventually it can become as effortless as (personal experience) *writing* in E-Prime. I know of the following people who have done so in varying degrees: myself, E. W. Kellogg, III, Risa Kaparo, Julie Evans, and Elizabeth Bourland. I put myself first only because I first tried this in public before the New York Society for General Semantics in 1969; I have gone in and out of focus on this matter over the years, but do better now that I have given up on "social is-iness."

9. It interested me greatly to learn, in the late 1950s, from one of Hemingway's sons whom I knew briefly (Gregory), that his father regarded *Across the River and Into the Trees* as his favorite of the novels he had written. I felt and feel the same way.

10. In New York City in November, 1992, I stopped in at the Corner Bookshop on Madison at East 93rd to see if I could obtain something by Bulwer-Lytton, widely regarded as the producer of "bad writing." They had nothing by him, poor soul, so I asked the manager to tell me what he regarded as the most poorly written book in his store. He immediately answered, "*Scarlett!*" I eventually obtained a copy, and found it, upon study, not all that uncrisp. Perhaps poorly written from a literary viewpoint, but at the very least professionally edited.

11. I want to express my appreciation to Earl Hautala, Paul D. Johnston, Russell Joyner, and Dr. E. W. Kellogg, III, for their extremely helpful comments on this paper (not all of which I have followed). Thanks, too, to my wife, Elizabeth J. Bourland, for her help in counting the sentences in the Welty material.

REFERENCES

1. D. David Bourland, Jr. "A Linguistic Note: Writing in E-Prime," *General Semantics Bulletin* Nos. 32 & 33, 1965.
2. E. W. Kellogg, III. "Speaking in E-Prime," *Et cetera: A Review of General Semantics*, Vol. 44, No. 2. 1987.
3. E. W. Kellogg, III, and D. David Bourland, Jr. "Working with E-Prime: Some Practical Notes," *Et cetera: A Review of General Semantics*, Vol. 47, No. 4. 1990.
4. D. David Bourland, Jr., and Paul D. Johnston, eds. *To Be or Not: An E-Prime Anthology*. San Francisco: International Society for General Semantics. 1991.
5. Theresa Parkinson, "Beyond E-Prime." *Et cetera: A Review of General Semantics*, Vol. 49, No. 2. 1992.
6. D. David Bourland, Jr. "E-Prime and Un-Sanity." *Et cetera: A Review of General Semantics*, Vol. 49, No. 2. 1992.
7. Earl Hautala. "General Semanticists and E-Prime." *Et cetera: A Review of General Semantics*, Vol. 49, No. 2. 1992.
8. Entry for *be*, Volume II, *The Oxford English Dictionary*. J. A. Simpson and E. S. C. Weiner, eds. Oxford: Clarendon Press. Second Edition, 1989.
9. Tom McArthur, ed. *The Oxford Companion to the English Language*. Oxford: Oxford University Press. 1992.
10. Thomas Hobbes. *Leviathan*. 1651.
11. Augustus de Morgan. *Formal Logic*. 1847. London: Open Court (reprinted 1926).
12. Bertrand Russell. *Our Knowledge of the External World*. Chicago: University of Chicago Press. 1914.
13. George Santayana. *Scepticism and Animal Faith*. New York: Scribner. 1923.

14. Alfred North Whitehead. *The Principle of Relativity with Applications to Physical Science.* Cambridge: Cambridge University Press. 1929. Reprinted in part in F. S. C. Northrop and Mason W. Gross, eds. *Alfred North Whitehead: An Anthology.* New York: Macmillan. 1961.
15. Alfred Korzybski. *Science and Sanity: An Introduction to Non-Aristotelian Systems and General Semantics.* Lakeville, Conn.: International Non-Aristotelian Library Publishing Co. 1933. Fourth edition, 1958.
16. D. David Bourland, Jr. "The Language of E-Prime," in D. E. Washburn and D. R. Smith, eds. *Coping With Increasing Complexity.* New York: Gordon & Breach. 1974.
17. Ernest Fenollosa. "The Chinese Written Character as a Medium for Poetry," in Ezra Pound, ed. *Instigations.* New York: Boni & Liveright. 1920.
18. E. W. Kellogg, III. "The Good, the Bad, and the Ugly," *Et cetera: A Review of General Semantics,* Vol. 49, No. 2.
19. William Dallmann. "Is Is Not Is Is Not Is, And Other Thoughts on E-Prime," *Et cetera: A Review of General Semantics,* Vol. 49, No. 2. 1992.
20. Emory Menefee. "'S Word Play at the Grammar Reform School," *Et cetera: A Review of General Semantics,* Vol. 49, No. 2. 1992.
21. D. David Bourland, Jr. "Introduction to a Structural Calculus: A Postulational Statement of Alfred Korzybski's Non-Aristotelian Linguistic System," *General Semantics Bulletin,* Nos. 8 & 9. 1952.
22. "Analysis: Differential Equations," *The New Encyclopedia Britannica,* 15th Edition (1986), Vol. 13, p. 477.

I admired Griffin's "The Rise of Nopanaceism" when it first appeared almost 30 years ago. However, at the time I thought of it only as a great example of non-allness in action...or, rather, a clearly stated study of how people can exercise an allness orientation trying to do intellectual violence to meritorious efforts. More recently I have perceived how even people supposedly familiar with Korzybski's non-Aristotelian revision can try to combat the benefits of E-Prime by attempts to apply Nopanaceism. You can find their efforts in several places in Parts I and II of this anthology. While one cannot reasonably expect this article to stop such misguided folks in their tracks, perhaps it will help them understand better what they really try to do. Unfortunately, the recognition of the dynamics of Nopanaceism does not provide us with a panacea! While some of the examples may seem dated (because they have in fact become *dated), it surprises me that so many of them still seem right on the money. Enjoy. — DDB*

C. W. Griffin, Jr.   # THE RISE OF NOPANACEISM *

H AVE YOU EVER WISHED for a simple argument to silence the perpetual din raised by radicals and reactionaries, do-gooders and do-badders, and all the restless mob that can't accept things as they are? Friends, there *is* such an argument, guaranteed to refute the most cunning peacemonger, draft-reformer, or smog-control crank. Its proponents are increasing, and they are practical men of affairs, guardians of the tried and true, defenders of trusted traditions. They preserve the elusive truth that the deepest wisdom is, with Hamlet, to "rather bear those ills we have than fly to others that we know not of." You will find these worldly metaphy-

* From *Atlantic*, September 1966. Copyright © 1966 by The Atlantic Monthly Company. Reprinted by kind permission.

sicians, whom I shall call Nopanaceists, everywhere from the corporate boardroom to the union hall.

One of the most prominent Nopanaceists is James M. Roche, president of General Motors, an organization whose welfare has been intimately associated with that of these United States. [This refers to a statement made by a previous president of General Motors, according to whom, "What's good for General Motors is good for the United States." He subsequently, in response to bitter criticism, denied having made the statement, or having made it in exactly that way, etc. — DDB] It has been Mr. Roche's harsh duty to awaken sentimentalists concerned with ways of reducing the 49,000 annual deaths on our highways. In response to proposals for structural improvements to increase the safety of automobiles, Mr. Roche denounced critics of the automobile industry's desultory safety program. "Safety is a highly complex problem and there are no simple solutions or pat panaceas," Mr. Roche is quoted as saying in the *Times*. No one, of course, had remotely hinted that structural safety devices were a panacea. The most optimistic claim was an annual saving of 25,000 lives. A system of air bags, instantly inflated on impact to cushion the collision shock sustained by the car's occupants, could cut annual highway fatalities in half, according to Dr. Carl Clark, a Martin Company bio-physicist. But the Nopanaceist seldom claims that your proposal won't achieve *your* goal; he claims that it won't achieve *his* goal. And since he will accept nothing less than a panacea, his goal, by definition, is impossible.

In its campaign against firearms-registration laws, the gun lobby relies heavily on Nopanaceism. Typical of the gun-boosting editorials is a disquisition in the McPherson, Kansas, *Sentinel*. "Stopping Mail Order Guns Won't Stop Crime," says the headline to this homey, prairie version of Nopanaceism. No one, of course, ever claimed such miraculous results from legislation regulating mail-order firearms sales. Proponents of firearms-control laws merely cite the demonstrable effect of such laws on the homicide rates. In Dallas, for example, where gun traffic is uncontrolled, the proportionate number of killings committed with guns is more than five times higher than the number of such crimes in New York City, which has a relatively stringent law requiring licensing of pistols. Other statistics cited by J. Edgar Hoover indicate the efficacy of gun control in reducing killings. Yet the National Rifle Association says, "The record is clear — firearms registration laws even on a national or state basis have had no effect in reducing crime." The Nopanaceist implication is equally clear: the saving of several hundred or several thousand lives annually lost because of the uncontrolled distribution of guns to madmen, criminals, and juveniles is a worthless endeavor.

Nopanaceism is an antidote to false hopes for the benefits of reapportioning rurally dominated state legislatures. Many political analysts believe that reapportionment on the one-man, one-vote principle, ordered by the Supreme Court in June, 1964, can make state legislatures more responsive to urban and suburban needs. In some states a farmer's vote counts 100 times as much as a city dweller's vote. Dominated by rural interests, state legislatures have proved dismal failures in controlling air and water pollution, providing urban mass transit, uprooting slums, and tackling other urban problems. Giving the city dweller equality with rural voters would make the state legislatures more responsive to urban needs.

Don't be deceived by such mischievous simplicity. Reapportionment is no panacea. In the words of a learned Nopanaceist, Karl A. Lamb, of the University of California: "The adoption of equal population districts will make no magical change in the ability of cities to resolve the problems that beset them." In recondite arguments I am unable to follow, Professor Lamb warns against "undue optimism" about "proposals for tinkering with the democratic machinery.... There are many problems created by the one-man, one-vote ruling." Consider the consternation in Vermont, for example, where the legislature has not been reapportioned since 1797. Imagine the chaos introduced into that farmer-run state by the sudden advent of democracy!

Lest you think that political conservatives hold a monopoly on Nopanaceism, let me disabuse you with an example from the liberal Washington *Post*. Several years ago, the *Post* denounced a Fauquier County, Virginia, program through which female welfare recipients were sterilized if they requested it. To those unendowed with the superior wisdom of Nopanaceism, this voluntary family-limiting appears to be a partial solution to several problems — limiting the burdens on poor families that may already be overrun with unwanted children and on the public as well. At the least, it seems to limit the scope of a vast social problem that requires infinitely more effort than it is getting. To the Nopanaceist eyes of the Washington *Post* editorial writer, however, a public agency promoting voluntary sterilization, or even voluntary birth control, is guilty of unsportsmanlike conduct. "The welfare problems of society do not spring totally from excessive fecundity or abnormal illegitimacy of the poor and will not be solved by an attack on these phenomena.... Contraception, vasectomy and sterilization are instruments of voluntary family planning about which citizens differ and the knowledge of which should not be suppressed. They certainly do not hold forth any reasonable hope as a general solution of the tax burdens induced by the costs of welfare."

New York City's illegal twelve-day transportation workers' strike in January, 1966, cost the local economy $1 billion and made life a daytime nightmare for millions of commuters. It inspired proposals for tightening existing laws against public employees' strikes. Fortunately, however, union official Jerome Wurf demonstrated the utter futility of such a move with a brilliant Nopanaceist refutation: "There is a tendency to seek a short cut, a panacea, a hastily drawn law, which its sponsors hope may somehow banish the problem."

The union leader's warning completes the irrefrangible logic of the Nopanaceist's reasons for doing nothing. By admonishing us against the tendency to seek a panacea, the Nopanaceist seems to chide us for attempting to achieve the impossible. Yet when he says of a proposal, "It's no panacea," he seems to chide us for *not* attempting the impossible. This ambivalence, however, merely displays the profound depths of Nopanaceist logic, which converges on its ineluctable conclusion from opposite directions. It is, of course, ridiculous to attempt the impossible. But can any red-blooded American settle for less? To ask this question is to answer it. Give me a panacea, or give me nothing. And thus, backed by a logic sublime in its stark simplicity — the impossibility of achieving the impossible, conjoined with the refusal to accept anything less — the Nopanaceist always exhorts us to do nothing.

Illuminating still another facet of Nopanaceist philosophy is a Wichita *Sunday Eagle* editorial entitled, "Federal Spending: A Panacea or the Road to Ruin?" Since Federal Spending is obviously no panacea, the dichotomy posed by the headline decrees that it must be the road to ruin, and the editorial leaves little doubt that it is. "If our managed economy continues, this generation and the next may thrive on borrowed prosperity. Only time will tell whether the Keynesians are right and the Federal government can spend us all into Easy Street.... If they are, well and good. If they aren't, this Nation and its people at some point in the future are doomed to a crash that may well prove fatal to the American system." Note how this passage drives home the Nopanaceist's ancillary reasons for opposing non-panaceas. They will not only fail, they may bring disaster. Discretion, in the Nopanaceist's eyes, is always the better part of valor.

As the reader has doubtless noted, there are no limits whatever to Nopanaceism; it rebuts any proposal for reform — anytime, anywhere. You want control of the spread of thermonuclear weapons through international agreements? Nonsense, old chap, it's no panacea. There have always been wars and rumors of wars, and there always will be. Maybe this isn't the best of all possible worlds, but it's the best of all probable worlds. Remember, Rome wasn't built in a day. Come to think of it, Rome should never have been built. It certainly was no panacea.

Would E-Prime work for mystery writing? By eliminating the passive voice, would E-Prime help achieve the tight, action-oriented style of many contemporary mysteries? Would E-Prime help you do what many writer's manuals recommend, to "show it, not tell it"? For example, instead of the saying "Steel was a good shot", you might say "From across the room, Steel shot Sanders between the eyes."

E-Prime has its limitations. You can't include "ordinary" conversation that uses is, was, am, are, were, *etc. On the other hand, people in actual conversation don't stick rigidly to the rules of grammar — they communicate in "uh-huhs," grunts, one-word utterances, verbless phrases, as well as "correct" sentences.*

I decided to write a mystery novel in E-Prime and see what happens. I'd hoped that the reader wouldn't really notice — that the absence of "to be" verbs might simply produce cleaner, less cluttered reading. But now I've given the game away....

—P.D.J.

BOILING CREEK:

PAUL DENNITHORNE
JOHNSTON
The G.S. Detective

Part One

1

ONCE IN A WHILE just to abuse myself I buy a mango. I get in a mood of sweet-and-sour memories.

The Boiling Creek case began at 5:30 p.m. on a Friday, a time when sensible people headed home. I'd stayed in my office, ostensibly to avoid the rush.

I dumped the mango on my desk, crushed the paper bag, and threw it in a wastebasket. I sat with an elbow on my blotter and my chin in one hand. With my free hand, I picked up a letter-opener and prodded the mango. From my window came the city's clamor: motors revving, horns blaring, drivers cussing, bells clanging, buskers bawling. Outside my window, fog settled over San Francisco like an abortive theatrical effect, unable to comfort, hide, or beautify the city's destitute.

My watch said five twenty-eight. I stared at the pretty blend of orange, green, and red streaks covering the mango's shiny skin. When I picked up the mango and hacked at it with the letter opener, the dull blade glanced off. Eventually I managed to pierce the skin with the point of my makeshift knife. Yellow juice dripped onto my green blotter. As I peeled back the skin and inhaled the sweet heady tropical mango aroma, memories exploded in my nervous system with such force that my feet burned....

Aboard the old cabin cruiser Testament, *the kid stands on the sun-parched foredeck, shifting his weight from one bare foot to the other. Squinting against the sea glare, he hitches up his shorts, without taking his eyes off a carpet of seaweed drifting toward him. Garbage floats among the weed: a liquor bottle, a green pawpaw, a brown banana, a hunk of gray lumber. The kid leans over the bow and looks down. Near the surface, tiny jellyfish sail by in the ebbing tide's swift current. As the seaweed carpet moves past, the cabin cruiser's anchor line bisects it. A strand of sargasso weed catches momentarily on the rope, then the flow pulls it off and it drifts on. The kid looks upstream again and sees a yellow-orange lump off to starboard, at the far edge of the drifting debris. As it moves closer, the shape resolves itself into a mango.*

He rises on his toes and dives. Weightless, he feels the hole of fear in the stomach. He braces for impact and water explodes in his ears. Underwater, he opens his eyes to a blue-green blur. Looking up, he sees the crinkled silver mirror of the underside of the of surface. He swims upward and breaks through into the air, spitting saltwater and gasping for breath.

At water level, a swimmer's eyes see a different world. He looks south, at low narrow Conch Island, its white and red lighthouse, lonely stands of wind-bent casuarina trees and spumes of white ocean spray. He turns north and sees Britannia City's waterfront with its rickety wooden wharves, dock-side straw market, stone warehouses, trading sloops, small cargo ships. From the water, the weathered hull of the cabin cruiser Testament *looks huge. A tethered dinghy trails off her stern, its painter taut from the current's drag. His view changes rapidly as the current carries him by — from off the bow to off the beam to off the starboard quarter.*

He grabs the mango. The fruit in one hand, he paddles frantically toward the Testament*. The current sweeps him past the cabin cruiser and past the trailing dinghy. With a desperate burst of energy, he swims forward and grabs the dinghy's gunnel. The current tugs violently at his aching arm, but he won't let go of the mango. His wet hand slips off the gunnel and he drifts away. The current carries him toward the harbor's mouth, the open sea....*

"Help! Franklin! Help!"

Aboard the Testament*, a boy's head appears from the aft-cabin hatch. Franklin stares a moment, then grabs a rope, stands on the transom and dives into the water. Franklin swims mightily. The kid feels his brother's strong hand around his wrist, a rope under his armpits, the rope snapping taut and cutting into his flesh.*

Slowly, they haul themselves hand-over-hand against the current.

They climb back aboard the cabin cruiser and collapse on the hot deck. The kid gasps: "We could have drowned, Franklin. You saved my life." Franklin grins. "Sure, Morgan. Save mine one day, okay?"

Franklin goes below. On deck, water still trickling down his body, the kid leans over the lifeline, peeling the mango with his rigging knife. The strips of red-orange skin curl back and fall into the sea. He plunges his face into the stringy pulpy sticky sweet juicy ripe mango flesh. Juice goes up his nose. Strings catch between his teeth. He eats in a frenzy, a fruit orgy under hot tropical sun, stepping from one foot to the other because the hot deck burns his feet. Blazing tropical sun dries mango juice on leather-brown skin, leaving a sticky shine that cracks when the skin moves. His feast over, he dives into the sea to wash and cool off. Holding onto a dangling rope ladder, he stays close to the boat he calls his home.

2

T HE CRASH OF MY OFFICE DOOR jarred me out of my reverie. I watched Spooks Logan lumber in, shove the door shut with his rear, and waddle rapidly toward my desk. Spooks' usual bow-wave of tobacco stink arrived before he did, destroying any mango fragrance that might have lingered. I dropped the mango and wiped my hands with a handkerchief. My fingers still felt sticky.

My watch said five thirty.

"We used to get free fruit," I said. "We'd swim out and grab it when it drifted by."

"When your preacher pop gave you time off from pushing Bibles on the heathen."

"On weekends the boat-traders threw their unsold produce in the sea before sailing home," I said. "They didn't want to ruin business by giving stuff away."

"She still hasn't called," cried Spooks in a rising wail. "You got to find her, Morgan."

Spooks tapped a crumpled cigarette from a scrunched package and lit it with a crooked paper match. I gazed past him at the backwards lettering on the frosted glass of my office door. From the corridor, people would read MORGAN MORPHUS, G.S. INQUIRIES. I'd once read in the *San Francisco Examiner* that Dashiell Hammett had worked for the Pinkerton Detective Agency in this same building beside the Powell and Market cable-car turnaround.

Spooks rubbed his thick neck and the motion brought my gaze back to his bloated rubbery face. He stared dolefully from cavernous eye-sockets.

"Ask questions," he said in a smoker's gasp, as a white cloud huffed from his behemothic gob. "Drink planters punch. I'll give you eight hundred a day."

"I don't want to go back."

"Plus expenses. Just get on a plane."

"Too many memories."

"You call yourself a pro. Ha."

"When I remember my childhood, I think of myself in the third person," I muttered. *"The kid stands on the sun-parched foredeck....* Why do I do that?"

"I'll give you a thousand a day."

"Most of the people I know probably died."

"She said she'd call, Morgan."

"You don't have a thousand a day for half a day. And if I went, I wouldn't charge you one cent. But I can't, okay?"

I opened a desk drawer, dragged out a bottle of Bushmills, an empty cheese-spread jar, a bottle of Guinness and an English one-pint dimpled glass mug. I shoved the whisky and the cheese jar at Spooks, opened the Guinness, poured the beautiful black liquid into the mug and admired the white, creamy head.

"Try to relax," I said. "Go over to Finnigan's, eat some corned beef and cabbage, play some darts."

The Bushmills label said "Original Grant to Distil 1608" in small black sans serif letters on a gold background. The label rose above my field of vision as Spooks lifted the bottle off my desk.

"How can I relax when Esme hasn't called. Please, Morgan."

Spooks slopped Irish whiskey into the cheese-spread jar, gulped it, grimaced, sighed noisily.

"You go," I said.

"You don't give a damn about your niece," he whined, trying to look pathetic.

"The daughter of my *distant* cousin, not my niece. You go."

"I can't. The Government down there put me on a list. A little matter of exports."

"Illegal substances...."

"Morgan, you know what killed my daughter's mother. Your esteemed next-of-kin deals, I do not, definitely do not. You know how I hate everything connected with drugs. I do conch shells, coral, sea fans, and such. Unfortunately some politico thought the reefs needed protection and put a bill through their parliament. Only I didn't agree, inasmuch as I'd already purchased a grand worth of tropical trinkets."

I leaned back in my creaking wooden chair, studied the yellowed water-stained ceiling and ruminated on how I should have stayed somewhere else. I sighed and took a deep swallow of Guinness, savored its lovely bitter bite as it reminded me of every lovely English pub I'd spent a beautiful evening in long ago when I still believed in things. I should have stayed over there where my relatives couldn't find me.

Spooks poured whiskey, sloshed it down, winced.

"Does Esme still eat rice and vegetables?" I asked cautiously.

"She got into fruit," replied Spooks evenly. "Bananas. Coconuts. Mangoes. She got heavily into mangoes. She must have got that from you."

"A veg head in the fast lane, it seems a contradiction," I muttered.

"What?"

"Nothing."

Outside a cable-car clanged. Inside, Spooks swallowed more whiskey and wiped the back of his hand across his chunky lips.

"You going to find your niece or what?" he growled. "She chartered a sailing sloop from Charlie Crawford."

"Who?"

"New guy down there, refugee from the Canadian snow. He runs Condo Yacht Charters."

"Phone him," I said.

"He only has a C. B. Can you believe it, in this day and age? I got patched through but he said he never heard of her. Pirates, drugs, hi-jacking, hurricanes...God knows what could happen to her."

"Spooks, the hurricane season hasn't started yet."

"They have deadly summer squalls when those big thunderhead clouds let loose. I've seen waterspouts suck up schools of pilchard so it rains fish like judgment day. Go and talk to Charlie Crawford."

"You worry too much."

"She should have come back last week, Morgan. She still hasn't phoned and I can't get anybody who's even seen her." Spook's voice had gone up an octave again.

"I can't. I got this important case coming up."

3

T HE ANCIENT DC-3 TOUCHED DOWN on the potholed runway, bounced, settled on lumpy tires and bumped along precariously. My seat tipped back suddenly as the aircraft's rear end sank onto its tail wheel. The scrub pine zooming by began to slow.

Through the window I watched the scene sliding past: tropical bush, dwarf palmettos, scrub pine, a burnt-out plane, a wrecked jeep, a saltwater pond edged with mangroves, mounds of bulldozed limestone. Our aircraft lurched into a right turn, then veered sharply left. My eyes followed the port wing-tip as it swung round. They'd built a new terminal: pink stucco with white toothing stones at the corners, the usual Caribbean British Colonial style. The old clapboard customs shed had gone. A plywood sign said "Welcome To Salt Harbor International Airport."

A white-faced pilot emerged from the cockpit, took his cap from an overhead locker and put it on. His hands shook. We followed him down the creaking steps. Heat blazed up from the asphalt, the sun's glare ricocheted off the parched scarred white limestone landscape where they'd ripped up the trees and thin soil and put nothing back. From the piles of bulldozed quarry earth skeletal roots of fallen trees poked into the stagnant air. The pilot lit a cigarette and threw his smoking match to the ground.

A dozen tired passengers, we trouped into the arrival building. A guy I didn't know lounged behind an unpainted pine immigration desk that looked like a down-home church pulpit. Beyond, a customs officer I didn't know stood with one foot on the low luggage table, drinking from a green-necked bottle in a brown paper bag. The sweat in the small of my back dripped down into my underpants. I stood in line behind a lanky middle-aged woman in sandals, jeans, beads, and a thin loose cotton blouse. I offered my California driver's license, return ticket, and entry card. The immigration officer stamped the card, kept half, and gave me back my documents. "Enjoy your visit, Sir."

I presented my bag for customs inspection and the officer drew a chalk mark on it before I could undo the zip. From the corner of my eye, I saw him turn and continue searching a bag belonging to the lanky woman in sandals. He took a hand-rolled cigarette from her make-up kit and held it up. The woman turned pale.

I grabbed my bag and hurried out into burning sunshine where I yanked off my tie and shoved it in my pocket. Still squinting at the sudden glare, I looked down at the immigration card in my hand. They'd given me two weeks. I'd once voted here. Now they give me two weeks like any other foreigner. So much for independence from British rule.

The taxi rank still had a black-painted plywood chalkboard nailed to a cork tree where the drivers scrawled their numbers as they arrived.

Happy Day, a tall cadaverous red-haired white guy with the world's gloomiest face, sat hunched under the big almond tree, holding his cards to his chest while the other boys slapped theirs down loudly on an upturned packing crate, whooping and hollering to his glum silence. Happy kept sneaking looks at the chalkboard so he wouldn't lose his turn. The taxi rank bequeathed me a beat-up minibus bus driven by a white kid dressed like a country singer. His sunken cheeks and green eyes told me which Loyalist family had begotten him.

"West End Marina," I said.

"You-all goin' on a charter?"

"You got to get away once in a while."

We drove along the flat through pine scrub, past a mangrove swamp, to partly-cleared flat land where the village began. I soon gave up trying to identify houses built since I'd left. We passed Key West-style clapboard cottages with gable roofs and new one-story stucco houses with hurricane roofs. We paused at a genuine factory-made stop sign at the so-called town center, a crossroads surrounded by Bilkeys' Bank, Amen's Corner Gas Station, Moxley's Liquor Store and the Church of the Endeavor. A church sign said "7502 Saved." The numbers slid into a track so the preacher could change them as he saved more souls. At the vacant lot next door stood another sign, this one with an architect's drawing of a

big modern church with tall steeple, flying buttresses, assorted wings and various arches. The wording said: "Future
home of the Church of the Endeavor. Please give to the
fund."

We moved off the paved road onto a dirt track that went
toward the harbor. Here, casuarina trees blocked my view of
the water, and I leaned forward impatiently. Nobody had
recognized me, so far. What had Spooks said to convince me
to take a case so filled with personal garbage? Or had I convinced myself because I wanted to wallow in the garbage a
little?

Spooks and I had got talking about the time we'd helped
Bondo Harry take his trawler across the gulf stream. We'd
spent a week cruising up the cays, spearing fish, trapping
crabs, and drinking Star beer. I'd longed for just one more
sunset, anchored miles out on the banks with the glassy evening sea reflecting those big purple cumulus clouds, not a
noise except water lapping on the hull or the plop of a jumping ray. We'd cook and eat our catch and when the stars
came out we'd sit on the flying bridge and lie about the fish
we should have caught and the women we should have
loved. The nostalgia had hurt so good I'd forgotten I'd sworn
I'd never go back.

Before leaving, I'd tried to phone Adelaide, my one-and-
only significant other, but she'd turned off her answer-phone,
as she does on even-numbered days as part of her plan to
organize her life. Since they'd discovered AIDS, I'd had to
cut back on the number of women I fell in love with. So now
I had a one-and-only, and I'd begun to like it that way, and I
felt bad about not telling her I'd gone away.

The old minibus dropped into a pothole so deep my head
hit the ceiling, effectively knocking me out of my daydreams.
I leaned forward in my seat again and watched the gravel
road ahead. We swung round a corner and I saw a glimmer
of sea between the trees.

When you finally emerge from the cottages and casuarina
trees after years away, the view of the harbor gives you a
feeling of sadness and joy — joy because you came back, sadness because you always blow it when you do. I valiantly
put my emotions in neutral. As we drove along the water-

front I watched the sailing yachts, cabin cruisers, and fishing boats anchored in turquoise water, all facing the southerly breeze. Who cares if moored boats face the wind, anyway? You don't have to travel across a continent and over the blue sea to learn that.

We drove along the waterfront toward a cove containing West End Marina. On the far side of the harbor stood a partly constructed radio tower. Some men moved about on the ground and up aloft as a crane swung another piece of tower into place.

We turned into the marina approach, I got out and took in the changes. White limestone landfill ran up to a steel retaining-wall that held in the reclaimed land. The last time I'd seen this place, land didn't exist here. You'd have sunk up to your waist in oolitic mud in the middle of a mangrove creek. They used to tie boats up here during hurricanes. Now I saw Florida-style condos, all plywood and louvered glass, at least five feet above sea level. In the next hurricane, both boats and buildings would head out to sea.

I asked the driver to wait. Outside the blue-and-white plywood office, a desiccated hibiscus struggled for survival in the sterile white ground. A circle of conch shells surrounded a gnarled sea grape tree. A young man desultorily picked up big brown dead sea grape leaves — one at a time — and put them in a black plastic bag. If I existed, the Haitian refugee didn't show it. The islands now had a whole new underclass that allowed the native underclass to move up a notch.

At the water's edge, two new docks jutted out into the harbor. I gazed at the jumble of masts and rigging, and listened to the ringing clank of a wind-blown halyard beating against a hollow aluminum mast. Something about the clank of rigging makes me sad these days. You shouldn't let it clang, it wears things out.

I walked into the office, dropped my bag on the counter, and wiped sweat from my forehead with a soggy handkerchief.

"We got your boat ready," said the dark-tanned yellow-haired youth behind the counter before I could give my name. "The *Lolita*. Dock number two." He wore a Yankees cap. In the old days, they wore hats made of palmetto straw.

My sweat made spots on the papers as I signed them.
"We stock our yachts with food and soft drinks. You-all got to get your own liquor."
"Can somebody put my bag aboard the *Lolita*?" I said. "I have to go back to town before the bank closes. Not to mention the liquor store. Can I use your phone?"
"Overseas call?"
"San Francisco."
"You'll have to wait 'til they finish the new radio tower, couple of days most likely."

4

I RODE BACK TO TOWN, wishing I'd mailed a note to Adelaide telling her about my trip. Not that it would have done much good. She only opens her mail on alternate Thursdays, as part of her plan to organize her life.

My taxi drove past Amos Place, an unpainted one-story clapboard bar and billiard room about the size of a one-car garage. Years ago, Amos Moxley had obtained the island's first liquor license, despite my Pop's valiant campaign against him. Last I heard, Amos owned a liquor warehouse, a restaurant, two bars, and two liquor stores.

I paid off the cab at Bilkeys' Bank, under a sign in Olde Englishe gold-and-black lettering that contrasted oddly with the coconut trees overhanging the pink-and-white stucco building. I strolled in, savoring the air conditioning, and asked for the manager. The staff paid me no mind, except for Conch Eye the senior teller, who stared blatantly with his one good peeper, then looked away. A pretty woman I'd never seen before showed me into the manager's office.

When I saw him my gut went tight but I kept a calm face.

"What can I do for you, Mr. Morphus, um...."

Franklin took off his glasses, peered at me and swallowed hard. He wore a suit, as usual, even though his town had only five miles of paved road and the temperature outside stood at ninety-five with the humidity of an equestrian's undergarments. Franklin still upheld the conservative tie, the clean-shaven square chin, the tall thin fit frame. He probably had his own high-tech gym in that big house on the hill. Along with his collection of Chinese jade.

"Morgan?" he asked querulously.

"Uh-huh."

He sat suddenly. His healthy brown face had grayed underneath.

"You came back?"

"For business purposes only."

"But your card says Morphus."

"I changed some things. Who'd hire a dick named Murphy?"

"You work for a living?"

"I get by."

"G.S. Inquiries? What's that mean?"

"I'll tell you sometime."

"I have to admit, I didn't recognize you at first."

"Head-on crash with a BMW full of drunken Stanford genius kids. When they started to reconstruct my face, I gave them somebody else's picture."

"You always hated us," said Franklin in a gritty voice. "You changed your face and your name because of it."

"You can think what you think," I said. "You always hated me because I embarrassed the family by hanging out with lowlife."

"Your birth embarrassed the family, Morgan."

I grabbed a chair, spun it round, straddled it, gripped the top of the back and leaned forward, spitting words. "I wore Afro hair and I drank and smoked and fornicated while you hoarded your virginity and sweated out your MBA at some hokey college in the frozen north. You married a third-rate off-island socialite and came back to big-fish-it in a small pond. And I still popped up to embarrass you when I didn't have anything else nefarious to do."

Franklin yanked his hands from the edge of his desk, took a deep breath, cracked his knuckles, sighed.

"You can't see him," he said eventually, hardly moving his lips.

"Big brother as usual, still protecting the senile old patriarch," I growled.

"He went out in the boat."

"Still looking for God out there?"

"You never could forgive him for growing old," retorted Franklin, and my gut tied itself in another knot.

"I like the sign you guys have outside your church now," I said sarcastically. " '7502 Served' it says."

"Saved," growled Franklin.

"Of course it doesn't say that the same people get saved every Sunday so they can get a free transistor radio."

"You know Poppa stopped giving away radios years ago," said Franklin indignantly.

"I hear he made you boss preacher now."

I put a cigarette in my mouth, turned over Franklin's THANK YOU FOR NOT SMOKING sign and lit up. Franklin glared and a vein pulsed below one eye. These days I only smoked for business, or to annoy people, or for pacing, or male bonding, that sort of crap, but he didn't know that.

"What do you want?" squeaked Franklin eventually.

"Depends...."

"On what?"

"I came here on a case. I want nothing to do with you hypocrites."

"What happened to your hair?"

"The chemo."

Franklin turned gray again. He never could stand pain, sickness, or death. "Cancer?"

"I got it in permission, according to the quack."

"Remission, you mean."

"Permission for a few more drinks and fornications before the axeman cometh. What do I care?"

"You talk tough," muttered Franklin. "You'll lose, as usual. You have to use the system if you want a house on the hill."

"Some guys round here would say you did different."

"What you want?"

"Nothing much, Dear Brother. Hardly anything. Some years ago I put two thousand dollars in a long-term CD in this very bank. Needless to say, I didn't know you'd leave your position up the street and take over Captainship of this worthy establishment. On checking by telephone recently, I find that this CD no longer exists. It would seem to have disappeared without trace. I assume that you took my minuscule nest egg to buy a few trinkets to add to your collection of Chinese jade in your humble cottage on the hill. A contribution of retribution, so to speak. You never could forget how I broke the hind leg off your priceless Chinese dragon."

Franklin coughed for a while. "I thought you'd died, the way you live."

"Sorry not to oblige."

"I'll pay you back."

"Today."

"Sure...cashier's check."

"Cash."

"Sure, sure."

"U.S. dollars, mon ami."

"I'll need your passport."

"No you won't. You fix it. You know how."

"All right," said Franklin with a sigh.

"You seem awfully eager to atone for your sins, Big Brother."

Franklin straightened up and gave me a cold hard look. His voice had a bite I'd never heard before. "Don't upset the balance of nature, Morgan. Don't rock the boat."

"I don't suppose you've seen Esme recently."

"Who?"

"Don't play dumb. Your cousin Spook's daughter Esmerelda."

Franklin fiddled distractedly with his tie. "Esme? Not for years."

"She always liked you. Your money, I suppose. She likes rice and vegetables and monied men."

"Jealous?"

"She likes the fast track. And mangoes. But, you'd know that, Franklin."

"The way you and Spooks enjoy the gutter, she probably wants something better."

Franklin's tie now had creases in it. I said I'd collect my money later and strolled out. Franklin had long held the habit of crumpling things distractedly when he lied.

5

A S I LEFT THE AIR-CONDITIONED BUILDING, the heat and sun hit me like a brick furnace. Squinting and sweating, I trudged half a block along a dirt road to the waterfront, where a light breeze blew in across the harbor.

I turned into the wind and sucked the delicious balmy salty moist sea air into my lungs. When you've stayed away from the islands too long, you forget how the sea breeze can caress your skin. In the city, you wrap your skin in clothes and it loses its feeling. Then you come back, and the soft sea breeze touches your cheeks like a lover welcoming you home.

In a while I looked around. At the water's edge, the sea had eroded the limestone sponge rock so that it overhung the water like a frozen curling wave. About a dozen small weathered wood cottages lined the low rocky shore. Further along lay a new wooden dock with gasoline pumps and a sign that said BILLY'S MARINA.

About a hundred yards to the west stood the Royal Family Restaurant Room, a clapboard shack on stilts partly over-hanging the water, built by Fred Moxley shortly before my last visit all those years ago. I walked along the shore and into the restaurant's cool shade, but didn't see anyone I rec-ognized. The harbor side of the room had wooden louvers that allowed visibility and ventilation but kept back the heat and glare. From my table, I could see a row of stakes in the eastern harbor, leading from the entrance to the government dock. *So they'd finally dredged Mud Bank,* I thought as a blue wooden fishing sloop came about near the new channel. I watched the locomotions of sailing and motor yachts, ding-hies, and a small freighter as I ate an afternoon breakfast of boiled grouper, Johnny cake, and coffee. Pensively contem-plating the harbor, I dragged out my meal. I hadn't tasted island food for so long I wanted to cry.

I paid for my meal with local dollars, returned to Bilkeys' Bank and got my money from a teller I didn't know. At Mox-leys Number 1 Likquer Store, I bought a bottle of Bushmills, a case of bottled Harp, two six-packs of Guinness, and a case of club soda. I took a cab back to the marina, borrowed a hand cart, and rolled my supplies out onto dock number two for a first look at the *Lolita*, the motor craft I'd chartered by phone from San Francisco.

I decided I'd classify the *Lolita* as a 40-foot fake lobsterman actually constructed as a cruising yacht. The only lobster she'd seen came thermidor. In their wisdom, the builders had given her an immaculate white fiberglass hull and cabin, an abundance of teak trim, and a wimpy mast suitable for flags, antennas and one small towel. In her hull they'd made neat grooves to represent the seams of a wooden boat, over-looking how in real wooden boats the putty bulges or falls out or the seams don't show at all. If they'd wanted realism, why hadn't they put red stains to represent the bleeding rust from old iron nails?

Jumping aboard a boat after a long stay ashore has its own special magic. Your feet hit the deck, you both feel and hear the echoey water-softened *thump* that only human feet strik-ing a floating hull can make. You can't talk about it to any-body. You can only feel it. If you haven't felt it for a long time, your throat catches.

The large cockpit had a roof over the forward half, and canvas curtains you can roll down in bad weather. The helm, a traditional varnished mahogany ship's wheel, stood to star-board, up against the cabin's aft bulkhead, with chrome single-lever engine controls convenient to the right hand. The *Lolita* had no dinghy; just a small white raft lashed to the cabin top. Despite my cynicism over the yacht's imitation of a working craft, I felt a thrill of anticipation as I stood at the helm and idly spun the wheel.

I loaded my liquor into the cockpit, then went below, opened a bottled Harp, and put some Harp on ice. I noted with satisfaction that someone from the marina had brought my bag aboard and left it on the galley table.

I sat on the companionway steps to drink my ale and ex-amine my temporary home. Looking forward, you saw to starboard a gimballed table and upholstered benches that probably converted to a double bunk; to port, a galley con-taining an alcohol stove, a small sink with water pump, a dual-voltage refrigerator, and assorted lockers. I got up and moved forward, keeping my head down. A mahogany bulkhead enclosed a head to starboard and clothes lockers to port. In the forepeak, two berths converged in a V. I returned to the main saloon, slid into a seat at the galley table and sighed with satisfaction. I liked the craft's interior: a lot of teak trim, varnished red mahogany, and soft burgundy-colored upholstery; overhead, a rack of rolled charts; in the aft bulkhead, a bookshelf holding a local cruising guide and some paperback novels.

I stripped off my city clothes, put on shorts and a T-shirt. I drank another beer while sitting in a fishing chair in the cockpit watching the comings and goings in the harbor. Something made me sleepy, so I went below and stretched out on the forward port bunk. I listened to the water lapping on the other side of the hull only a few inches from my ear. I got up a moment to prop the fore-hatch open so it would funnel the breeze down over me, then lay down again. The next thing I knew, I woke up in the dark.

I put on a loud Hawaiian shirt and a pair of wild Bermuda shorts, clothes I never wear, and strolled ashore. Somebody had opened a bar and restaurant in a plywood cabaña a quarter-mile down the beach. I walked along the water's edge and strolled in, glancing at the occupants, two middle-aged white male tourists sitting dejectedly at the bar. I sniffed the fragrance of frying fish and smiled.

"Morgan, my man!"

Had I really thought I could stay incognito?

"Hey Stanley."

I shook hands with Stanley, who seemed to have grown even taller and lankier than before.

"You look bad, man," said Stanley. "You come home to stay?"

"Just visiting. You work here now, eh?"

"You want Old Oak and water?"

"Just a Harp."

Stanley put a cold bottle of Harp on the bar. Condensation beaded on the brown glass, but the blue, red, and gold label remained dry. Stanley ducked out from behind the bar, limped over to the pool table, and dropped in a quarter. When he let go the coin lever, the thud, clack and rumble of dropping pool balls took me back a dozen years.

"You look like your dog done died," said Stanley sympathetically.

"Remember the old days, Stan?"

"Why you want to remember what make you feel sad?"

"We had some good times, eh Stan? We used to raise hell."

Stanley handed me a cue. "You break, Morgan."

My break didn't sink one ball. I watched as Stanley sank the seven, the three, the five, the two, the four, the one, the six. He banked the eight off the end cushion into the near middle pocket.

"Thanks for the game," I said, putting my cue back in its rack. Stanley hobbled back to the bar to make planter's punch for the two tourists. We played several more games of pool. I won once, but didn't have my heart in it.

"Cousin Spooks could play a mean game," I said reflectively as Stanley put two cold beers on the counter.

"I heard Spooks done got himself bankrupt," said Stanley, slowly wiping the counter with a filthy rag.

"They call him Spooks because he got no neck, just like a ghost," I said for no reason.

"You see Spooks out in Frisco California?"

"Spooks done got himself bankrupt more times than you've et fried porgy but he always comes up smelling sweet. He does imports now. You know those Afro statues they sell in the straw market. He can get them for you hand-carved by machine in Taiwan."

"I seen his little girl other day."

"He told me she'd planned a holiday," I said noncommittally.

"Up to your brother's house."

"You don't say?"

"She growed up now."

"Uh-huh."

"Your brother don't associate with my kind. Boss Moxley, he done sent me up to deliver two cases of French wine."

"Stanley, you got any cracked conch and peas and rice? I don't know how long since I tasted conch."

Stanley looked at me sadly. "How you live without crack conch?"

"In San Francisco they got abalone. It costs like uranium and tastes like baby food."

"I tell the cook. You want a table on the patio?"

Stanley wrote something on my check; he looked thoughtful for a moment, then tore my check in half. I ate beaten breaded deep-fried cracked conch while sitting on the patio, watching the moon come up over the Eastern shore, sending its reflection in ripples across the harbor. From the anchored yachts a few dinghies came and went. So Esme or somebody looking like her had visited my brother not long ago, I thought. Now what would Charlie Crawfish, owner of Condo Yacht Charters of Faithful Harbor, have to say? But that would have to wait until tomorrow, owing to my falling asleep in the afternoon instead of going out detecting like Spooks had told me to. On the other hand, if I hadn't run into Stanley....

6

A T DAWN, I started up *Lolita's* engines, hauled up anchor with an electric winch operated by a push button near the helm, and motored slowly out of Salt Harbor. It gave me pure joy standing at the wheel, feeling the engine vibration through my feet, watching the moored yachts slip past in the gray morning light. What a difference from that waterlogged tub Poppa had used dragging us through dangerous seas to take the Word to the ungodly.

When I'd left the moored yachts behind, I opened the throttles, listened to the fuel-hungry growl of the twin high-speed diesels and the rising whine of the turbochargers picking up speed. *Lolita's* stern lowered momentarily and her bow rose as she climbed up onto the plane, then she leveled out and began to *move*. I watched the digital knotmeter...and my eyes stung. When you've stayed on land too long, your spirit tends to go arthritic.

The narrow exit channel approached faster than I'd anticipated. In the morning light, the glassy water reflected the sky like a mirror, and I couldn't see a thing below the surface. I yanked back the throttles, *Lolita* tucked her nose under, scuttled down off the plane and wallowed in her own wake.

I steered towards Poor Boy's Point, a low strip of scrub and jagged limestone that formed the southern side of the harbor. A one-foot chop come sliding round the point, the waves cresting a little in the southeast wind. Lolita began to pitch a little and below decks a piece of china hit the floor and smashed. The land moved aside, opening up my view of the sound. Seeing open water, I felt like I'd just got out of jail. I slammed the throttles full ahead and *Lolita* climbed back up onto the plane.

Coming round the point, *Lolita* took a wave over the bow and I got a face full of cold water. Without thinking, I began to cuss. I cussed the bastards who'd made me hate the islands and the beautiful wind, water, and banks that made me love them, and I cussed the bastards that made me hate the city and the bastards that made me want it, and I mostly cussed myself for never getting it right wherever I went because I always loved and hated things at the same time. And then I cussed cussing because cussing does about as much for you as praying.

I eased back on the throttles so that *Lolita* stayed up on the step but threw most of the spray to each side of her flared bow. I sucked warm breeze into my lungs and tasted the salt on my lips and sighed. A great peace settled over me. What did I care? Whatever they did, they couldn't take away the sea.

As Poor Boy's Point came abeam I glared angrily at the shore. Here stood six acres of beach-front property lined with coconut trees that would still belong to me if Franklin hadn't made me sell it to him before he'd pay my bail. Then I thanked the bastard, because if he hadn't screwed me I'd have probably wound up just like him, trapped in respectability on a tiny island without the memory of one pub, taverna, bar, bistro, or other foreign watering hole inside my aging head, without the memory of all the beautiful women of different nationalities that I'd loved and inadvertently left behind.

I cruised into Faithful Harbor at about four in the afternoon. Residue from the dredging had left white mud banks on each side of the channel, now visible because of the low tide. Closer inshore you could see tips of the green-brown sea grass emerging from the shallow water near the beach.

The last time I'd visited Faithful Harbor the mangroves had covered half the eastern shore. Now none remained there. They'd built a seawall, a pine dock, and plywood condos. To the north, Slow Mangrove Creek still had mangroves on both sides, but they'd dredged the creek and filled it with yachts.

According to Spooks, Canadian snow refugee Charlie Crawford now chartered out production sloops on some kind of time-share tax-dodge deal which allowed their owners to sail them one week a year and own what the landlubbers and the local reefs had left after seven years. The locals called him Crawfish. Like a lot of other phenomena, he'd arrived after I'd left.

I tied up at a T-shaped wooden dock on the western shore. A sign said CONDO YACHT CHARTERS. I shut off the engines, climbed onto the dock, walked ashore and up the hill to an octagonal thatch cabaña, where I saw a man tidying up the bar. I climbed onto a fake bamboo stool, trying to figure out the man's features and coloring: aquiline nose, high cheekbones, gaunt, angular, red-brown face.

"Charlie Crawfish, at your service," he said with a grin, as he dried a wine glass with a white towel. "Quarter Cherokee, eighth Ivory coast, eighth New Orleans Creole, five-eighths Glasgow Irish," he added, putting down the glass and flipping the towel onto his shoulder.

"Can't argue with mathematics," I said. "Wouldn't have a bottle of Harp would you now?"

Crawfish grinned. He turned to a rusting propane refrigerator and took out two bottles of Harp lager. I watched the condensation make beautiful liquid beads on the cold brown glass. I didn't mention I'd seen some cases of Harp on the dock.

"You look kind of multi-cultural yourself," said Crawfish.

I lifted the cool bottle to my lips, tipped it back and felt the lovely bubbles caress my lonely throat. On a hot tropical day, a cold lager has its own poetry, such that words cannot describe.

I swallowed half a beer before speaking. "When the nubiles got the spirit, Poppa gave them Gabriel's horn."

"Sired by a preacher, no less," said Crawfish meditatively, and he took a long drink of beer. "You poor bastard."

"Too true," I said quietly. "Poppa had himself a white woman for a time. His wife didn't exactly approve, but she tried to raise me like a Christian woman should. What can you do with an outside child? It makes the heathens gossip. I can't call myself black and I can't call myself white."

"So?"

Crawfish stared, then we both grinned and drank.

I glanced across the lagoon at the village of Faithful Harbor, at the old cottages of weathered pine clapboards and silvered cedar shingle roofs, at the new two-story cement-block stuccoed houses with glass windows and the three-story white painted plywood Faithful Hotel. The beer and the sea breeze gave me a good feeling and suddenly I wanted to talk about the old days, and all the changes, about who'd bred and who'd died and who hadn't. I almost bit my tongue. I didn't want more people to know I'd come back so I couldn't say a damn thing.

As I gazed wistfully at the village across the water, I heard an engine noise that didn't sound like a boat because boats don't shift gears like cars and trucks do. A red pickup came out of the palms and drove along the shore just above the high-tide line. The sods had brought a truck over! I stared hard. I couldn't see that pretty little white crescent of beach that used to make a quarter circle round the harbor ending under that big grove of palms by Casper's boat shed. They'd built a sea wall and filled in the land and built a bloody road there. I looked glumly back at Crawfish.

"You all right?" he asked.

"Kind of hot."

"Arrive today?"

"Yesterday. Spent the night at Salt Harbor."

"Fishing?"

"To tell the truth, I came on business. A missing person."

"You don't look like a cop."

"I do private inquiries. Out of San Francisco just now."

I gave Crawfish my card and he stared at it, rubbing his big aquiline nose between left thumb and forefinger.

"G.S. Inquiries. How about that?"

"G.S. stands for general semantics," I explained.

"Exactly."

"You see, the G.S. Detective uses non-Aristotelian logic."

"Sure," said Crawfish with a grin. "Non-Aristotelian, some-times called Non-A or Null-A."

"Hey, nobody knows that stuff," I yelled.

"The Non-A thinker goes beyond Aristotle by also includ-ing a logic of multiple values."

"You've read Korzybski?" I gasped.

"You got to read something on these long tropical nights."

"You read *Science and Sanity*?"

"Charter people leave all sorts of things aboard my boats. On the *Captain Slocum* I found a science fiction novel called *The World of Null-A* by a guy named A. E. van Vogt. The pro-tagonist used what the author called Null-A logic. It im-pressed me because he could think so damn smart."

"I read the same book," I said. "And the other two in the series. I heard that a lot of people got interested in general semantics through reading the Null-A trilogy."

Crawfish bent down behind the bar, then straightened up holding a big well-thumbed dog-eared book.

"The author gave the address of the International Society for General Semantics, so I sent off for more reading material. When I start getting island fever, I go over to a little cabaña I built on the eastern beach and have a good read."

"One of these days it'll help me solve a case," I grumbled.

"It probably has," retorted Crawfish. "General semantics can give you some powerful tools for evaluating your life. The principle of non-identity helped me adjust to the fact that because of my mixed ancestry I don't belong to any recognized social or cultural group."

"I should remember that. Actually, I use G.S. methods a lot," I admitted. "And they have helped me solve several apparently hopeless cases. I try to remember to go beyond Aristotle's law of the excluded middle...."

"Yes, looking at the middle ground between yes and no. You know about the idea of evaluational calculus? You evaluate your problem in a series of very small steps, instead of one big overwhelming lump."

"Yeah," I cried enthusiastically. "And I try to treat so-called 'facts' as probabilities. I give each 'fact' a number between one and a hundred that represents the degree of probability. I call it the percentage-of-probability rule."

Crawfish grinned. "I notice you held up two fingers of each hand as you said the word *facts*. I read about people doing that — a sort of gestured quote marks to indicate some distrust of that word."

"If I held them another way, it could mean give me some whiskey."

"Or something less polite in certain parts of the world. I'd give it about ninety-nine percent you'd like another beer."

"A good working hypothesis, Mr. Crawfish, uh, Crawford."

"Call me Crawfish, everybody does."

Crawfish got two beers from the refrigerator, poured, and we drank in silence for a few moments to show our respect for the golden ale.

"Tell me about this missing person, Mr. Morphus. I don't recall anybody visiting here from San Francisco recently."

"My friends call me Morgan," I said. "Or they would if I had any."

Crawfish picked up a towel and a glass and began polishing. I gazed at the harbor. Years ago you'd have seen one or two schooner-rigged wooden fishing smacks moored there. Now dozens of fiberglass motor and sailing yachts crammed the harbor. I couldn't see one working craft.

"My cousin's daughter's gone missing," I said eventually, putting my bottle on a Watney's bar mat. "At least he thinks she has. She lives in Silicon Valley where she had some kind of genius job programming until her company went bust. She got involved in robotics, making those animated figures move for movies and theme parks. I can still see her five-years-old, eating ice cream I bought because she'd scraped her knees when she fell off her tricycle. Now she has a Ph.D. in computer science and I got a degree in gassing in the wind."

"Just a minute, Morgan."

"She got so she liked the good life. It kind of hit her when she lost her job. Or so they say."

Crawfish loped over to a hand-made pine desk, came back with an exercise book, and laid it on the counter. The cover had a picture of Queen Elizabeth the Second. He opened the book and ran a dirty thumbnail down the page.

"What name did your missing person go by?"

"Logan. Esmerelda. She loved to sail so much I gave her my rigging knife."

Crawfish squinted at the page. His face drained, he swore quietly, then raised his eyes to mine. I didn't like the look on his face, too much like sympathy. "We had an Ester Loran from Cape Cod, it says here. She chartered the *Salty Dove* along with a party named Lindquest. Paid cash, including the deposit which I still have because they wrecked the *Salty Dove* at Love Reef. Drowned, both of them."

7

I LIT A CIGARETTE, one of those I smoke for business purposes.
"Some guy from California called a couple of days ago,"
said Crawfish. "The Salt Harbor operator patched him
through to my C.B. I never made the connection between
the two names 'til now."

"Her father called you. Assuming that *Ester Loran* and *Esmerelda Logan* amount to two names for the same person."

"The commissioner informed the authorities," said Crawfish in a low voice. "You should have heard."

"The authorities in Cape Cod, I suppose."

"I guess you didn't hear."

"I'd had something special engraved on it," I said.

"Eh?"

"The rigging knife I gave her. My knife. Because she loved
sailing so much."

I could still see her — yellow hair, pink dress, eating vanil-
la ice cream, tricycle on its side in the brown sun-burned
grass of Silicon Park. And later, a beautiful young woman,
dinghy sailing in San Francisco Bay. The pictures mixed
themselves together.

"You got a photo, Mr. Morphus?"

From my shirt pocket I took out the photo of Esmerelda
that Spooks had given me. I flipped the picture so Crawfish
could see it. He tried to keep a neutral face.

"Looks like the same person, if memory serves me right.
Man, I feel bad...."

"How could you know? But where'd they send the remains?"

"Nowhere. They only found one body, the man called
Lindquest," said Crawfish, putting two short glasses on the
counter. He filled both with dark Old Oak rum. "Air and Sea
Rescue searched for two days, but never found the others."

"Others?"

"A third party joined up with them. At least some people
on another charter of mine reported seeing three people on
board the *Salty Dove.*"

More E-Prime: To Be or Not II

The 150-proof rum kicked me where I needed kicking. "Tides, currents, you never know," I mused.

"Now a follower of general semantics would call this idea of three drownings an inference, not a fact," said Crawfish pointedly. "Except for the one body they found. They cremated him when they couldn't reach any next of kin."

I put my elbow on the bar, hunched over, held my forehead and mumbled some useless cuss words.

"A G.S. detective wouldn't jump to conclusions," said Crawfish quietly. "He'd investigate for himself."

I straightened up and took a deep breath.

"He'd pause a moment," I said. "He'd try to make some observations. He'd visit the scene of the alleged event."

"That you can do, Morphus. Love Reef lies down the sound a ways. All the bodies should have drifted up the shore into Curving Cove. But we only found that one."

"You said 'we'?"

"A lot of guys belong to Air and Sea Rescue."

"Got a chart I could look at?"

Crawfish bent down and brought a rolled-up chart from under the bar. We spread the chart on the bar and weighted down the curling edges with seashell ashtrays.

"Love Reef," said Crawfish, pointing with a swizzle stick. "It usually takes a day to get there from here because you can only cross Treacherous Bank at high tide. I call it the worst hazard in Queen's Bay, at least for the people who charter my boats, but everybody just *has* to see the sea gardens and the boiling holes. 'Course, if you know the waters around here, you know what to expect."

Because I wanted to stay incognito, I didn't tell Crawfish I knew every reef around, owing to the fact that my old man in his missionary zeal had personally discovered each one.

"The bay runs about thirty miles east-west, and ten miles north-south," continued Crawfish in a sing-song that sounded like his spiel for orienting his customers. "You have about a three-fathom average depth over the grassy bottom, and anything from a foot to a fathom over the yellow banks. The bay gets protection to the west from a line of reefs and narrow islands that stand between it and the Atlantic Ocean.

Big Island's long concave shoreline provides shelter to the west."

Crawfish rubbed his aquiline nose. The beer and the rum had given me a warmth that contrasted badly with the cold news. I wanted to tell Crawfish how as a kid I'd sailed my dinghy all over Queen's Bay, but I kept my mouth shut. Crawfish put down his glass, belched reverently, continued talking as if I didn't know a damn thing.

"To the south, Big Island makes a dog-leg toward the northwest, and the line of reefs and islands follow it about five miles out, providing continued shelter for another thirty miles in an area known as Pink Sound. Many yachting people consider both areas particularly good cruising ground. A relative landlubber can charter one of my sloops and generally do no worse than run aground on soft sand."

"Some idiots can lose a mast anywhere," I growled, and Crawfish gave me a quizzical look.

I guzzled beer and ranted on, wishing I had the sense to shut up.

"Take the average American male who drives a desk all year, put him behind the helm, and suddenly you've got Captain Bligh, the Marquis de Sade, John Wayne, King Kong, Evel Knievel, and the Red Baron all in one robotic self-destructive Pavlovian Humpty Dumpty psychotic Captain from Hell. Wives wish they'd gone to Reno. Husbands wish they'd bring back keel-hauling of disobedient female crew. When a man hears the call of the sea, the wife hears divorce bells ring."

Crawfish grinned. "You can love the sea or love your wife, but you can't love both." Then he looked solemn. "You used to live here, right?"

"My mother deposited me in this world during a gale in the middle of the Gulf Stream, but yes I lived here once. She tried to make it to the States so I'd get born American, but she didn't make it in time. I got no hunk of national real estate to call my place of birth."

"So?"

Crawfish frowned. "You got family over at Salt Harbor. Your half-brother runs Bilkeys' bank."

I sipped beer. So much for incognitoness.

8

W ITH A PAIR OF PARALLEL RULERS, Crawfish drew pencil lines on the chart, showing me a course to the location of the wreck.

"From outside Faithful Harbor, you take Bluebeard's Channel between these two cays here. Keep to the west until you get half-way through, then jog over to the east. I'll write in the compass readings. Or do I need to?"

"It wouldn't hurt," I replied noncommittally.

Crawfish pencilled in compass courses all the way to the site of the wrecked *Salty Dove*, which lay near some outlying cays along the shore of Big Island.

"You'll find a lot of mangrove creeks between these cays and Big Island," continued Crawfish. "Most people consider them good creeks for bone fishing. Back there in Boiling Creek you'll find the boiling holes, or blue holes as the Americans call them. You can spear some grouper down in the holes but don't go down during the ebb tide, you might get sucked in."

"I've swum in the boiling holes," I admitted. "Some go down hundreds of feet, with subterranean passages leading all the way out to sea. Or so they say. When the tide comes in, water gushes up, making a boiling on the surface, hence the name boiling hole. With the ebb tide, a strong current goes down into the hole and it can pull you down and you'll never get out before you've breathed up all your air."

Crawfish grimaced, stabbed a forefinger at the chart. "I once had the pleasure of retrieving the corpse of a tourist from down a boiling hole in Boiling Creek."

"What do you call the opposite of boiling? When the tide ebbs and the water goes down instead of boiling up...."

"I don't know. How about dangerous?"

"It doesn't go fast enough to make a vortex. You can't even tell until it's got you."

"You'll find the *Salty Dove* here," continued Crawfish, pencilling an X on the chart. "What they left of her, anyway. The locals think of it as their right to salvage anything abandoned more than a few hours."

"In the old days they'd extinguish the lighthouse and carry a lantern along the shore to disorient the ship's master."

"Rum running paid better."

"Do you rent scuba gear, Mr. Crawford?"

"Sure."

We walked down to a weathered clapboard shed at the foot of the dock. Crawfish took some keys from his jeans and undid a padlock on a rusty hasp in the dutch door.

"You have to lock it now," I muttered.

Crawfish gave me a curious look but said nothing. We ducked in the low door, out of the bright sunlight and into cool gloom. Sunlight shone through cracks in the wall, lighting up dust in the still air. As my eyes got used to the shadows I saw an assortment of diving equipment hanging from hooks in the wall: masks, snorkels, flippers, regulators, hoses, weight belts, knives. On the floor, a row of scuba tanks leaned against the wall. Crawfish selected some diving gear which we lugged out onto the dock and loaded aboard the *Lolita*. Back in the shed, I gave him a deposit of two hundred dollars and he gave me a receipt.

"You got no spear guns?"

"The government made power guns illegal five years ago. Try this Hawaiian sling. It'll spear you a grouper if she's not too big."

"Anywhere around here I can get a good grouper dinner?"

"A woman called Aunty Tam's got a shack on her dock over in Slow Mangrove Creek. You can't get there on foot, have to take a dinghy."

"The boat I chartered only has a raft."

"Use one of my dinghies, the red one at the foot of the dock with a Seagull on it. And take a bottle. Tam's got no liquor license but she'll provide the mixers."

"Can I use the shower?"

"Sure. Bring some quarters."

I jumped aboard *Lolita* to get a robe and towel, then squeezed into a plywood shower stall beside the dock house where I took short shower, four quarters' worth. Faithful Harbor had no wells; the islanders hoarded rainwater in concrete cisterns. The coin-operated timer discouraged waste, but left me soapy. I dressed in khaki shorts, a white short-sleeved shirt, and leather boating shoes, and sat in *Lolita's* cockpit to watch the sun go down.

You can't buy a good sunset, but you can borrow one occasionally. Especially at Faithful Harbor. The wind dies about this time. The unruffled water looks like glass. You can look due west through the harbor entrance, through the notch between mangrove-lined Big Bluff and the seawall along Faithful Village's harbor road. Through that gap you see nothing but open water all the way to the horizon, mirror-smooth silver water reflecting distant low pink cumulus clouds and the increasingly red setting sun. With the wind gone, and the locals indoors eating their dinner, a silence falls, a silence of nature's rest, of gentle sky and peaceful water, of peace in your heart. It makes you think what a wonderful world we'd have if the sods didn't procreate.

If I hadn't had a few beers, I wouldn't have gone. I clambered into Crawfish's red dinghy, wound a piece of clothesline around the flywheel of the old Seagull, cranked it up, and headed up Slow Mangrove Creek toward Aunty Tam's. In the old days Aunty Tam, a brown-skinned woman of indeterminate age, had lived at Salt Harbor. Between my eighth and tenth years, Aunty Tam had looked after us. She'd done the ironing, the cleaning, and the best ever fried porgy, conch salad, peas and rice, and stone-oven bread. Aunty Tam would recognize me even if I had no face.

I tied up at a rickety dock and went into Aunty Tam Best Food, a dilapidated, careening, driftwood, corrugated iron, plywood and thatch shanty that defied tides, gravity, and architectural logic. A dozen tourists ate, drank, and yelled conversation at one another. A pretty gum-chewing white girl wearing no bra and a T-shirt that said "This Side Up" showed me to my table. I ate conch salad, broiled grouper, peas and rice, coleslaw, coconut pie with coconut ice cream. Aunty Tam, a hundred pounds heavier than I remembered, spent the evening behind the cash register, drinking from a rose teacup. When I paid my bill, our eyes met for a long moment, she gave me a face-full of rummy breath, and showed no sign of recognition. As Heraclitus said, you can't step in the same swamp twice.

9

NEXT MORNING, I paid my dockage, started the twin diesels, and motored out the harbor channel. A white four-by-four foot plywood hand-scrawled sign said 5 MPH. In the old days, when you sculled or sailed or had an old British Seagull outboard or a three-horse air-cooled inboard, you never got much more than three or four knots. Now they had boats with two-hundred horse outboards on the stern that could go from Salt Harbor to Faithful Harbor in the time it used to take to bail your dinghy.

The channel made a right angle turn, then another one. I faced east now, the rising sun in my eyes, the water's surface a wrinkled mirror of red-gold light. In the old days, if you couldn't see the bottom you had trouble. Now, you saw white stakes on each side of the channel. You didn't even have to know your way around.

I cruised east for about quarter an hour, then turned south, taking a shortcut across Old Tay's Bank. Here, you lined up the end of Leeward Cay with the Bird Rock, and if you kept them in line you stayed in water deep enough to take you across the bank if you had at least half tide. You used to, anyway. If the banks hadn't shifted too much, perhaps I'd make it.

As I stood at the wheel, I ruminated on how Non-A thinkers take into account that the entire world, like shifting sand banks, undergoes constant change. Non-A thinkers accept change as part of their method of thought. They employ certain techniques to remind them of the uniqueness in space-time of all things or events — giving each a mental date or an index number, for example. But what had I done since I'd arrived? I'd ranted and railed to myself because of changes: a creek filled in, new buildings, dredged channels, a new road, a truck, a lost beach. If I wanted to keep my sanity, I should start putting some of my Non-A theory into practice and include the changes I observed in a revised mental map, instead of wishing the territory had stayed the way my precious nostalgia said it should.

I anchored for lunch just off Dirt Point, noticeable for its stand of casuarina trees and long white beach. Here a line of coral heads runs some two hundred yards out into the sound, so you have to keep well offshore.

By my reckoning, the tide had ebbed for about an hour. I'd reach Treacherous Bank at about 2 p.m. with the tide about half down and falling. I'd have to take the long way round.

I ate a sandwich made with tuna from a can. The charter outfit had stocked *Lolita* with a week's worth of food for four. Oddly enough, the sandwich tasted great. I took some snapper from the freezer to thaw, climbed back on deck, munched my food and drank a Harp as I watched a dark thunderhead cloud growing in the sky far to the south, sending its big black anvil high into the sky. I daydreamed of Adelaide sitting in the other fishing chair, drinking her tall milky-looking Pernod, her red hair catching the sun.

Lunch over, I started the diesels, winched up the hook and got underway. Along here the shoreline looks much the same for the many miles. No land rises more than fifty feet above sea level. A string of rocks and small cays stands silhouetted against distant pines of Big Island. As sun or cloud shadows pass over them, the cays stand out or disappear into the background low land. Behind the outer cays and rocks lies a maze of mangrove-lined creeks and tide-swept channels. Back in those uncharted creeks you'll find some of the boiling holes which Crawfish and I had discussed so philosophically.

Dusk had fallen by the time I'd reached Bluebeard's Channel, lined on each side by coral reefs. I could not risk crossing between those reefs in a low light, so I anchored a few hundred yards offshore. The wind had died, once again leaving the water like glass. My position would put me on a lee shore if a summer squall came up from the west, but it looked like a clear night in store. The thunderhead had moved south and dissipated. I set the anchor by reversing back on it, cut the engines, went below, and lit the alcohol stove in the little galley. I'd chosen a boat with an alcohol stove in preference to one with a propane stove because of leaking propane's propensity to sink into the bilge, turning your pleasure craft into a small bomb. I'd once seen a boat explode and I didn't want to see another, especially as a participant observer.

I sat in the cockpit, eating fried gray snapper and boiled white grits, watching darkness fall over the silver water. I drank Bushmills and soda, and tried to figure out a few things.

A G.S. detective would treat his conclusions as hypotheses, not facts. Such a method can help you, if you have some observations to evaluate. I had little to go on. I'd made unacknowledged assumptions all down the line. I should at least have recognized some of those assumptions as assumptions.

In San Francisco, Spooks had told me his daughter Esme had gone missing. Assumption: Spooks had reported to me honestly. Could he have had some other motive for getting me to the islands? Assumption: Esme would have called Spooks if she could, because in the past she usually has. Assumption built on that assumption: she hasn't phoned, therefore something bad has happened to her. Assumption: Esme, who I hadn't seen for three years, still fitted the idealized picture I had of her as my "Little Esme," who called me Uncle Murph, and when she fell off her tricycle usually stopped crying if I bought her ice cream. Observation: the last time I saw Esme, then aged 27, after our lunch at Fisherman's Wharf she'd driven away in a fast car worth some forty grand. She'd had the sniffles, hay fever, she'd said. Although we'd dined indoors, she hadn't removed her sunglasses.

On these assumptions, and for certain obligations I have to Spooks, and for other personal reasons, I have traveled from California to the Caribbean in search of the missing woman. I have gathered two other pieces of "evidence." I observed the records of a boat charter company which says that a person who bears the same initials as Esme — E. L. — chartered one of their sloops. I have no reason at this time to believe that the boat owner lied to me or faked his records. Observation three, a para-observation, the hearing of a verbal report: the boat owner has told me his sloop sank and that the locals have decided that both those aboard drowned although they found only one body.

I must not treat assumptions, mine or other people's, as fact. I must remember the percentage-of-probability rule. So

far, I've seen no bodies and no wreck. In the morning, I'll lo-
cate the wreck, if it exists, dive down and investigate. Mean-
while, I can do nothing.

What had Esme done? I kept having the feeling that she'd
got involved in criminal activities because she needed
money. But my old pictures of her wouldn't let me confront
this idea. In my search for answers, why hadn't I used the
general semantics technique of dating? Using this method,
you put dates to your data. You do this because the external
world changes continually, but your inner world of descriptions and evaluations tends to get stuck in the past. Esme
1974 certainly did not equal Esme 1994. Why couldn't I get
my bogged down evaluational-system to stop perceiving
Esme as a permanent child?

In the cold fog of many a San Francisco night I'd longed for
another evening anchored out in this very sound, miles from
civilization, enjoying the water's tranquility and the deep
peace. Tonight the beauty of stars over quiet water brings
me little peace, but the whiskey helps me live with the disap-
pointment.

10

I N THE MORNING, I shaved my face while standing in the cockpit in front of a little mirror I'd leaned against a fishing chair, savoring the feel of breeze on my torso. I looked at the other fishing chair and imagined a bikini clad Adelaide sitting in it, her sleek black hair catching the morning sun. Assuming she had sleek black hair this week. I pondered shaving my cranium again, then decided not to bother. The disguise had failed, but at least I'd had the satisfaction of seeing my brother look sick when I'd told him that lie about chemotherapy in the family.

I ate a light breakfast of stone-oven white bread and tea sweetened with condensed milk, as I watched the sun emerge from the horizon between Quarter and Hunchback Cays. A light west wind gave the water enough ripple to break the mirror surface and let you see the bottom, unless you looked into the sun. The day before yesterday I'd entered Faithful Harbor at low tide at about 4 p.m. Today the low would occur at about 6 p.m., with a high some six hours earlier, at about noon.

I tried to get the local marine operator on the ship-to-shore but gave up after about five minutes. Not that Adelaide worried about such insignificant things as why I hadn't called. I started the diesels, hauled up the anchor and headed south through Bluebeard's Channel, hugging the eastern side until I got halfway through, then I turned forty-five degrees to starboard until I'd come up close to the western shore, where I resumed a course of 180 degrees.

I followed Crawford's directions: go northeast across Yellow Bank until you've lined up the notch in Death Rock with the lone casuarina on Loveless Cay, then turn 80 degrees to starboard, to head towards Loveless Cay. I approached the shore cautiously looking for the clues that would indicate Love Reef. Looking southwest, you line up three rocks off the eastern edge of Turtle Cay. To the northwest, you line up the tall coconut tree on Bad Rock with the Sugarloaf Hill on the Big Island.

Creeping forward at dead throttle, I strained my eyes for a sign of the wrecked craft that had allegedly taken the lives of two people, perhaps three. I kept a hundred yards offshore so the reef wouldn't lie to my east where I couldn't see it because of morning sun on the water. I knew this area well because as a kid I'd once spent a night listening to this same reef pound a hole in our old wooden tub, the *Testament*.

Then I saw a small post slanting up out of the water, the *Salty Dove's* mast, if I'd navigated right.

I cruised slowly by the mast, keeping it to starboard, as I leaned out and looked down. From below came a murky watery image of an elongated white something, probably a white hull. The wreck did not lie on the reef as I'd expected. She lay half her length to the west on sea-grass covered mud bottom. A light breeze now came from the east, making a light chop only a few inches high. I turned *Lolita* into the wind, reversed the engines, dropped anchor with the cockpit winch switch when she began to move sternwards, set the anchor, and shut off engines. I left the helm and scurried forward along the narrow starboard side-deck. From the bow, with the sun in the east, I couldn't see anything of the wreck below water because of the reflected sky.

I decided not to wear a wet suit because I hate that claustrophobic feeling. On deck, I changed into swimming trunks, then put on air tank, canvas and lead weight belt, fins, and shark knife. I spit in my face mask to keep it from fogging, rinsed the mask in a bucket of sea water and put it on, shoved my snorkel under the mask's strap, turned on my air, grabbed my waterproof flashlight, bit down on my mouthpiece, and jumped overboard.

When you go under, you enter another world. The water in your ears makes both a noise and a silence. Over the reefs, the beauty shocks you, no matter how many times you've dived there. Below, you see pink brain coral and golden antler coral; bright purple and yellow finger coral next to lumpy coral of soft earth colors. You swim down until you float at eye level with coral that looks like sponges and sponges that look like cactus. Purple sea fans sway in the residual swell. A green moray eel peers out of a crevice, opens its mouth and gulps at you, and you backpaddle away fast. Schools of schoolmaster, porgy, and pilchard sway in unison. A three-foot red-brown grouper turns sideways and shows you one large eye.

When I stopped swimming, I sank to the bottom. My weight belt had too many weights on it. This belt had two kinds of weights, eight removable weights secured with buckles, and a number of other weights sewn into canvas pockets. I unbuckled and jettisoned weights until I had achieved neutral buoyancy. I told myself to remember to retrieve the weights when I returned.

The sloop lay on her port side, her bow facing me as I approached. Swimming over the hull, I peered down, observing details: a single cabin forward of a small cockpit, chrome throttle and clutch controls mounted on the aft cockpit wall, a long wooden tiller. A small domed barbecue still remained attached to bracket on the transom. Sails, ropes, anchors, winches, halyards, running lights, in fact almost everything removable except the barbecue, had gone. The aluminum mast remained, but the boom had disappeared.

I swam on beyond her stern and dove to look at the transom. Four empty screw holes in the white fiberglass suggested that somebody had removed the name plate. My heart started pounding anyway. I reached out, grabbed a life-rail and pulled myself along it hand over hand. Down in the cockpit, the engine hatch had gone and somebody had hacked away part of the cockpit deck, probably to remove the engine.

I swam to the main hatch and peered in. Grasping the hatch combing, I pulled myself down into the dim interior. Filled with water instead of air, the cabin seemed an eerie place now. Here, gravity didn't exist for me as I hovered over the galley table and looked around. The rush of my own breathing and the sudden clank of my air tank hitting a beam made the loudest noise for miles.

Scavengers had also ransacked the cabin: locker doors ripped off, floorboards torn up, a wall mirror smashed, the companionway ladder gone, but mattresses and sheets still there.

Looking around, I suddenly heard a different noise, the clanging of my assumption alarm, an imaginary bell but nev-

ertheless loud inside my head. Assumption: the locals had
plundered the interior of this craft. Had Esme and her unknown partner done the damage? Had someone torn the
interior apart looking for something? Had another party entered the equation, perhaps modern pirates who'd stripped
the craft before scuttling it? I'd heard reports of hijackings at
sea recently, and of unsuspecting tourists accidentally sailing
into a drug drop, and paying the price.

I turned and looked aft, through the opening once covered
by the companionway ladder, at the space once occupied by
the craft's auxiliary engine. The aft half of a bronze and rubber propshaft coupling stared back at me. Somebody had
undone the mounting bolts, disconnected the coupling, the
fuel line and the wiring and taken away the engine. These
sloops usually carried a thirty- or forty-horsepower four-
cylinder marine gasoline engine...worth a few dollars if you
washed it out with freshwater then diesel fuel.

I turned back toward the cabin interior. Some rolled charts
remained in an overhead rack under the cabin roof. A varnished mahogany shelf on a port forward bulkhead held a
few books: *The Yachtsman's Guide to the Caribbean, The British
Colonial Shopper's Guide, The AAA Road Atlas of the USA, The
Chrysler Marine Engine Repair Manual*, and a Gideon Bible. I
pulled out the publications and opened them one by one,
hoping to find documents that might tell me something...air
tickets, a diary or log, a passport, whatever, but found nothing that seemed significant. The pages waved lazily in the
water as the books sank slowly to the cabin floor.

I peered into a locker under the two-burner stainless steel
propane stove. Strangely, the stove remained. The locker
contained canned bacon, tuna, oysters, string beans, sauer-
kraut, caviar, liver pate, corn, salted Spanish peanuts. The
top-opening refrigerator had no lid; presumably it had
floated away. Inside, I found containers of once-frozen peas,
corn, cauliflower, strawberries, ice cream, and chocolate cake;
cans of cola and ginger ale, and some shreds of plastic wrap
that once might have contained frozen meat. The sharks or
barracuda had no doubt eaten the meat. Styrofoam packag-
ing had floated up to trap itself under the cabin roof beside
an empty bottle labeled Bacardi Rum. Looking forward, I

saw more floating things caught between the cabin-top beams: a yellow pencil, a red plastic float with an ignition key on it, an orange life jacket, a plastic cola bottle.

I swam slowly forward, into a small passageway between the head to port and a small hanging locker to starboard, paused, opened the head door and pulled myself half inside. A roll of swollen pink toilet paper remained on its hanger, its tail-end swaying in the water's ebb and flow. When I opened the medicine cabinet a bottle floated out and up. Inside, I saw aspirin, toothpaste, two toothbrushes, waxed cinnamon-flavored dental floss, contact lens cleaner, seasick pills, a red plastic hair curler, Vaseline, sun block, a bottle of Grecian Formula, two disposable razors. Trying to float upwards, the air-filled containers hugged the underside of the cabinet's shelves.

I backed out of the cramped head, grabbed one of the remaining floorboards, and pulled myself down to examine a hole in the bilge. White gashes showed through the oil-stained fiberglass, gashes that looked like marks left by an axe. Had something made the hole from the *inside*? A hole from a reef outside should have pushed the hull skin inward.

I swam further forward, pulled back the door to the fore-peak, and stared into the jaws of a huge grouper. The big fish hung motionless, like a gigantic galactic battleship. Only its mouth and gills moved. Then it swam regally up and out the forward hatch. After a moment to calm myself, I examined the forepeak.

One of the bunks had sheets tucked in neatly all round. Overhead, some objects floated against the underside of the foredeck, trapped between the beams: a blue can labeled Coffee, a tennis ball, a champagne cork, a plastic zip bag containing folded paper. As I grabbed for the bag, the stirred up water pushed it away from me. I reached out slowly, grasped the bag, and brought it close for inspection. The folded paper had no writing or printing on the visible surfaces. I went to open the bag, then thought better of it, and pushed it into my trunks.

I yanked open a drawer under the port berth and poked through the waterlogged contents: men's socks, skinny briefs, trunks, T-shirts, a single rubber sandal, a condom. The thought of Esme and an unknown man made me angry. What had I expected to find, a hymn book? Would I never let her grow up in my mind?

I twisted round, my air tank clanging against a beam, opened the starboard drawer and found woman's boating shoes, panties, shorts, a bikini top, two limp postcards of tropical palm and sea scenes. Released from the drawer, two small plastic bottles floated up. I pulled out shirts, jeans, a belt, sunglasses. A rigging knife fell in slow motion from one of the jeans and I caught it. I examined the knife miserably. The stainless-steel handle had some words on it: "My Favorite Sailor." I recognized the words without really reading them owing to the fact that I'd paid for the engraving.

11

I REACHED UP, grabbed the hatch combing, and hauled myself up and out of there. Kicking violently, I shot to the surface. I dove again and circled round the wreck as fast as I could swim, my breath coming in big rasping gasps. I didn't know what the hell I wanted, I just kept swimming....

When you don't know what to do, go in circles.

I didn't know what I expected to find but I found something: a rut in the seabed heading off into the distance.

It looked as if the yacht had dragged her keel, cutting through the sea grass to expose the white oolitic mud beneath. I dove and examined the groove closely. It looked like a keel mark, but not from this sloop. It stopped some ten feet from the *Salty Dove's* keel. And it looked too wide. Had some sort of wide keel from another craft done this?

At high tide, the water by the wreck had a depth of some twelve feet. Even at a dead low spring tide, most of the yachts that cruised these banks didn't draw enough to run aground here.

I followed the rut a short distance, then surfaced. I saw that if it continued in the same direction, the rut would go between two small cays and into the maze of mangroves, backwaters, and boiling holes of Boiling Creek.

I used to go fishing in these creeks. With the ebb tide you can get bonefish. Or you can drop a line into those virtually bottomless boiling holes and catch grouper, snapper, and barracuda. I used to dive down and spear fish in the boiling holes, but I never much cared for it, and I stopped after I heard a tourist got himself drowned down there. Some said the ebbing tide sucked him down. Others said he'd used contaminated air from a gasoline-powered compressor with an air intake beside the exhaust pipe.

I swam along the surface for a while so I could observe the direction of the rut in relation to the nearby land. As I'd expected, the rut went between the two cays and into Boiling Creek. Passing between the cays, I found no current in either direction. High tide had peaked, or soon would. I looked at my watch, which said eleven ten, but it didn't mean a lot.

Back in the creeks, nature's tides don't always follow the tide tables the way they should.

The rut took a right turn and followed a channel some fifty yards wide between the outlying cays and a row of high mangroves. It looked a bit like the groove a dragging anchor makes, but that didn't make any sense. The seabed remained covered in short sea grass. Here and there I saw a conch or a starfish. I passed a huge mound of empty conch shells, dark with age at the bottom, fresh pink at the top. I surfaced and looked toward the shore of a nearby barrier cay. Surrounded by weeds, a thatched-roof driftwood hut sat decaying under a grove of tall coconut trees. The crisscrossed sticks of a fish-drying rack held no salted fish. The sand beach showed no sign of footprints or a dinghy's keel.

It seemed as if, once I'd stopped swimming, the current had carried me backwards. I swam on, looking for something, I didn't know what. A G.S. detective thinks in terms of ranges of accuracy of the information he has obtained. He doesn't say just right-wrong, true-untrue. But what the hell did I have in the way of info? I kicked up my feet and dove. The trail continued ahead of me along the sea floor. I still couldn't decide what had caused it, a wide-keeled craft? a dragging anchor? the Lock Ness monster? or something completely different?

After a while, I returned to the surface, and took visual bearings by lining up a distant casuarina tree with a notch in the nearby mangroves. As I treaded water, the casuarina moved out of sight behind the mangroves. Yes, the tide had begun to ebb. I put my face down and swam on. A mango floated by.

When you don't know what you look for, how do you know when you've found it?

You follow the keel mark, or rut from a dragged object, or whatever. You keep swimming. When you look up at the surface from down below, it looks like wrinkled, silver foil. A small patch of uprooted dead sea grass hangs suspended just below surface level, swaying slightly.

She loved fruit, did Esmerelda.

To my left, the dark disk of a boiling hole came into view. I swam to the hole and looked down. The blackness down

there gives me the creeps, water so deep you can't see bottom, even in the crystal clear waters of the islands. Down
there you'll find hungry sharks eying hungry barracudas and
licking their lips.

I turned, swam back to the rut, and continued following it.
Three stingrays overtook me silently on my right, cruising in
formation like stealth bombers.

Ahead in the murk I saw a black blur, another boiling hole.
A ray of sunlight penetrated a little way down into the blackness, illuminating tiny floating things like dust in a sunbeam.
The rut went up to the edge of this boiling hole. I swam
across, expecting to pick up the trail on the other side. The
grassy bottom on the far side of the boiling holes showed no
sign of disturbance. No rut or keel mark. Nothing.

Had the boat waited here until high tide, and then moved
out without touching bottom?

It didn't make sense.

The depth had changed from about twelve feet where the
keel mark had started, to about six feet here by the boiling
hole. Yet the keel mark had gone steadily on, no matter
what the depth. Why had I inferred from this evidence that
a boat had dragged its keel into Boiling Creek? What had
actually happened?

Why would anyone deliberately drag their anchor along
this route? A storm would drag an anchor erratically. Aside
from one turn upon entering the creeks, this rut went in a
relatively straight line. Could someone have dragged a
heavy object? A mooring? Or the motor that someone had
taken from the *Salty Dove*?

I dove down a few feet into the boiling hole. The thought
of going deeper made my heart pound. A beam of sunlight
illuminated small organisms in the water like motes of dust.
The swirling specks moved slowly downward. The tide had
definitely begun to fall, pulling water down into the boiling
hole. The column of water descended slowly now, but it
would pick up speed as the minutes went by.

I knew I had to go down into that dark hole. And quickly.
Before the current made such a powerful downdraft I
couldn't get back out.

How else could I find out what somebody had hidden down there?

Looking down, I could see nothing but dark water. My heart still thumped in my ears. With an effort, I slowed my breathing. I kicked my feet up and dove down another fathom. Here the gloom only presaged the gloom to come. That weakening shaft of sunlight still dimly illuminated numerous small organisms in the water. As I descended, I looked back up occasionally, to see the faint disk of sunlight above me grow smaller and weaker. From deep down in the murk, something floated past me, momentarily catching the beam of my underwater flashlight, an ovoid thing, orange in color, covered in black spots — an overripe mango.

I stopped moving my arms and legs, but continued to descend. A white shape came toward me and I grabbed it as it went by, shone my light and saw a gallon plastic bottle. Somebody had tied a quarter-inch rope to the handle. I'd found an air-filled bleach bottle unable to float to the surface because of a rope that dropped down into the depths. The buoyancy of the bottle kept me from sinking further. I tugged experimentally but the rope wouldn't give.

I'd discovered an underwater buoy. Not a bad way to mark something you don't want people to find. On the surface, you take some shore bearings so you can find the right boiling hole again. You stash your treasure and hide your marker under water. Except you don't think that some over-curious idiot like me might follow the drag marks you've left behind in the sea bed.

A five-foot nurse shark cruised by but I ignored it. Nurse sharks have no teeth, they say.

I let go the bottle and pulled myself down the rope, my light flashing its beam wildly on the jagged rocky sides of the boiling hole as I fumbled with the rope. The downdraft had picked up speed, so I didn't have to pull very hard. Soon, I'd have to wait for a rising tide, a mere six hours or so, assuming I wanted to get back up to the surface.

I had enough air for about thirty minutes.

The water got darker and murkier as I descended. Too bad I hadn't worn a depth gauge. Down here, you can black out, or just panic. Or you start acting looney, take out your mouthpiece, and feed your air to the nearest grouper.

Something light-colored below me caught the beam of my flashlight, offering a meager brightness in the gloom. I pulled myself further down and hovered above a patch of white sand. I'd actually reached the bottom of this boiling hole. Circling, I saw that the rope went off to one side, into a little cave.

The current pulled me against the side of the cave and I spread my legs to keep from going in.

I shone my light into the cave.

I found them there, two figures in wet suits, with air tanks, fins, and weighted belts.

A knife-handle protruded from the stomach of the male. The female seemed unscathed, except her airline ended in a jagged cut and her mouthpiece and regulator had disappeared.

She held the male's mouthpiece in her hand.

Both figures had their arms and legs tangled in the braided nylon rope I'd followed to reach the scene. The female had a net bag tied to one wrist, floating upward at a slant, the flotation provided by an air-filled sandwich bag and one rotting mango.

12

O N THE CAVE'S FLOOR lay an aluminum chest. I eased into the
cave and tied a lanyard from my belt to the chest to keep
the current from dragging me off. Floundering, I opened the
chest. It contained some bundles of hundred dollar bills, a
plastic bag of white powder, and a small jade dragon.

I'd seen the dragon before.

A rubbery thing brushed my shoulder, a hand belonging to
the female corpse. I turned to the corpse and lifted up the
face mask. My niece or cousin once removed Esmerelda Logan had looked much prettier alive. I put the mask back
carefully.

My insides felt dead, cold, hot, miserable, and angry all at
once.

Some bastard would pay for this.

I turned to the chest again, grabbed the jade dragon, and
examined it with my flashlight. Yes, somebody had broken
off the right rear leg — me — long ago, when I'd dropped the
dragon on Franklin's imported tile floor after drinking too
much of his expensive French wine.

My dear brother Franklin had taken great pride in his jade
collection, but he wouldn't enjoy seeing this particular piece
again.

I'd get Franklin for this.

I shut the chest, laughing aloud, inadvertently spitting out
my mouthpiece. I'd show that sanctimonious hypocritical,
holier-than-thou, do-gooding bastard brother of mine. I now
had proof of his link with drug dealing, and I'd drag him off
his high perch with it. Even if they didn't send him to jail, a
prosecution would destroy his good name, and his antiseptic
wife would leave him because of the scandal.

I inserted my mouthpiece back between my lips and took a
slow careful breath.

Why had someone put that jade dragon in there? Esmerelda, for insurance, perhaps.

I opened the chest again. The plastic bag of white stuff
drifted out and I grabbed it, shoved it under an elastic strap
in the trunk's lid. I took out a bundle of money and ex-

amined it with my flashlight. The brown paper band around this stack of one hundred U.S. dollar bills bore the name Bilkeys' Bank, the bank that employed Franklin. I let go the bundle and the current carried it away. I lifted out another and saw something yellow underneath. I clawed out more bundles, letting them drift away, revealing what lay underneath — a layer of yellow metal rectangles. I pried one out with my fingers and held up it to my mask. The gold brick felt heavy, even under water. Now I knew why that chest had dragged such a deep rut in the mud.

Gold has its advantages. You can trace money if somebody recorded the serial numbers, but gold you can melt down. People kill for gold, of course. It gives some humans a certain fever.

Somebody's drug deal had gone wrong, I thought, and my inference alarm went off again. Drug dealing, bank robbing, money laundering, embezzling — I didn't know what had happened, I only knew what I'd found.

With my shark knife, I cut open one of the pockets in my canvas weight belt, no easy task with the current tugging at me and my flashlight shaking all over the place. I pulled a lead weight from its pocket in the canvas belt and dropped it on the seabed. I picked up one gold brick and shoved it into the canvas pocket in place of the lead weight.

I could think of no way of getting the heavy chest up out of the boiling hole without hoisting equipment.

I kept my back to the corpses. It wouldn't do Esme any good for me to look at her now.

I put Franklin's jade dragon back in the chest. The police would find it there when I sent them back here. Let them make an inference about that and then call it a fact.

I untied my safety lanyard and hauled myself out of the cave. The water pushed hard against me, trying to force me back in. Could I make it to the surface against this powerful descending tide? Did I have enough air left? I sidled along to a piece of vertical wall, put my back against it and my feet on the bottom. Sharp rock cut my fingers where I gripped the coral encrusted wall. I watched blood floating downward in the tidal stream and reflected on how they say blood attracts hungry sharks. I bent my knees, kicked off the bottom and swam hard. I found I could just make slow vertical headway against the current. The effort made me breathe fast, using up more air.

Occasionally I stopped swimming and clung to small out-croppings on the walls of the boiling hole. As I moved slowly toward the surface, my air felt thinner and thinner. I tried climbing up the rock wall, but the resulting lacerations in my hands made me return to swimming. Eventually it occurred to me to jettison some of my lead weights. With bleeding fingers, I unbuckled the removable leads on my weight belt and let them drop. I kept the belt in order to continue carry-ing the gold brick.

Above me, the disk of light began to brighten.

As the hole widened, the downward current seemed to lessen. Why hadn't I thought to use that air-filled plastic bleach bottle for buoyancy? I turned on my reserve air and swam on, feeling increasingly dizzy and increasingly distant from it all.

I broke through the surface, spit out my mouthpiece and gasped real air. I swam slowly to a little beach and lay in the shallow water while my breathing slowly returned to nor-mal. When I eventually took a pull at my mouthpiece, I couldn't get any air; it had all run out.

When I'd got my strength back, I swam back to the *Lolita* on the surface, breathing through my snorkel.

When I reached the *Lolita* I realized I'd forgotten to hang the boarding ladder over the side. I had to doff my scuba equipment, haul myself aboard by way of the anchor line, then dive down and retrieve my gear from the bottom.

Back aboard the *Lolita*, I changed into shorts and T-shirt, started the diesels, winched up the anchor, and headed back to Salt Harbor at full throttle, relishing my forthcoming talk with the local law.

My imagination went into overtime, visualizing Franklin in court, the judge in British white wig handing down a twenty-year sentence, Franklin sitting in a hot tropical jail. The scan-dal would hurt him more than the jail, of course. People wouldn't go to his church anymore.

Yes, I had something to look forward to.

13

T HEY'D BUILT A NEW POLICE STATION in the usual British Colonial style: pink stuccoed concrete block with white toothing stones, green shutters, a white hurricane roof. I went in and asked for Inspector Moxley.

"He done retired," said the constable, a tall young man in white helmet, white tunic, and black trousers.

"Oh," I said in my usual crisp witty style.

"Can I help you, Sir?"

"Ah...no. Just a social call. Just visiting."

I hurried out, got in my taxi, and rode back to the marina. I should have asked for the current man in charge, but I didn't.

I spent one last night on the *Lolita*. I ate canned beans, drank Bushmills and soda, and watched the sunset. I didn't go ashore to the Marina restaurant for a meal, I didn't go to the bar to socialize. In the morning, I walked over to the dive shop, bought one small sail-repair kit and two canvas diving belts similar to the belt I'd rented from Charlie Crawfish.

I gave a kid at the dive shop fifty bucks to take the scuba equipment I'd rented back to Crawford at Faithful Harbor. He agreed to come and get the stuff in a couple of hours.

Aboard *Lolita*, I began work cutting and sewing on the weight belts. I cut some weights out of one belt I'd just bought and used them to replace the weights I'd jettisoned from the belt I'd rented from Charlie Crawford. Shortly after I'd finished, the kid came out on the dock to collect Charlie's gear.

I sat at the galley table with the other new weight belt in front of me and carefully unpicked the stitches of one pocket. I removed the lead weight, put the gold brick in its place and sewed it in, using the same needle holes. It took a while, but I did a reasonably neat job. The gold brick fitted somewhat loosely in its pocket. I hoped nobody would have reason to notice that.

14

I GOT AN AFTERNOON FLIGHT TO MIAMI and a midnight flight to San Francisco. On the plane I drew a map in my notebook showing the location of the boiling hole where I'd found the bodies. I wrote down how I'd discovered the bleach bottle tethered several fathoms under, how I'd followed the rope down into the deep hole to the bodies, the aluminium chest containing paper money, gold bricks, a plastic bag of white stuff, and a jade Chinese dragon with a missing right hind leg. I decided I'd mail the incriminating details to the Salt Harbor police. I'd nail that hypocritical brother of mine.

I put away my notes, sipped whiskey and soda, closed my eyes, and tried not to think. My mind kept going round and round, thinking of the pleasure and the pain of sweet revenge.

My mind wouldn't stop.

The G.S. thinker acknowledges that a person has more than one *value-cum-evaluational* system. Such systems sometimes conflict with one another, causing all sorts of pain, anguish, and general confusion. In that sense, I had more than one *me*. Among all the *me-s* competing for attention, two threw the meanest punches: from one corner of the ring came the one-way *me*, the either-or, yes-no, for me or against me, no alternatives *me*; from the other corner came another *me*, the multi-choice *me*, the seeker of multiple possibilities, methods, responses, and alternatives. No medication can cure you when these two guys start slugging it out. You yourself, you the referee, the meta-*me*, the guy who overhears and oversees the conversations you have with yourself, this poor mug has to make the decision of the day.

Revenge tastes sweet. I'd bring that sanctimonious, holier-than-thou, well-to-do brother of mine down from his lofty perch. I'd expose his dirty dealings and he'd never stand in his village pulpit again. Nobody loved vicious gossip better than the saved sinners of Salt Harbor. They'd ostracize Franklin and his wife. They wouldn't speak to him in the street, and in the small shops they'd refuse to serve him. A few faithful would keep going to his little church. Most would not. And a secondary war would break out between the faithful Franklin supporters and the heathen who'd turned aside when their god had fallen. Sweet revenge, the great leveler.

Except the one-way *me* and the multi-choice *me* couldn't stop arguing.

To some degree, going beyond Aristotle's law of the excluded middle had helped me accept my multiple *me-s*. I didn't *have* to have a hundred percent consistency in my feelings, thoughts, or behavior. I could change my demands to preferences, most of the time. And this time, I sure needed to modify my demands on myself because my demands said revenge, revenge, revenge... I sure as hell didn't want to modify anything. Screw reason, let extreme revenge take its nutri-sweet course.

In fantasy, hurting my brother seemed just great.

When I thought of actually hurting him, it made *me* hurt. One of the *me-s* inside me could feel the tears struggling to get out. It seemed as if the years and the adult betrayals didn't matter when compared to two scared kids on a leaky boat protecting each other from the sea and a reckless landlubber missionary-mad father who relied on God instead of charts to show him a course between the reefs.

I had no proof my brother had had anything to do with these events, I only had a memory of a jade dragon with a missing leg. I only had the inferences *I* had made that connected the two. I had no proof of a drug deal, I only had a new memory of corpses and a chest full of various stuff. I had no proof, only my own inferences. I had no proof that Spooks' daughter Esmerelda had died because of her involvement in dealing substances prohibited by most governments. I only had a grisly memory of her water-swollen face.

Spooks hated drugs because drugs had taken the mother of his only child. It would hurt Spooks if he heard from me what I thought constituted some sort of representation of reality about his daughter Esmerelda. He'd take it to heart. He might even decide it constituted some sort of truth.

Screw Spooks.

If I hurt Franklin, I'd hurt Spooks.

Screw Franklin.

The only way to keep Spooks from finding out lay in the unacceptable possibility of not sending Franklin to the justice he deserved. Or would they get Franklin anyway? Whoever had bankrolled that abortive business would come looking for somebody.

After a sufficient quantity of airline miniatures, I dozed a fitful half-sleep filled with tortured dreams — the islands, the turquoise water, a mango floating by, an older brother wrapping a rope under the kid's arms to save him from the ebbing tide....

Slowly, they haul themselves hand-over-hand against the current. They climb back aboard the cabin cruiser and collapse on the hot deck. The kid gasps: "You could have drowned, Franklin. You saved my life." Franklin grins. "Sure, kid. Save mine one day, okay?"

I woke up with a start and heard the stewardess say we'd just begun our descent for San Francisco. My fuzzy mind kept thinking how I'd prided myself that Morgan Murphy always paid his debts.

I landed at SFO and walked the long concourse past the weird sculpture and the shops selling San Francisco sourdough, carrying my hand luggage, my weight belt slung over my shoulder. Eventually, I found a taxi to take me home.

My apartment welcomed me with its familiar though not necessarily desirable medley of stenches: the sour effluvium of damp carpet and unwashed laundry; the vile stink of un-emptied garbage; the almost tangible essence of cat urine from the ancient sofa which had once lived in a cat-inhabited residence; the acrid smell of ancient charcoaled food that encrusted various parts of my kitchen stove.

I dropped my baggage on the kitchen's curling lino and sighed wearily as olfactory, tactile, and visual sensory impulses congealed in my tired brain which then compiled the hallowed abstraction — *home.*

I opened the sacrosanct cold white box called *refrigerator* and took out a bottle of sacred fluid called *beer.* I pried off the cap and poured a glass of clear, yellow ale. I sat at the 1950s formica-and-chrome kitchen-nook table, drank the holy brew, dripped beer on my yellow legal pad, chewed on a yellow 2B pencil, and continued writing notes for The Case Of The Missing Niece. Through the window, the Golden Gate Bridge gave its impersonation of permanence, much as did the hanging gardens of Babylon in their day. Below the golden-red span, some white-sailed yachts gave their impression of impermanence. After twenty minutes of pencil chewing, I shoved the notes in my pocket. I grabbed the San Francisco yellow pages and browsed, looking for a place to take a jewelry-making class — gold jewelry, where you learn to melt gold down and cast things.

I cooked a breakfast of scrambled eggs and toast. I didn't call Spooks. I didn't call Adelaide. I didn't play back the messages on my phone answering machine. I circumnavigated my FAX and its accumulation of limp paper on the floor, found the location of my bedroom, and crawled wearily into bed.

15

I WOKE UP IN THE LATE AFTERNOON to a persistent ringing of my doorbell, plodded down, and let Spooks in. Theoretically, I'd slept.

"You look like hell," gasped Spooks as we climbed the steep stairs.

"Thanks."

"What'd you find out?"

"Want a beer?"

"You offer me a beer when I got the most important thing in my life on my mind," yelled Spooks as he followed me into the kitchen. "Why didn't you call me? When'd you get back? You went to find my daughter, remember? Didn't you do nothing but drink planters punch and skinny dip? Didn't you find her? She died, didn't she. I know it. She drowned, didn't she? Her, who could sail better than Captain Cook, drowned because of drugs and stuff."

"Wait a minute, Spooks."

"What you mean wait? Give me the bad news."

"Okay."

Spooks sat suddenly on a creaking chrome-and-vinyl chair, looking like a man who just ate poison. His bulbous face turned pale and the sweat shone all over it and down his no-neck neck so he looked like a lumpy yellow squash somebody at the supermarket had just sprayed down.

"I can take it," he said hoarsely.

"I couldn't tell you on the phone," I said. "Man, I hate this. She died, Spooks."

"I knew she died. I knew it. Didn't I tell you? I knew she died. But how? Where? What happened? I can't believe this, Morphus. Tell me, man, tell me I got it wrong."

"Some kind of bad deal."

Spooks sagged even more. His breathing had stopped. "Deal?"

"Bad choice of words," I blurted. "I mean a bad bargain. Fate dealt her a bad hand. She drowned. They had a local storm. Summer squall. Worst of the century. A bad wind

blows nobody good.   They wrecked their chartered sloop.
She and this guy."
    "A guy? You think I don't know she had guys? Don't pa-
tronize me, man."
    "Something like that.   They'd registered with the charter
company as coming from Cape Cod, so nobody knew to contact her kin in California. They'd used phony names."
    "Uh-huh."
    Spooks got up, plodded across to a kitchen cupboard,
grabbed my bottle of Bushmills and drank thoughtfully. He
trudged over to the sofa and dropped into it. The force of his
impact sent a volley of sour sofa smell across the room.
    "The bodies, man. What'd they do? I can't believe this. I
mean, they had bodies that they had to do something with."
    "They couldn't find any next of kin."
    "Yeah, yeah."
    "They cremated them."
    Spooks took a long draft of whiskey.
    "It doesn't really matter, does it, Morphus? I mean, what
does it matter what they do with the remains once the life
has gone. She died. So it ends. She gave *me* life, Morphus.
When her mother died, she kept me going. So it ends. My
own Esmerelda. Nothing more to tell."
    "You got to reclaim your life," I said, and wished I hadn't
because it sounded so stupid.
    I turned my back to Spooks, took my notes of the so-called
case from my pocket and dropped them into the garbage dis-
posal.
    "Hey!" yelled Spooks as the garbage grinder roared.
    "Just some junk from the islands," I said casually.
    I sat on the sofa with Spooks, took the bottle from him, and
swallowed a little whiskey. Just to keep him company.
    "Nothing more to tell," repeated Spooks in a punch-drunk
voice.
    "When I found out she'd died, I really wanted to smash
somebody. That won't bring her back, will it Spooks?" I said
slowly.
    "If it would, I'd do it."
    "I wanted to write up some case notes, but I don't see any
point," I added cautiously.

"Why waste the paper? If I believed in anything, I'd light a candle or something. Perhaps I'll do it anyway."

"Can't hurt."

"Man, I feel sorry for myself," mumbled Spooks. He drank again, then turned abruptly toward me, eyes wide. "You had to go through all that garbage. She belonged to you, too, man. You must feel like hell."

"Don't hog the bottle, Spooks."

Spooks handed me the bottle and pondered a while, then he looked at me again and his face looked a little more alive. "Finnigan's does corned beef and cabbage on Thursdays. My treat, okay?"

"They got Guinness back on tap?"

"Since Tuesday."

"Just a couple of pints for the digestion."

"A man's got to look after his digestion."

"Not to mention his stomach."

"I telephoned your Adelaide for you Morphus. I told her where you'd gone."

We went down to the street and I saw the fog had come in, making the street lamps fuzzy, and muffling the bells of the cable cars. I took a deep breath. The San Francisco fog always tastes good when you haven't breathed it for a week or two.

Etc.

There you have it: Part One of an E-Prime mystery. What happens next? Please stay tuned.

— P.D.J.

D. DAVID BOURLAND, JR.   *CHANGING "HUMAN NATURE"* *

1. *Introduction*

I DON'T KNOW WHETHER you folks experienced this — how could I? — but when I grew up in Smalltown, U.S.A., I heard bore after bore saying to one another, "Well, you just can't change human nature." Shaking of heads, in wonderment, out of respect for the presence of one of the eternal verities: "Yup. Thas ri'." They offered this observation as a blazing insight, as an explanation for various distressing happenings, as a semi-sanctimonious explanation for conflicts with the local mores or laws, etc.

Then along came that old tease, Alfred Korzybski, who said, "We *need not* blind ourselves with the old dogma that 'human nature cannot be changed,' for we find that it *can be changed.* We must begin to realize our potentialities as humans, then we may approach the future with some hope. We may feel with Galileo, as he stamped his foot on the ground after recanting the Copernican theory before the Holy Inquisition, '*Eppur si muove!*' The evolution of our human development may be retarded, but it cannot be stopped." (1; p. xxiii)   He repeated that assertion in almost the same words in the conclusion to "What I Believe," reprinted in reference (2; p. lxiii).   In the latter version, however, he added a proviso after his first sentence: "[if we know how]."

2. A Centenary Celebration

A friend and advisor of mine in the Department of Philosophy at the Universidad de Costa Rica, Dr. Luis Camacho Naranjo, invited me to give an address before the (quite small) Philosophical Society of that university in the fall of 1979, which I did. (3) We had just passed the exact date of Korzybski's centenary (on July 3), but I took this occasion for my modest contribution to the celebration of that event. In addition to the usual recitation of the biographical details of his extraordinary life, plus optimistic aspects of past and potential developments of general semantics and the various organizations that support the field, I tried to offer something a little novel.

Despite the obvious importance of the matter of "human nature," *changing* "human nature," and *how* to change it... Korzybski had not collected his views on these issues into one convenient place. So I tried to do so, and to include the fruits of this search in my presentation. The steps involved: (1) Write the material in English; (2) Translate to Spanish; (3) Have typed by bi-lingual secretary who unfortunately knew more English than Spanish, from a philological point of view; (4) Edit, removing obvious goofs;   (5) Have re-typed. I felt reasonably proud of the final version.

When the evening came (why did I get myself into this?), I read from the manuscript, always a thrilling way to present material.   Probably in places the intonation contours conveyed a less-than-complete understanding of some nuances by the reader. At the end, inviting questions, only one professor wanted more information: "What relevance did Korzybski's thought have for the class struggle?" A spirited discussion ensued, at the completion of which we all felt that the others needed some serious counseling, and, as we say in Texas, nobody should try to operate any heavy machinery. Some days later I forwarded a copy of the address to Dr.

Allen Walker Read, who eventually replied that he did not read Spanish.

I have continued to feel that Korzybski's views on the matter of changing "human nature" have some importance; I want to share them with you.

3. How to Do It

I assume that we do not need to belabor the point as to whether we should at least *try* to change what we generally regard as "human nature." At this point please allow me to invite attention to the *quotes* that encase the terms "human" and "nature." This amounts to a serious issue: the *quotes* say, "Watch out! These words belong to the group of high order abstractions that may stimulate very different semantic processes in different people" (due to their multiordinality (1; p. 14)). The material given below includes the results of continuing to reflect on these issues, and hence goes rather beyond that given in reference (3).

Korzybski's suggestions, or directions, or his recipe, for changing "human nature" fall into four general categories: (i) Stop copying animals; (ii) Become conscious of abstracting; (iii) Eliminate identifications in our semantic processes; and (iv) Change the [semantic] structure of our language. Let us take them up one by one.

Stop copying animals. We need to make two main points here. The first consists of Korzybski's time-binding definition of humanity. (2) This will help us to understand more clearly what we have to deal with. In 1921 Alfred Korzybski presented us with what he called a *functional* definition of "humanity," basing it on unique human capabilities, rather than on reasoning which proceeds from, as he put it, either a zoological basis ("an animal plus something") or a mythological basis ("an angel minus something"). (2; p. 86ff)

After first observing that plants combine the minerals, moisture, sunlight, etc., in their immediate environment to make it possible for them to live, Korzybski characterized them as belonging to a *chemistry-binding* class of life. Animals, having an ability to enhance their possibilities of survival by moving about, he allocated to a *space-binding* class of life. Finally, Korzybski recognized the unique ability of humans to act over various periods of time through the use of symbols, and hence he assigned humans to a *time-binding* class of life.

We can readily see the major consequences that result from the time-binding definition of humanity: (i) Important ethical implications stem from the clear-cut dimensional discrimination between animals and humans. (ii) Emphasis becomes focused on the importance of the symbolic means whereby each generation can potentially begin where the preceding one left off, without the need to re-invent every "wheel." These "symbolic means" include speech, writing systems, mathematical, musical, and dance notations, etc. (iii) In order to operate effectively, time-binding requires a high degree of structural correspondence between language processes and the non-language processes described, which Korzybski went on to explore in his subsequent work. (1, 4) The preceding discussion of time-binding came largely from reference (5; p. 2).

The other point we must make here consists of a psychophysiological one, relating to the great complexity and potential of the human cortex, and involving the different degrees of conditionality associated with humans and with animals. Korzybski offered the following "structural observations": "1) That reactions in animals and humans exhibit *different degrees of conditionality;* 2) That the signals and symbols may have *different orders,* indicating superimposition of stimuli; 3) That animals cannot extend their responses to signals of higher order indefinitely; 4) That humans can extend their semantic responses to higher order symbols indefinitely, and in fact, have done so through language which is always connected with *some* response, be it only repression or some other neurotic or psychotic manifestations." (1; p. 333f)

In other words, after some point you may have trouble teaching that dog (young *or* old) additional tricks, but we humans retain a potentially unlimited conditional ability to respond differently, and more appropriately, in response to new situations. Thus the difference between an animalistic *signal* reaction and the contrasting humanistic, conditional *symbol* reaction. (1; p. 334, etc.) This material provides the psychophysiological basis for suggesting that we *can* change "human nature." Of course some harsh "educational" practices could interfere with our conditionality: knowing about the possibilities helps us to prevent precisely this kind of "dead level abstracting," as Wendell Johnson put it. (6; p. 270ff)

Become conscious of abstracting. Korzybski's second directive takes us to the heart of his non-Aristotelian system, for he stated that, "The consciousness of abstracting, or the remembering that we abstract in different orders with omission of characteristics, depends on the denial of the 'is' of identity and is connected with limitations or 'non-allness,' so characteristic of the new non-systems. [He referred here to the non-Euclidean geometries and non-Newtonian physics.] The consciousness of abstracting eliminates *automatically* identification or 'confusion of orders of abstractions,' both applying to the semantic confusion on all levels." (1; p. 471)

He tied this issue into our present concerns in the following way: "The consciousness of abstracting, which involves, among others, the full instinctive semantic realization of nonidentity and the stratification of human knowledge, and so the multiordinality of the most important terms we use solves these weighty and complex problems [produced by semantic blockages] because it gives us structural methods for semantic evaluation, for orientation, and for handling them. By passing to higher orders, these states which involve inhibition or negative excitation become reversed. Some of them on higher levels become culturally important; and some of them become morbid. Now consciousness of abstracting in all cases gives us the semantic *freedom* of all levels and so helps *evaluation* and selection, thus removing the possibility of remaining animalistically fixed or blocked on any one level. Here we find the mechanism of the 'change of human nature.'" (1; p. 441)

Eliminate identifications in our semantic processes. Let no one minimize the difficulty, and some would say the near impossibility, of accomplishing this aim. It may amount to an impossibility for many of us, especially for those who do not understand why all the shouting, or who do not even try to do something about it. Nevertheless, we must realize that this way lie greater "sanity," greater creativity, inner tranquillity, etc. Identification has many roots that may entwine us without our even realizing it.

Suppose I ask you to visualize my holding in my hand a bright yellow, perfect lemon. After cutting it in half, I bite deep into it, and suck the lemon juice. If, as a consequence of this described demonstration, you feel a slight (or more) amount of saliva in your mouth, you have *identified* organismically the words (structures on the symbolic level) with concentrated citric acid (a structure on the silent levels).

In Korzybski's terms, we will begin here in accordance with the natural order, and present his view on identifying silent level happenings with structures on the symbolic level. Subsequently (in the next section) we will address these issues with a focus more specifically on the symbolic level.

A key step in retraining the nervous systems of persons embedded in an Aristotelian culture consists in eliminating identification in so far as possible from their semantic processes, and particularly the identification of the silent levels (i.e., the event and object levels) with the symbolic level. From an educational point of view, Korzybski made the following suggestions: "In the older days, all 'wisdom' was taught to us by purely 'intellectual,' 'verbal,' classical Aristotelian and elementalistic methods. We had no simple psycho-*physiological* method of *complete* generality, which could be taught in a non-elementalistic way affecting *all* nerve centers. It is known how difficult it is to 'change human nature,' which simply means that the older verbal educational methods could not properly affect the lower centers. It seems that the first step in developing a method to accomplish these ends is to use the Structural Differential, without which it is practically impossible to teach 'silence on the objective level' and 'delayed action' and to train through *all* centers in non-identity, 'stratification,' natural order, and so in appropriate semantic reactions." (1; p. 446)

Continuing to present material on the non-Aristotelian training of children, Korzybski suggested that, "Once the child is thoroughly aware of the absence of identity between words and objects, we may attempt the expanding of the notion 'object' to the 'objective levels.' Such training requires persistence, even though it seems fundamentally simple. We

demonstrate and explain that action, actual bodily performance, and all objective happenings, *are not* words. At a later
stage we explain that a toothache, or demonstrate that the
actual pain of a prick, etc., *are not* words, and belong to the
objective un-speakable levels. Still later, we enlarge this notion
to cover all ordinary objects, all actions, functions, performances, processes going on outside our skin, and also all immediate feelings, 'emotions,' 'moods,' etc., going on inside our
skins which also *are not* words. We enlarge the 'silence' to all
happenings on the objective levels and the animalistic, 'human nature' begins to be 'changed' into quite a different *human* nature." (1; p. 477)

I regret that it seems necessary in this paper to include the
lengthy quotations from *Science and Sanity* given above.
However, the need to do so proceeds from the unfortunate
circumstance that for far too long the insights and proposals
of Korzybski remained on the back shelves of somebody
else's library, while watered down versions of tiny aspects of
his system received great prominence. And, whether we like
it or not, the pallid material often received short shrift, quite
appropriately, from some in the scientific and academic communities, with the blame for the inadequacies remaining as a
present for Korzybski!

Change the [semantic] structure of our language. This student
of Korzybski's feels it necessary to emphasize "semantic" in
the name of this section. While some linguists, such as the
late Uriel Weinreich and I, reject an elementalistic split between syntax and semantics, most linguists would tend to
become so syntactically energized (without the emphasis on
"semantics") that they might miss the whole point of the discussion. Korzybski expected that sometime soon after the
publication of his major work that "we will discover more
about the dependence of 'human nature' on the structure of
our languages, doctrines, institutions, etc., and will conclude
that for adjustment, stability, etc., we must adjust these man-
made and man-invented semantic and other conditions in
conformity with that newly discovered 'human nature.' " (1;
p. 547) Some 15 years and World War II later, he stated in his
seminars that he believed that his most important personal
contribution consisted of developing the *extensional devices*

which, he asserted, made it possible to "change the structure of language without changing the language itself." More specifically, he wished to change the Aristotelian, elementalistic, allness-filled, two-valued, etc., language whose semantic structure hearkened back to much earlier times, to a non-Aristotelian one. To this noble end, he suggested that we apply the following devices: (a) Dates; (b) Indexes; (c) Chain-indexes; (d) Etc.; (e) Quotes; and (f) Hyphens. Various popular texts have provided excellent material on those devices, in particular Wendell Johnson's *People in Quandaries.* (6)

In more recent years, some of Korzybski's students have come to regard the application of E-Prime (English without any form of the verb *to be*) as a particularly valuable addition to the other extensional devices. (7) This proceeds from an understanding of Korzybski's important statement: "The subject-predicate form, the 'is' of identity, and the elementalism of the Aristotelian system are perhaps the main semantic factors in need of revision, as they are found to be the foundation of the insufficiency of this system and represent the mechanism of semantic disturbances, making general adjustment and sanity impossible." (1; p. 371)   Oddly enough, some of Korzybski's supposedly most dedicated students seem unable to understand the preceding sentence. E-Prime offers a straightforward way to do away completely with the first two problems and helps significantly in dealing with the third, but nevertheless some heel-draggers show no enthusiasm for making the E-Prime revision.

4. *Concluding Remarks*

There you have my road map for how to get from here to a variety of desirable goals. If you want to go backward, and some perversely nearly always do, start with E-Prime as a first step, and just stop using forms of *to be* in your writing and speech.   Use the other extensional devices as much as possible. Work on yourself to try to stamp out identifications, remaining silent on the silent levels.   Check yourself for unconditional responses, when greater conditionality might produce greater payoffs. Have your experiences and someone else's dicta set limits on how you perceive the world about you and how you react to it?   Once, one of Korzybski's "senior grade" students said to him that, "Together we can change the world!" She told me that he replied, "Well, we might change *you* a little." If you really have an interest in changing "human nature," perhaps it would work best if you begin with yourself. Good luck! Let me know how you and the world turn out!

REFERENCES

1. Alfred Korzybski. *Science and Sanity: An Introduction to Non-Aristotelian Systems and General Semantics.* Lakeville, Conn.: International Non-Aristotelian Library Publishing Co., 1933. Fourth edition, 1958.
2. Alfred Korzybski. *Manhood of Humanity.* New York: E. P. Dutton & Co., 1921. Lakeville, Conn.: International Non-Aristotelian Library Publishing Co. Second edition, 1950.
3. D. David Bourland, Jr. "Alfred Korzybski y su revisión no-Aristotélica," Presentación frente a la Sociedad Filosófica de la Universidad de Costa Rica, Noviembre de 1979.
4. Alfred Korzybski. *Collected Writings: 1920 - 1950.* M. Kendig, ed. Englewood, N.J.: International Non-Aristotelian Library Publishing Co., 1990.
5. D. David Bourland, Jr., and Elizabeth J. Bourland. *A Course in Advanced Squirrelly Semantics.* San Francisco: International Society for General Semantics, 1993.
6. Wendell Johnson. *People in Quandaries: The Semantics of Personal Adjustment.* New York: Harper & Bros., 1946. San Francisco: International Society for General Semantics, Fourth printing, 1989.
7. D. David Bourland, Jr., and Paul Dennithorne Johnston, eds. *To Be or Not: An E-Prime Anthology.* San Francisco: International Society for General Semantics, 1991.

THE EDITORS

PAUL DENNITHORNE JOHNSTON, a graduate of the City of London (England) Polytechnic, serves as Executive Director of the International Society for General Semantics and Managing Editor of *ETC.: A Review of General Semantics.* Mr. Johnston has worked as newspaper reporter and editor, and has published fiction and nonfiction in the U.S.A. and Britain.

D. DAVID BOURLAND, JR., graduated from Culver Military Academy (1946), Harvard College (A.B. Mathematics, 1951), Harvard Graduate School of Business Administration (M.B.A. 1953), and the Universidad de Costa Rica (Licenciatura in English Linguistics, 1973). Mr. Bourland, who held a fellowship for study at the Institute for General Semantics, 1949-1950, has participated in many of the Institute's seminars, edited the General Semantics Bulletin, 1964-1970, and acted as a trustee of the Institute, 1964-1989. He served on the Staff, Commander Naval Forces Far East, as a Lieutenant, Junior Grade, 1953-1955, and worked in naval operations research, 1955-1971. Mr. Bourland taught at the Universidad de Costa Rica from 1971 to 1980, retiring as Associate Professor of Linguistics.

JEREMY KLEIN, a graduate of the University of Chicago, has served since 1990 as Editor-in-Chief of *ETC.: A Review of General Semantics,* and since 1991 as President of the San Francisco Bay Area chapter of the International Society for General Semantics. Mr. Klein also holds the position of Associate Editor with a major West Coast commercial real estate trade journal.